Modern Language Association of America

Approaches to Teaching
World Literature

Joseph Gibaldi, Series Editor

26. Robin Riley Fast and Christine Mack Gordon, eds. *Approaches to Teaching Dickinson's Poetry.* 1989.

27. Spencer Hall, ed. *Approaches to Teaching Shelley's Poetry.* 1990.

28. Sidney Gottlieb, ed. *Approaches to Teaching the Metaphysical Poets.* 1990.

29. Richard K. Emmerson, ed. *Approaches to Teaching Medieval English Drama.* 1990.

30. Kathleen Blake, ed. *Approaches to Teaching Eliot's* Middlemarch. 1990.

31. María Elena de Valdés and Mario J. Valdés, eds. *Approaches to Teaching García Márquez's* One Hundred Years of Solitude. 1990.

32. Donald D. Kummings, ed. *Approaches to Teaching Whitman's* Leaves of Grass. 1990.

33. Stephen C. Behrendt, ed. *Approaches to Teaching Shelley's* Frankenstein. 1990.

34. June Schlueter and Enoch Brater, eds. *Approaches to Teaching Beckett's* Waiting for Godot. 1991.

35. Walter H. Evert and Jack W. Rhodes, eds. *Approaches to Teaching Keats's Poetry.* 1991.

36. Frederick W. Shilstone, ed. *Approaches to Teaching Byron's Poetry.* 1991.

Approaches to Teaching Byron's Poetry

Edited by
Frederick W. Shilstone

The Modern Language Association of America
New York   1991

© 1991 by The Modern Language Association of America

Library of Congress Cataloging-in-Publication Data

Approaches to teaching Byron's poetry / edited by Frederick W.
  Shilstone.
      p.   cm. — (Approaches to teaching world literature ; 36)
    Includes bibliographical references and index.
    ISBN 0-87352-545-0 (cloth)   ISBN 0-87352-546-9 (paper)
    1. Byron, George Gordon Byron, Baron, 1788–1824—Criticism and
  interpretation.   2. Byron, George Gordon Byron, Baron 1788–1824—
  Study and teaching.   I. Shilstone, Frederick W., 1948–
  II. Series.
  PR4388.A6   1991
  821'.7—dc20   91-10780

Cover illustration of the paperback edition: Eugène Delacroix, *The Giaour and
the Pasha*, Petit Palais, Paris, 1835. Photograph: Draeger Frères/Art Resource,
New York.

Published by The Modern Language Association of America
10 Astor Place, New York, New York 10003-6981

CONTENTS

The Satires, "Romantic" Poems, and Plays

Don Juan

PREFACE TO THE SERIES

In *The Art of Teaching* Gilbert Highet wrote, "Bad teaching wastes a great deal of effort, and spoils many lives which might have been full of energy and happiness." All too many teachers have failed in their work, Highet argued, simply "because they have not thought about it." We hope that the Approaches to Teaching World Literature series, sponsored by the Modern Language Association Publications Committee, will not only improve the craft—as well as the art—of teaching but also encourage serious and continuing discussion of the aims and methods of teaching literature.

The principal objective of the series is to collect within each volume different points of view on teaching a specific literary work, a literary tradition, or a writer widely taught at the undergraduate level. The preparation of each volume begins with a wide-ranging survey of instructors, thus enabling us to include in the volume the philosophies and approaches, thoughts and methods of scores of experienced teachers. The result is a sourcebook of material, information, and ideas on teaching the subject of the volume to undergraduates.

The series is intended to serve nonspecialists as well as specialists, inexperienced as well as experienced teachers, graduate students who wish to learn effective ways of teaching as well as senior professors who wish to compare their own approaches with the approaches of colleagues in other schools. Of course, no volume in the series can ever substitute for erudition, intelligence, creativity, and sensitivity in teaching. We hope merely that each book will point readers in useful directions; at most, each will offer only a first step in the long journey to successful teaching.

Joseph Gibaldi
Series Editor

PREFACE TO THE VOLUME

This book originated, in the purest sense of that term, in conversations—in hallways, at conferences—with colleagues who share my enthusiasm for Byron yet consider his works, especially when taught in survey courses, problematic; and in classrooms, where students have shaped my approach to Byron through subtle patterns of question and response, leading naturally to a curiosity about others' pedagogical experiences and the conclusions to which they have led. In both these forums, consensus opinions have emerged about key issues in Byron pedagogy and criticism. There is the intriguing paradox in the way Byron combines a multiplicity of poetic guises, from the outraged Augustan arbiter of taste in the couplet satires to the most extreme of Romantic gloomy egotists in *Childe Harold* and *Manfred*, with a tenacious personal intrusion into even his most ostensibly "dramatic" productions (a tendency noted by Stendhal, among others), an intrusion that brings biography into discussions of his works in a fashion that is as inevitable, and frequently as unwelcome, as the manner in which King Charles's head rolls into Mr. Dick's memorial. There is the question of Byron's "place" among his contemporaries, an issue that is especially prominent in surveys of first-generation Romantics such as Wordsworth and Blake as well as of Keats and Shelley, Byron's fellows in the younger set, where opinions regard Byron as everything from Romanticism's essence to his age's chief anomaly. And there is, to include only one more item in a long list, the relation between Byron's status as a poet and a given teacher's theoretical or ideological orientation. These and many other issues are repeatedly addressed in this book in the hope that teachers who read the selections will profit as greatly as I have in editing them.

This volume pursues the goal of the Approaches series to represent the widest possible range of pedagogical issues in two major ways. First, in the "Materials" section, I amalgamate opinions on the most important primary and secondary sources available to the student and teacher of Byron. Drawing mainly from responses to the questionnaire circulated as the initial step in the preparation of this volume, a resource complemented by more informal suggestions from colleagues and useful amendments offered by the manuscript's readers, that essay aims to guide readers to the sources most closely related to a given critical issue or specific work. At the heart of this project, however, are the essays in part 2, "Approaches." There, contributors exploit a range of interests in critical issues in Byron—philosophical, textual, biographical, social, historical, aesthetic—and offer pedagogical applications of insights that have already, in many instances, at least implicitly enriched our teaching. Although such a collection can go only so far in covering the relevant issues, the essays suggest a program for teaching Byron in a comprehensive manner. The authors discuss the poems most frequently and successfully taught in undergraduate curricula and represent them in proportion to students' positive response—hence the inclusion of a separate section on *Don Juan*. The approaches described for presenting a specific work can easily be adapted for other poems or even for an entire unit on Byron. In sum, the volume provides a detailed map of what the best teachers of Byron are doing to keep their classes lively and flexible.

This project is intended to serve many audiences. While individual sections may address those teaching Byron in junior-college, undergraduate survey, or specialized upper-level classes, no essay or suggestion for reading is without implication for other groups studying or teaching the poet. Throughout, it seems clear that interest in Byron, formal criticism of his works, and teaching of him are inseparable components of the professional vigor reflected in the essays in this volume.

As editor of *Approaches to Teaching Byron's Poetry*, I express special thanks to my colleagues who responded to the project questionnaire, frequently in a detailed manner indicative of their selfless commitment to helping others improve their teaching. I am grateful to Joseph Gibaldi, Adrienne Marie Ward, and Elizabeth Holland at the Modern Language Association, for their sympathy with the project and energetic pursuit of measures to ensure its success and quality. Closer to home, I thank Frank Day, who offered both moral and practical support during his tenure as acting head of Clemson's English Department, and Leslie Robinson, whose assistance with details during the long, hot summers was indispensable.

FWS

Part One

MATERIALS

Editions

As the current, raging debate over the nature, even validity, of the traditional literary canon amply indicates, acts of selection, excerpting, and annotating (what and how) are in themselves as indicative of a critical or pedagogical orientation as one's choice of a scholarly model or mentor. Thus, while teachers frequently select texts of Byron on the basis of economics ("McGann's Oxford Authors is clearly the best, but who can justify individual volumes for each poet [in a Romantics survey] these days?") or typography ("I need a complete Byron to teach what I want to, but the current choices condemn me and my students to blindness"), they appear to find compatible editions for every level of instruction and pattern of critical emphasis. Indeed, respondents to the survey conducted in preparation for this volume generally agree about editions of the poetry and even about what should be considered the "classic" readings of Byron's career and character.

Teachers report including Byron in a wide range of course offerings. Some undergraduate curricula place the poet in interdisciplinary contexts, in, for instance, a course entitled The Romantic Mind: Goethe, Byron, Delacroix, Berlioz. More commonly, the poet is taught in the standard world humanities survey; in comparative literature studies with Russians such as Pushkin and Dostoyevski and the Americans Melville and Poe; in specialized courses with an English counterpart, most often Shelley but recently also Blake and Keats (reflecting a changing sense of Romantic affinities); and even all by himself, in a senior honors seminar. Increasingly, too, teachers include Byron in thematic courses that reflect emerging critical interests: Romanticism and Feminism, Romanticism and the Politics of Regency. Most frequently, though, Byron is a staple part of the standard second-half British survey and the upper-division Romantic poets course, usually focused on the "Big Six" or, in very specialized curricula, solely on Byron, Shelley, and Keats. Along with preferring, as the level of specialization increases, *The Norton Anthology*, edited by M. H. Abrams, David Perkins's *English Romantic Writers*, and Jerome J. McGann's and Leslie A. Marchand's single-volume selections of the poems and prose, teachers concur on what texts work best, while lodging individual complaints based on favorite poems or critical viewpoints.

I progress in this section from selected and complete teaching editions, through anthologies that include Byron, to the now-standard complete editions most useful to students in advanced and graduate courses. Throughout the entire "Materials" section, I integrate commentary, based on the survey questionnaires, on critical issues as they relate to the summary of texts and readings. From favored edition to favored critic, a teacher's sense of how to present Byron is frequently clearest in his or her principles of selection.

Teaching Editions: Selections, Don Juan, and Complete Works

While still recent and thus not yet fully incorporated into many instructors' syllabi, Jerome McGann's Oxford Authors edition of Byron is clearly destined to become the most popular collection in courses where a single-volume text is warranted. McGann, unlike any previous editor of a selected Byron, has included the complete texts of *Childe Harold's Pilgrimage* and *Don Juan*— in, of course, his own now-authoritative editions—as well as the plays *Manfred* and *Cain*, the satires *Beppo* and *The Vision of Judgment*, and selections from *English Bards and Scotch Reviewers*, the lyrics, and the informal prose. McGann's notes, culled and adapted from his Oxford *Complete Poetical Works*, explain topical references and thus remove one major obstacle (in Byron perhaps more than any of his contemporaries) to students' access to his often subtly allusive style. Some teachers lament omissions necessitated by McGann's inclusion of the complete *Harold* and *Don Juan*, chiefly of more Augustan satire (represented only by the *English Bards* excerpt) and of a more "representative" Oriental tale: *The Giaour* and *Mazeppa*, which are present, strike some as atypical, while *The Corsair* and *Lara* are here condensed to their famous portraits of the Byronic hero. Nonetheless, the editorial principles used here clearly provide the most complete overview of Byron's canon possible in the space available, as well as readable, authoritative texts and apparatus especially helpful to advanced undergraduates.

Several other selected editions of Byron exist. While teachers are far more divided on their usefulness, and the majority are periodically unavailable, they each have their advocates. Most often mentioned among this group is William H. Marshall's Riverside edition, *Lord Byron: Selected Poems and Letters*. Because there is a Riverside edition devoted solely to *Don Juan*, edited by Marchand, Marshall's has space for all of *Childe Harold*, a generous selection of other works from the entire span of Byron's career, and selected letters and generally useful textual notes. Survey respondents are most divided on Frank D. McConnell's Norton Critical Edition, ranking it from "quite good" to "nearly useless." Forced to excerpt both *Childe Harold* and *Don Juan* (always a thankless task, especially in the latter case), McConnell is nonetheless able to include several well-chosen, if now somewhat outdated critical articles, as well as a section called "Images of Byron," which gives students a sense of the cult of Byronism, or personality worship and contempt, as it evolved throughout the nineteenth and early twentieth centuries.

The selected poetry list is completed by three volumes with more limited appeal than the above. Edward E. Bostetter's Rinehart edition presents more extensive selections from *Don Juan* and the prose than McConnell's, yet still suffers from jagged excerpting of the longer works and gaps in representing the couplet satires and early Oriental narratives. Finally, W. H. Auden's *Selected Poetry and Prose of Byron* and A. S. B. Glover's *Poems* are smaller-format paperbacks that are useful primarily for their terse, generally sound introductions. Especially in the Auden selection, which heavily emphasizes the satires and prose, these books offer no more comprehensive menu of Byronic voices than one finds in the standard anthologies.

As Byron's informal prose has become available in greater abundance and less bowdlerized form, the result primarily of Leslie Marchand's efforts in recent years, teaching it as autobiography and as a fascinating if not always reliable commentary on the poems has become more and more common, even "as essential as including Keats's best letters." For the specialized course, Marchand has issued a one-volume paperback edition of well-chosen journal and letter entries, complemented by a judicious selection of bons mots and sketches of the poet's chief correspondents. Peter Gunn's *Byron: Selected Prose* also provides a good overview of Byron the letter writer. Still unavailable in any collection are Byron's parliamentary speeches and formal critical essays; because of the increasing emphasis on history and politics in our age of the new historicism, these gaps, especially the former, are ones many would like to see quickly filled.

It is almost a "truth universally acknowledged" (and without Austen's irony) that the most successful Byronic text in undergraduate courses at every level is *Don Juan*: as one survey respondent noted, "Students find Byron [in *Don Juan*] a delightful change of pace . . . from the pontifical obscurities [of his Romantic predecessors]." Not surprisingly, then, the ottava rima masterpiece is the one work readily available in an inexpensive volume of its own. The Riverside *Don Juan*, edited by Marchand, most often appears in syllabi where there is room for extensive treatment. A superior text, based on the *Variorum Edition* of *Don Juan* (discussed below), has been edited by T. G. Steffan, E. Steffan, and Willis W. Pratt; having lapsed out of print in its Yale paperback edition, it is fortunately available again through Penguin Books. Finally, a Modern Library issue of *Don Juan* (ed. Kronenberger) is still in print, though it is not considered the equal of the others in text or editorial apparatus.

None of the poetry collections described in the beginning of this section completely suits everyone's pedagogical aims; recent incisive criticism has fueled greater interest in, among other texts, Byron's early Oriental tales and late historical tragedies, the latter of which the poet claimed as among his very best achievements. Since these works are sparsely represented in all the collected Byrons, many teachers order one of two relatively inexpensive complete editions: the Oxford Standard Authors *Byron: Poetical*

Works, edited by Frederick Page and updated in 1970, or Paul E. More's Cambridge edition, revised by Robert Gleckner in 1975. Each benefits from completeness and suffers from too-small print. Still, these books are essential to teachers presenting Byron in detail and in all his poetic guises.

Anthologies

Teachers consider anthologies a necessary evil in presenting Byron in English survey and Romantic period courses; they provide the only reasonably comprehensive and affordable texts, yet by nature restrict editors even more severely than collected editions. And respondents differ on the usefulness of the editorial material presented in the available anthologies, as well as on what are the essential inclusions: some abandon hope of accurately presenting the "gutted" longer works and thus prize anthologies that emphasize the lyrics and complete, if in some instances less essential (in their estimate) poems such as *The Prisoner of Chillon* and *Manfred*. Others believe that excerpted segments of early portraits of the Byronic hero and a two-to-four canto selection of *Don Juan* are preferable, especially given the traditional but now somewhat disputed estimate of the inferiority and atypicality of Byron's lyric effusions. Some demand all of *English Bards*; others want many more letters, which are excluded entirely from some anthologies. Most insist on *Don Juan* in some decipherable form, though, but generally bemoan editorial decisions that opt to reconstruct the bare narrative line of that poem (and also, to some degree, of *Childe Harold*) at the expense of the work's essence, the narrator's embodiment of stylistic *mobilité* and Romantic irony. The following brief survey summarizes only widely noted strengths and limitations, first of anthologies appropriate for a broad historical survey, then of those used in a specialized Romantic-era course.

No other general anthology even remotely approaches the popularity of the two-volume *Norton*, whose Romantic-period section was edited by M. H. Abrams and Jack Stillinger. Teachers praise the background essay on the period and, even more, the brief introductory discussions of the poet's career and major works included there. On the latter, a few teachers find some segments, especially allusive ones, a bit too esoteric for beginning students, while others bemoan the lack of any discussion of Romantic irony, "what really distinguishes Byron from the earlier Romantics," especially in the discussion that precedes *Don Juan*—"though that does," says one, "leave the teacher some room to look cleverly familiar with the current views." Notes to the poems are marked "serviceable," if not always complete enough for students utterly innocent of Byron's historical and literary contexts. The scope of the *Norton* exacerbates many of the problems noted above in the collected editions: only *Manfred* and *The Vision of Judgment*, among the most frequently taught works, are represented in full; no section of *Childe Harold* is wholly present (teachers think canto 3, at least, works well as an independent piece); and some judge the poem "virtually unteachable" in the form printed here, despite the editors' attempt to retain at least a sense of the itinerary of Byron's second European sojourn. *Don Juan* lives only in severed pieces of the opening four cantos and in narrative summaries, which most teachers feel compelled to supplement with readings from other parts. And the letters and journals are omitted entirely, despite an introductory description of their "wonderfully vivacious" character. In short, those who wish to emphasize Byron in a British literature survey—and who thus were likely respondents to the project questionnaire—"make do" with the *Norton*, a feeling yet more intense in those forced to employ the one-volume Major Authors edition, in which *Manfred* is dropped. Despite these restrictions, teachers still regard the *Norton* as the best-available choice at this level, perhaps ultimately a testament to Byron's resistance to being anthologized as well as, in his own words, to having himself pinned down to a poetical or philosophical "system." (Teachers should also note Alfred David's recent guide *Teaching with the Norton Anthology*, which includes some useful suggestions for approaching the Byron selections.)

The distant second choice among survey anthologies is the fourth volume of *The Oxford Anthology of English Literature*, edited by Harold Bloom and Lionel Trilling. Even more jagged in its excerpting than the *Norton*, the *Oxford* is also passed over by some Byron teachers because of its "sometimes quirky editorial comments." It does, however, present a brief early segment of the last, or "English," cantos of *Don Juan*, preferred by some over the more commonly included opening ones, and it offers plates of paintings, by John Martin, Thomas Phillips, and J. M. W. Turner (twice), as bound-in visual aids illustrating Byronic scenes and moods. In comparative literature surveys, teachers have two choices. One is *The Norton Anthology of World Masterpieces*, under the general editorship of Maynard Mack, which represents Byron solely by the second canto of *Don Juan*. The other is the second edition of Brian Wilkie and James Hurt's *Literature of the Western World*, though the editors there have unwisely replaced their original Byron selections—some of *Don Juan* and all of *Manfred* (possibly the most potent influence on the European contemporaries with whom Byron shares this anthology)—with only the somewhat atypical *Vision of Judgment*. Finally, those teaching the poet in a humanities survey find him briefly represented, primarily in the "Ode to Napoleon Buonaparte" and "Prometheus," in the second volume of Robert C. Lamm and Neal M. Cross's *Humanities in Western Culture* and, similarly briefly, in Mary Ann Frese Witt's *Humanities*.

Teachers of advanced Romantic-period courses continue to express a reserved preference for Perkins's *English Romantic Writers*. While voicing some of the same minor reservations about the advanced assumptions made in the introductory material as those lodged against the *Norton* and *Oxford* anthologies, as well as a few objections to the now-dated bibliography and principle of text selection, respondents feel Perkins does well, given the recurrent difficulty of adequately anthologizing Byron. The selections here are, in fact, similar to those in the *Norton*, with the addition of a healthy excerpt from the English cantos of *Don Juan*, to complement the usual early sections, and a fairly large and well-selected section of letters, though one compiled too early to incorporate Marchand's voluminous efforts and the totally new materials discovered in 1976 in the Scrope Davies trunk. Again here, the usual complaints about excerpting *Childe Harold* and *Don Juan* obtain, though Perkins is himself aware of the great difficulty in capturing the essence of those kaleidoscopic works as only "exhibited in extracts."

Other comparable anthologies, mentioned sparingly by survey respondents, differ from Perkins in various ways. William Heath's *Major British Poets of the Romantic Period*, by confining its scope to the six major poets (Perkins includes several prose writers and minor poets), is able to offer the most extensive selection of Byron's verse. Included are far more lyrics than are available elsewhere; all of *The Giaour*, the most frequently discussed of the Oriental tales in recent years; *Manfred*; and a selection of *Don Juan* similar to Perkins's in its concentration on the opening and English episodes. Heath also offers the complete third canto of *Childe Harold* (as noted above, the most self-contained of the poem's segments, though one quite different in kind from the earlier cantos) and *The Prisoner of Chillon*, curiously absent from many anthologies. Prose excerpts are strangely confined to a few journal entries, though those from the 1816 diary addressed to Byron's half-sister, Augusta, reflect extremely well the state of mind that produced the tormented poems of that first exile year. In John L. Mahoney's *English Romantics: Major Poetry and Critical Theory*, available in paperback, the Byron selections are traditional but are invigorated by the inclusion of William Hazlitt's portrait of the poet, as well as by three classic essays, by Marchand, Peter Thorslev, and Paul G. Trueblood, of modern Byron criticism. Russell Noyes's *English Romantic Poetry and Prose* is now considered dated in its critical apparatus, but it nonetheless offers a serviceable selection of Byron's verse and prose.

Standard Editions

The imminent completion of Jerome McGann's monumental *Lord Byron: The Complete Poetical Works* makes it the unquestioned standard reference for the verse, and its notes, especially, should be consulted by any teacher seeking the background and textual history of a work being taught on all but the most elementary level. Not only does McGann argue convincingly for the authority of his editions of the poems, he also illustrates the validity of his own recent theories of textual criticism and contextual placement of the poetic statement (discussed later in this essay). While the volumes in this series are far too dear to be considered as teaching editions on any level, they are, for now, the authority for scholarly reference and debate. Still useful, though, is E. H. Coleridge's long-standard *Works of Lord Byron: Poetry*; many of Coleridge's insightful annotations complement McGann's. As an additional textual source, teachers might consult the Byron entries in the Garland Manuscripts of the Younger Romantics series, so far represented in facsimiles and drafts of *Miscellaneous Poems* (ed. Levine and McGann), *The Draft Manuscripts of Cantos VI and VII of* Don Juan (ed. Nicholson), and two volumes devoted to *Childe Harold* (ed. Burnett; Erdman and Worrall).

As suggested above, Marchand's twelve-volume *Letters and Journals* provides the prose counterpart to McGann's edition of the verse. These volumes are enriched by recent discoveries, freed of mysteries introduced by the timidity of earlier editors, and illuminated by sage commentary and a comprehensive index. Teachers should not, however, ignore Rowland E. Prothero's earlier *Letters and Journals*, if only because Prothero's appendixes still include the most accessible reprintings of Byron's parliamentary speeches and formal critical epistles, especially those related to the Bowles controversy; on this issue Prothero also includes key documents penned by the other participants. Until these papers are more readily available, the editions in Prothero should be kept near at hand.

In a similar category are published versions of Byron's "Conversations," products of his contemporaries' attempts to link their names with his notoriety. While many such works exist—for a further listing, consult the bibliographic sources described below—a teacher probably need not go beyond the most famous, those of Thomas Medwin and Lady Blessington, authoritatively edited by Ernest J. Lovell, Jr., and Lovell's compendium of similar accounts, *His Very Self and Voice*. (In a much less comprehensive vein is Norman Page's collection *Byron: Interviews and Recollections*, whose approach is something like that in the "Images of Byron" section in McConnell's Norton Critical Edition of his verse.) While we should remain skeptical of the veracity of their contributors' recollections—as well as Byron's own duplicity in presenting an image to them—these volumes nonetheless add an important voice to the standard edition of the "informal" Byron.

A final note to this segment: while McGann's texts have effectively superseded all other editions of the poems, a few individual volumes remain useful for their introductory material and textual commentary. These include

Steffan and Pratt's *Variorum* Don Juan, Steffan's *Lord Byron's* Cain: *Twelve Essays and a Text*, and, indicating a rise in Byron's reputation as a lyric poet, Thomas L. Ashton's *Byron's* Hebrew Melodies, with two fine introductory essays, and the recent edition of the same collection by Frederick Burwick and Paul Douglass, one greatly enriched by an accompanying audiocassette of several of the *Melodies* set to their proper airs (see the "Teaching Aids" section below).

Readings for Students and Teachers

The following pages describe what a consensus of respondents to the survey questionnaire regard as the central documents students and teachers should consult in their attempts to understand the background of and essential critical issues in Byron's verse. By its very nature selective and only briefly descriptive, the survey aims at acquainting readers with those classic sources most appropriate to different pedagogical aims and levels of study. The division of materials into various categories—for instance, those appropriate for undergraduate students rather than preparing teachers—is a convenience that should not prevent anyone from adapting or ignoring its boundaries. In fact, one should read the following essay entire and determine the applicability of its sections to a given teaching level or environment.

I progress in this section from bibliographic and major reference readings to a discussion of those sources, primarily secondary, that appear again and again in teachers' descriptions of their readings and syllabi. In the second category, I first approach works frequently cited as especially useful and comprehensible to undergraduate (especially upper-level) students, in those cases in which teachers feel it valuable to guide their classes beyond the primary texts. The last and most specialized section is primarily directed to teachers preparing their classroom approach to Byron, whether for the first or the fiftieth time. My tack there is to unfold a thematically oriented account of books and essays focused on key critical elements in the discussion of Byron: for instance, the poet's relation to his English contemporaries, the place of biography, and the importance of history and politics. There follows a list of popular studies of individual poems that do not appear in other contexts in the "Materials" section. The segment concludes with a brief summary of recent collections of criticism focused on Byron; while many of these are too new to gauge their pedagogical implications, they surely indicate directions that research, and thus teaching of the poet, will be taking in the coming years.

Bibliographic and Reference Readings

The starting point for anyone wanting a brief yet incisive overview of Byron criticism is John Clubbe's fine bibliographic essay in the fourth edition of the MLA's *English Romantic Poets: A Review of Research and Criticism*, edited by Frank Jordan. Clubbe's essay recounts the entire history of Byron criticism from the poet's day to our own, offers capsule discussions of modern critical responses to different works and major areas of inquiry, and includes unstintingly perceptive and just evaluative comments on the important major studies of the poet published in recent decades. Readers should also consult Jordan's opening segment of the volume for its discussion of major background sources and central controversies, such as that between the "natural supernaturalists" and the "romantic ironists," important to any figure in or facet of the English Romantic age. I make reference to these essays more than once in the ensuing discussion, and I urge all teachers of Byron to make even more frequent reference of their own.

The most important annotated bibliography of Byron and his fellow Romantics is that which appeared in *ELH* from 1937 to 1949, then in *Philological Quarterly* until 1964, followed, until 1978, by a residence in *English Language Notes*. In recent years, David Erdman has edited the bibliography in individual volumes issued by Garland Press through 1987 and currently by Locust Hill. A sometimes fuller yet only briefly annotated listing of studies of Byron and his (broadly defined) circle occupies the latter section of the annual *Keats-Shelley Journal*; reviews of major studies are also noted there. Robert A. Hartley has compiled and usefully indexed the 1 July 1962– 31 December 1974 segments of this bibliography in a volume available from the University of Nebraska Press; his book may be complemented by reference to Ronald B. Hearn's *Byron Criticism since 1952: A Bibliography*. The most generally complete unannotated listing is that in the annual *MLA International Bibliography*, now available on computer through DIALOG online search in many libraries. For older sources, teachers may consult Oscar José Santucho's *George Gordon, Lord Byron: A Comprehensive Bibliography of Secondary Materials in English, 1807–1974*, which contains a prefatory narrative by Clement Goode describing the evolution of Byron criticism, and H. G. Pollard's Byron section in the third volume of *The New Cambridge Bibliography of English Literature* (1969). Students may still find R. H. Fogle's Goldentree bibliography on the Romantics useful, though its listings are now seriously dated. For a catalog of more specialized Byron bibliographies, consult pages 466–71 of John Clubbe's essay, noted above.

Contemporary views and reviews are available in Donald H. Reiman's volumes of *The Romantics Reviewed: Contemporary Reviews of British Romantic Writers* and, in less comprehensive format, in Andrew Rutherford's volume on Byron in the Critical Heritage Series. Also, a single-volume compendium, *Romantic Bards and British Reviewers: A Selected Edition of Contemporary Reviews of the Works of Wordsworth, Coleridge, Byron, Keats, and Shelley*, has been prepared by John O. Hayden.

Teachers may follow current trends in Byron criticism by consulting the relevant notices in the special review issue of the *Wordsworth Circle* and, for briefer remarks, in the annual *Byron Journal*, the official publication of the British Byron Society. Readers should keep current on both reviews and essays contained in such specialized journals as *Studies in Romanticism;*

Studies in English Literature, which devotes an entire quarterly issue to the nineteenth century; *Nineteenth-Century Contexts* (formerly *Romanticism Past and Present*); and *Nineteenth-Century Studies*, an annual published by the Southeastern Nineteenth-Century Studies Association; as well as those that appear in more general periodicals, such as *Criticism, Genre,* and *Colby Library Quarterly*, that encourage and frequently publish submissions on Byron and the other Romantics.

For an accurate, almost day-to-day calendar of Byron's activities, useful in establishing the exact circumstances in which individual works were produced, teachers may consult Norman Page's *Byron Chronology*. Two useful concordances to Byron are available: Ione Dodson Young's, keyed to the Houghton Mifflin Cambridge edition of the poems, which covers references in all the verse; and Charles Hagelman and Robert J. Barnes's *Concordance to Byron's Don Juan*, which benefits from reference to the 1957 first edition of Steffan and Pratt's *Variorum*.

Those interested in viewing original manuscripts and other Byronic artifacts should visit the Humanities Research Center at the University of Texas, Austin, home of the largest American collection of such materials. Smaller collections are housed at the Carl H. Pforzheimer Library in New York and at the University of Pennsylvania.

Fundamental Student Readings

For the most part, teachers find little room in their syllabi for secondary readings except in the most specialized courses at the undergraduate level. Nonetheless, there is wide agreement on what the indispensable sources are when materials beyond Byron's poems themselves are requested or warranted. Most cited are influential autobiographical and biographical documents, solid general introductions to Byron and the Romantic age, essay collections that contain classic readings of Byron's verse, and major (and, to undergraduates, accessible) studies of the poet's career.

One survey respondent summarizes the general sentiment about ancillary readings: "For God's sake, read Byron first; then, if there's time, Marchand." "Reading Byron first" means getting into the private prose writings, either in Marchand's selection from his definitive edition or in Peter Quennell's *Byron, a Self-Portrait: Letters and Diaries*. These documents provide fascinating if not altogether reliable commentary on the poems, as well as glimpses of Byron's facility at projecting images to his various correspondents. More fascinating and even less reliable are the "conversations," interviews, and recollections cited above.

"Marchand" is, of course, the standard three-volume biography, though undergraduate students will be more likely to read the abridged (and available in paperback) *Byron: A Portrait*, a revision as well as a condensation of the earlier text. No life engages students' interest in a Romantics course more readily or intensely than Byron's—so much so that it frequently makes nonbiographical discussion of the works extremely difficult—and Marchand's narrative is swift and richly detailed, even in its shorter version. Some teachers like to supplement Marchand's modern estimate with those of Byron's contemporaries—for instance, Hazlitt's portrait in *The Spirit of the Age* or Shelley's in *Julian and Maddalo*. Other, frequently more specialized biographical sources are too numerous to mention here; among them, teachers most frequently cite Quennell's *Byron: The Years of Fame* and *Byron in Italy*, for their readability, and Doris Langley Moore's *Late Lord Byron* and *Lord Byron: Accounts Rendered*, for their intriguing narratives of the poet's postmortem notoriety and the economic intricacies of his daily life. Clubbe (480–506 in the MLA *Review of Research*) provides a detailed listing of other biographical sources to which the inquisitive student may be led.

In the category of critical overview and background sources for Byron and his age, teachers consistently cite solid traditional texts and a few enthusiastically welcome new arrivals. Given the increased emphasis on historical and political contexts in Romantic (and other) studies, three of the most frequently praised recent books emphasize the importance of that material: Marilyn Gaull's *English Romanticism: The Human Context*—"a wonderful gift to us all"—Marilyn Butler's *Romantics, Rebels and Reactionaries*, and Malcolm Kelsall's *Byron's Politics*, especially its opening chapter. These volumes establish the day-to-day circumstances in which Byron and his counterparts functioned and composed and also provide an exciting social narrative that frequently illuminates textual analysis in many classrooms. Repeatedly mentioned as a companion to these volumes is J. R. Watson's *English Poetry of the Romantic Period, 1789–1830*; more general and comprehensive than the other works mentioned, Watson provides an overview of the background and major themes of Romantic poetry, as well as a solid if safe essay on Byron and a brief bibliography of well-selected major studies for further consultation.

Other frequently cited resources in the background-overview category vary somewhat in the scope of their coverage but all offer solid general surveys of Romantic currents essential to teaching Byron. The most longstanding of these include Samuel Chew's essay *The Nineteenth Century and After*; Ernest Bernbaum's *Guide through the Romantic Movement*; the Romantics section of David Daiches's *Critical History of English Literature*; and the general introduction and John Jump's essay on Byron in volume 5 of *The Pelican Guide to English Literature*, edited by Boris Ford. More detailed information is available in volume 10 of *The Oxford History of English Literature*, by Ian Jack and covering the years 1815–32. This survey is, to the advantage of Byron teachers, universally praised as superior to its companion volume on the early Romantics and can thus confidently be recommended to students. Complementary primary readings are available in Leonard Trawick's *Backgrounds of Romanticism* and Karl Kroeber's *Backgrounds to British Romantic Literature*, though both to a degree emphasize documents more relevant to the other Romantics than to Byron.

Useful in establishing the Romantic aesthetic context are Quennell's *Romantic England: Writing and Painting* and Kenneth Clark's *Romantic Rebellion*. Both of these offer art reproductions that many teachers employ in their classroom presentations; they are also a feature of a more specialized "studio book," Derek Parker's *Byron and His World*. A more recent similar tool is *William Wordsworth and the Age of English Romanticism* (J. Wordsworth et al.), the companion volume to the 1987–88 exhibit, displayed at the New York Public Library and Indiana University, among other venues, of the same name. Especially among teachers who viewed the exhibit, reference to it and the companion volume appear frequently in syllabi.

As mentioned previously, political and social background has become an essential component of most advanced courses that feature Byron, and many of the cited studies feature at least some discussion of that subject. I will offer fuller examination of more specialized sources of this nature later. However, survey respondents agree that three sources in particular— Edward J. Hobsbawm's *Age of Revolution: 1789–1848* and A. D. Harvey's companion studies *Britain in the Early Nineteenth Century* and *English Poetry in a Changing Society, 1780–1825*—are especially rich and clear, particularly the Harvey volumes, on the vital connection between poetry and politics.

Perhaps most feasible as secondary readings in undergraduate courses are several classic essays on Byron and Romanticism, some (though unfortunately not all) of which appear in still-available essay collections. I note here only those few studies that teachers repeatedly cite as useful student readings. (Other, more specialized essay collections are gathered below as more appropriate for the teacher's bookshelf.) All students should begin with the classic confrontation between A. O. Lovejoy ("On the Discrimination of Romanticisms") and Morse Peckham (his two "Toward a Theory of Romanticism" essays); Lovejoy's piece and Peckham's first essay are reprinted in *Romanticism: Points of View*, edited by Robert Gleckner and Gerald Enscoe, and elsewhere. Peckham's designation of Byron as a "negative Romantic," as well as the ideas presented in his subsequent collections such as *The Triumph of Romanticism*, has been the springboard for many current, sometimes contrary studies, especially those on Byron's Romantic irony (see below). Harold Bloom's "The Internalization of Quest Romance," reprinted in his collection *Romanticism and Consciousness*, is a key study in linking the

"Romantic" Byron, especially in *Childe Harold*, to a central feature, the subjective mental quest, in the works of his often-contrasted contemporaries. Bloom's volume also contains an edited-down reprint of Alvin B. Kernan's essay on *Don Juan* from his *Plot of Satire*, still mentioned as a seminal study in the contemporary revaluation of Byron's ottava rima masterpiece. M. H. Abrams's *English Romantic Poets: Modern Essays in Criticism* makes available the Lovejoy essay, two classic studies by Abrams and W. K. Wimsatt of Romantic imagery—perhaps a bit more relevant to the other Romantics than to Byron—and three studies, by T. S. Eliot, Ronald Bottrall, and E. J. Lovell, Jr., that are still respected in Byron criticism. Shiv Kumar's *British Romantic Poets: Recent Revaluations* reprints Peckham's first "Romanticism" essay but is weak and outdated in its section on Byron. The Twentieth Century Views volume on Byron (ed. West) contains a good cross section of early- and mid-century criticism, including Mario Praz's influential, hostile segment from his *Romantic Agony*, which solidified the critical link between the Byronic hero and satanism. The briefer *Twentieth Century Interpretations of* Don Juan (ed. Bostetter), again seriously dated by its 1969 publication, still includes a judicious selection of criticism, including Kernan's essay; however, the brief format of the volume necessitates the heavy condensation of articles in a way that dilutes its value as a resource on the poem.

Three additional essays appear frequently in responses to the project survey: L. J. Swingle's "On Reading Romantic Poetry," which again provides a program for not regarding Byron as an anomaly in his age; Abrams's "English Romanticism: The Spirit of the Age" (reprinted in Northrop Frye's collection *Romanticism Reconsidered*); and the essay on Byron in Frye's own *Fables of Identity*. Some teachers also report using excerpts from more recent criticism contained in the Salem Press series *Critical Survey of Poetry* (ed. Magill). While questionnaire respondents feel that no available collection truly represents the range of modern, and especially recent, Byron criticism, that void is beginning to be filled by the collections edited by Jump, Alan Bold, and Bernard Beatty and Vincent Newey, as well as by the special 1988 Byron issue of *Studies in Romanticism*, which I discuss more fully below.

I conclude this segment on student readings with a brief mention of what teachers and scholars regard as the most currently influential major studies of the poet's career. While only the most ambitious students will likely have the time to consult these, they are the books they should be led to if their interests extend to the current critical debate on Byron. M. K. Joseph's *Byron the Poet* is a fine starting point for students; a comprehensive career study of Byron, Joseph's work offers background information and textual analysis that has maintained its authority throughout the ebb and flow of critical currents that have succeeded its publication. Jerome McGann's *Fiery Dust* and Don Juan *in Context*, despite their author's recanting of some conclusions reached in the earlier study, remain central interpretations of the autobiographical and social dimensions of Byron's art. (They may, however, be a bit difficult for undergraduate students.) Peter Manning's fine psychological exegesis, *Byron and His Fictions*, carefully and eloquently traces the evolution of the poet's playfulness in *Don Juan* from its origins in the tense psychodrama of the earlier works. From a different angle, Frederick L. Beaty's *Byron the Satirist*, whose purview extends well beyond what its title indicates, reveals a continuity extending from *English Bards* to the conclusion of Byron's career and uncovers the persistently satirical essence that runs through the poet's entire oeuvre. Also mentioned among useful career studies are Gleckner's *Byron and the Ruins of Paradise*, with the caveat that it offers an unremittingly gloomy view of the poet that has been seriously questioned in more recent criticism; Peter Thorslev's *Byronic Hero: Types and Prototypes*, for the literary precedents of Byron's gift to the archetype; and Andrew Rutherford's *Byron: A Critical Study*, a good introduction, though one whose view of Byron is occasionally slanted by its pervasively Christian humanist perspective. Rounding out this category are Marchand's *Byron's Poetry: A Critical Introduction* and P. G. Trueblood's *Lord Byron*, generally considered one of the better Twayne studies on the Romantics, as well as three briefer and more general introductions: Francis M. Doherty's *Byron*, Jump's Routledge Authors Guide, and Beatty's *Byron: Don Juan and Other Poems: A Critical Study*.

I look finally at books containing useful sections on Byron that relate him to the aims and techniques of his contemporaries. Anne Mellor's *English Romantic Irony* provides a definitive corrective to Gleckner's pessimistic view, especially of *Don Juan*. E. E. Bostetter's chapter in *The Romantic Ventriloquists* offers a largely existential reading of Byron that holds him out as the only English Romantic to have successfully worked through the failed idealism and *Sehnsucht* of his contemporaries to emerge with a modern and sustaining vision. Further, Brian Wilkie's *Romantic Poets and Epic Tradition* offers a chapter on *Don Juan* as an "epic of negation," while Karl Kroeber's *Romantic Narrative Art* places Byron in the context of his fellow poets' experiments in narrative. Finally, the relevant sections of Bloom's *Visionary Company* hold their authority and maintain an image of Byron that does not, as many other studies do, exile him from the mainstream of Romanticism.

Specialized Readings for Teachers

I take my cue in this section from the introduction to and essays within *Beginning Byron's Third Century*, edited by Karl Kroeber, a special issue of *Studies in Romanticism*. An eclectic gathering, the essays, as Kroeber notes, respond to the "historical, not formalistic" emphasis in current criticism by "endeavor[ing] to place specific poems and passages within [a] dense . . . description of the extra-aesthetic context." Yet they also consistently illustrate "how recent romantic criticism builds upon . . . both the original biographical-historical traditions of American literary scholarship and the formalistic developments, beginning with the New Criticism, that replaced it" (475). A journey through these essays is indeed a gratifying glimpse into the synthesis of the traditional and critically chic, and it serves to show how Byron scholarship, inheriting a valuable legacy, has consistently exploited the richest of critical methodologies; likewise, these writers reflect that legacy with the New Critical tradition in their pursuit of the most current scholarly interests. The ensuing remarks reveal, I believe, that many facets of Byron criticism, especially the biographical and historical-social, have never completely disappeared from the tradition and that the most recent studies evolve from rather than reject that tradition. In outlining more specialized studies appropriate for the teacher of Byron, I progress from a thematic overview of works related to major segments of the critical tradition, as cited by survey respondents, through descriptions of a few key analyses of individual works not mentioned earlier, and on to a brief survey of recent essay collections, such as the *Studies in Romanticism* special issue, that hint at the future direction of Byron criticism. Only the quickest reference to works mentioned earlier in this account is included here, and only when teachers' mention of their importance is virtually unanimous.

Perhaps most fundamental and controversial are the studies related to Byron's place in Romanticism; opinions range from locating Byron as the central symbol of his age's consciousness to exiling him from it entirely. Most obviously, M. H. Abrams's monumental *Mirror and the Lamp* and *Natural Supernaturalism*—the latter of which contains the author's open admission that "Byron I omit altogether"—regard the poet as an "ironic counter-voice" to the vatic mythopoesis of his contemporaries. Byron is similarly, though for different reasons, almost totally absent from James Engell's encyclopedic analysis of the Romantic aesthetic, *The Creative Imagination: Enlightenment to Romanticism*. And many other studies, for all of which David Perkins's *Quest for Permanence* may speak here, echo Abrams's and Engell's stances through simple yet complete omission of Byron from their purview. The more recent trend toward identifying romantic irony as a significant contribution to the history of ideas has, however, done much to reacquaint Byron with his fellow poets and with the spirit of his age. Chief among these are Mellor's *English Romantic Irony*, which identifies the traditionally contrasted Byron and Keats as the central practitioners of its title's vision; Lilian Furst's *Fictions of Romantic Irony*, with an international perspective; David Simpson's *Irony and Authority in Romantic Poetry*; the relevant sections of D. C. Muecke's *Compass of Irony*; and Tilottama Rajan's *Dark Interpreter: The Discourse of Romanticism*, a probing examination of the linguistic features of Romantic irony effected through the methods of critical deconstruction (a theory whose origins may in fact extend back to the Germanic probings of *die romantische Ironie*). Frederick Garber's recent *Self, Text, and Romantic Irony: The Example of Byron* continues the merger of textual, phenomenological, and deconstructive methodologies that has moved Byron, for many, to the very center of the Romantic movement. A teacher may also consult John Francis Fetzer's terse and lucid account, "The Evolution of a Revolution: Romantic Irony." And I urge all to read Frank Jordan's segment "Natural Supernaturalism and Romantic Irony" in *The English Romantic Poets* for a clear summary of the critical controversy fundamental to one's sense of Byron's intellectual position in his age.

Implicit in many of these studies is an interest in the connection between Byron, his age, and literary modernism and postmodernism. While the "new historicism" (discussed below) emphasizes the period-specific constraints on Romantic expression, some studies concur with those examiners of Romantic irony who trace to it many features of twentieth-century literature and criticism. Other angles on this argument are offered in Hermione de Almeida's *Byron and Joyce through Homer:* Don Juan *and* Ulysses, which takes a largely formalistic approach; Bostetter's *Romantic Ventriloquists*, whose thesis assumes a direct line from Romanticism to existentialism; and, most broadly, Carlos Baker's *Echoing Green*, which defines a theory of literary "transference" that facilitates a lucid juxtaposition of Byron and his contemporaries with representative major voices among the modern poets.

In "The Study of Poetry," Matthew Arnold warns against fallaciously valuing an author through application of the "personal estimate" or "historical estimate" to his or her works, propounding instead that a "true classic" exhibits philosophical "truth and seriousness" and stylistic grace, "the high poetic stamp of diction and movement" that leads Arnold to articulate the eccentric "touchstone" theory, his ragged premonition of twentieth-century New Criticism and formalism. The central documents in Byron studies, judging from the consensus of survey respondents, emphasize both Arnold's blamed and praised features in their approaches to the poet's works. Thus the ensuing discussion, while necessarily oversimplifying the complex nature of lengthy critical arguments, exploits Arnold's definitions to group studies that cohere as related responses to the Byron canon.

As contributions—and eminently valuable ones, despite Arnold's caveat —to the "personal estimate" of Byron, I include studies that add in a broadly defined way to our understanding of the poet's life and character, especially as they illuminate elements of his verse. Preeminent here is, again, McGann's *Fiery Dust*, whose central thesis is Byron's increasing confidence in his own individuality as the valid source of his literary voice. This book of course includes many more insights, including textual ones, and never mind that McGann has subsequently rejected some of its conclusions: *Fiery Dust* resoundingly reestablished, in the aftermath of the New Criticism, the utter necessity of *not* divorcing Byron's works from his life, and it is therefore the progenitor of much of the best criticism since the 1970s. Among the more intriguing heirs of *Fiery Dust* is Bernard Blackstone's *Byron: A Survey*, an eclectic if often quirky study that wisely emphasizes the environments in which various works were produced, what Blackstone denotes "topocriticism," yet whose biographical essence is nicely pinpointed in a comment from one survey respondent: "[Blackstone's is a] useful overview focusing upon the psychology of/in Byron's work and its deliberate assaults upon conventionality." Manning's *Byron and His Fictions* is also ever acute in its psychological approach to the verse. Teachers continue to cite G. Wilson Knight's two books *Lord Byron: Christian Virtues* and *Byron and Shakespeare* as engaging if not always reliable character studies. Most recently, Louis Crompton's *Byron and Greek Love* combines biography, textual analysis, and social history into "the best-informed treatment of sexuality and homophobia in Byron, his milieu, and his age." Finally, Jerome Christensen's ongoing work on Byron's character, especially the poet's sense of his literary identity and career, promises to add a significant voice to the "personal estimate" of him. Christensen's "Byron's Career: The Speculative Stage" stands as an early chapter in what should be a comprehensive and new apprehension of its subject.

Also trustworthy among the older biographical and character studies are William Calvert's *Byron: Romantic Paradox*, though its bifurcated vision of the poet as half Enlightenment and half Romantic man has undergone extensive revision; John Drinkwater's *Pilgrim of Eternity*, a lucid account with a thesis similar to Calvert's; and the French studies by Robert Escarpit, *Lord Byron, un tempérament littéraire*, and Charles du Bos, *Byron et le besoin de la fatalité*, for, among many other insights, their continental view of the impact of Byron's personality. Special perspectives on Byron's life are offered, finally, in Malcolm Elwin's *Lord Byron's Wife*—and the sensationalistic *Lady Byron Vindicated*, by Harriet Beecher Stowe, to which Elwin is in a degree responding—as well as Samuel Smiles's *Publisher and His Friends*, which sketches in the details of Byron's literary circle through a focus on his publisher John Murray, and Charles Robinson's *Shelley and Byron: The Snake and Eagle Wreathed in Fight*, including much on the personal and literary friendship of those fellow poets.

Related to these analyses of Byron's life and personality are those that discuss him as a thinker, that attempt to establish his place within the history of ideas. In this area, Bertrand Russell's *History of Western Philosophy* gave the first serious if brief recognition to Byron as a significant thinker. More recent and comprehensive studies have seconded Russell's judgment, seeing Byron as a poet attuned to the intellectual currents of his age and those that preceded it and as a thinker prophetic of modern concepts such as existentialism and absurdism. Primary texts using this approach are Rolf Lessenich's *Lord Byron and the Nature of Man*; Michael Cooke's *Blind Man Traces the Circle* and *Acts of Inclusion*, the former devoted exclusively to Byron; Peter Thorslev's *Romantic Contraries: Freedom versus Destiny*, which highlights Byron's central role in defining the Romantic sensibility; relevant segments of Donald Reiman's recent *Intervals of Inspiration: The Skeptical Tradition and the Psychology of Romanticism*; Bostetter's *Romantic Ventriloquists* (again); and Frederick W. Shilstone's *Byron and the Myth of Tradition*, whose focus is the evolution of the poet's Romantic irony from the intellectual circumstances of his life and times.

More specialized studies are Ernest J. Lovell's *Byron: The Record of a Quest*, which gives a full if somewhat dated account of the poet's attitudes toward nature; relevant sections of Douglas Bush's *Mythology and the Romantic Tradition in English Poetry*; James D. Wilson's *Romantic Heroic Ideal*, which places the Byronic hero in an international intellectual context; and two books on the presence and interpretation of Christian ideas in the poet's writings: E. W. Marjarum's *Byron as Skeptic and Believer* and Travis Looper's compendium *Byron and the Bible*, which includes a good summary introduction. Teachers should also consult Clubbe and Lovell's *English Romanticism: The Grounds of Belief* for a careful, probing chapter on Byron's thought and its relation to that of his contemporaries.

The resurgence of historical criticism, like so many similar movements in recent decades, originated in large degree among students of the Romantic period, and Byron studies reflect that resurgence in materials appearing even as I write this essay. Nonetheless, the cyclical and dialectical nature of the critical agora emerges clearly in the fact that among the best and most frequently cited historical-political analyses are David Erdman's classic essays, published from the early 1940s on into the 1960s: "Lord Byron and the Genteel Reformers," "Lord Byron as Rinaldo," "Byron and Revolt in England," and "Byron and 'the New Force of the People.' " A similar focus informs Carl Woodring's Byron chapter in the slightly more recent *Politics in English Romantic Poetry*. Erdman's and Woodring's main successor in present criticism is, of course, McGann, whose *Don Juan in Context* hinted strongly at the insistence on historically sensitive reading of Byron and his contemporaries contained in the more openly polemical *Romantic Ideology*. McGann also perceptively combines methods of textual editing with sensitivity to context in his notes to the standard *Complete Poetical Works* and the Oxford Authors *Byron*, in the chapter on Byron in *The Beauty of In-*

flections: Literary Investigations in Historical Method and Theory, and in A Critique of Modern Textual Criticism—a connection also illuminated in Peter Manning's essay "Tales and Politics: The Corsair, Lara, and The White Doe of Rylstone" (in Stürzl and Hogg's Byron: Poetry and Politics, noted below). Recent major studies that answer McGann's call for contextually based readings are Kelsall's Byron's Politics, Kurt Heinzelman's "Byron's Poetry of Politics: The Economic Basis of the 'Poetical Character,' " and— more directly cast in the mold set by McGann—Daniel P. Watkins's Social Relations in Byron's Eastern Tales, as well as Watkins's series of proto-Marxist essays focused mainly on the late plays: "Violence, Class Consciousness, and Ideology in Byron's History Plays," "Politics and Religion in Byron's Heaven and Earth," "The Ideological Dimensions of Byron's The Deformed Transformed," and "Byron and the Poetics of Revolution." While these various studies approach the political and social context of Byron's canon piecemeal, together they add up to a reasonably comprehensive program to guide teachers wishing to integrate the new historicism into their pedagogy. On a related note: survey respondents counsel those seeking more sophisticated historical background than that offered in books chronicled earlier in this essay to go to Raymond Williams's Country and the City and Culture and Society, 1780–1950, Donald A. Low's That Sunny Dome: A Portrait of Regency England, Roger Sales's English Literature in History, 1780–1830: Pastoral and Politics, and Carolly Erickson's Our Tempestuous Day.

The branch of political-social criticism focused on feminist concerns has not yet produced a significant number of responses to Byron and his canon, a gap that I hope is at least partially filled by the relevant essays in the "Approaches" section of this volume. Susan Wolfson's " 'Their She Condition': Cross-Dressing and the Politics of Gender in Don Juan" and Joanna Rapf's "Byronic Heroine: Incest and the Creative Process" provide the sort of specific program for this approach that Watkins's studies of the tales and plays, which incidentally touch on women's issues, do for the broader social perspective. Byron is also reasonably well represented in Anne Mellor's collection Romanticism and Feminism, implicitly in the general theoretical essays and explicitly in Sonia Hofkosh's "Women and the Romantic Author: The Example of Byron." A teacher might also look to the occasional commentary on Byron in Nathaniel Brown's Sexuality and Feminism in Shelley, something of a "sexual politics" counterpart to Robinson's Shelley and Byron in places, and, again, for a related but different view, to Crompton's Byron and Greek Love. Feminist studies of Byron should begin to appear with more frequency, and teachers would do well to follow the noted bibliographies and book reviews to keep current on this vital but fledgling branch of his critical tradition.

As Brian Wilkie observes in his essay in the "Approaches" section of this volume, close textual analysis, especially along the lines dictated by the New Criticism, has never been a dominant methodology in Byron studies, though the general denigration of the poet's texts by readers guided by that methodology has been seriously questioned by McGann's work and by other students of Byron's style in individual poems. Nonetheless, the relative dearth of close textual analysis in the history of Byron criticism requires that one look carefully to identify readings cast primarily in that critical mold. Preeminent among older works are W. Paul Elledge's *Byron and the Dynamics of Metaphor*, an imagery study along the lines of R. H. Fogle's work on Keats and Shelley, and William H. Marshall's *Structure of Byron's Major Poems*, whose selective analyses of several works are still common referents in studies touching on the verses' architectonics. Many sections of Joseph's *Byron the Poet* qualify as close readings of the poems, especially the lengthy treatment of *Don Juan*. For analysis of the structural and stylistic nuances of other individual works, the teacher can go to two articles that focus on Byron's most seemingly symmetrical poem, *Childe Harold* 3: John A. Hodgson's "Structures of *Childe Harold* III" and Sheila Emerson's "Byron's 'one word': The Language of Self-Expression in *Childe Harold* III." Also shedding light on the specifically linguistic features of Byron's verse are Peter Manning's superb "*Don Juan* and Byron's Imperceptiveness to the English Word," disputing T. S. Eliot's charge that Byron was grossly careless in his use of language, and L. E. Marshall's " 'Words Are Things': Byron and the Prophetic Efficacy of Language." The case for Byron's skill as a lyric poet is argued well in Michael Cooke's "Byron and the Romantic Lyric," the opening chapter of *The Blind Man Traces the Circle*—a text that, like Joseph's, is interspersed with linguistic and structural analysis—as well as in recent criticism of the collection *Hebrew Melodies*: the introductory materials in Ashton's and Burwick and Douglass's editions of those poems and articles by Shilstone ("The Lyric Collection as Genre") and Heinzelman ("Politics, Memory, and the Lyric"). Another relevant study is George Ridenour's *Style of Don Juan*. Close readings, though primarily not guided by the New Critical ideology, are scattered throughout the major studies discussed above, but the summary here should provide hints on where to go to rescue Byron from his older reputation as a fascinating soul with a sloppy sense of poetic craftsmanship.

I turn now, briefly, to frequently cited interpretations of individual works, as an aid to teachers seeking authoritative commentary beyond that in the major studies and critical categories described above. I refer to sources already mentioned only where questionnaire respondents noted their clear usefulness in undergraduate pedagogy.

A good starting point for teachers of *Childe Harold's Pilgrimage*, in whole or part, is Francis Berry's "Poet of *Childe Harold*," cited by John Clubbe in the MLA *Review of Research* as indicative of the "critical turnabout" in regarding the Spenserian stanzas and one of the strongest appreciations of the force and currency of the Romantic Byron. Highly perceptive and useful to anyone teaching the first part of Byron's poem is Bernard A. Hirsch's "Erosion of the Narrator's World View in *Childe Harold's Pilgrimage*, I–II," a stanza-by-stanza analysis of how the poem's confident, reactionary narrator succumbs to the painful ironies and ambiguities of his journey. Also, McGann's chapters on *Childe Harold* in *Fiery Dust* are among the best parts of that important study, while Woodring offers a lucid program for discussing the vision of the poem, one he sees as ultimately dominated by reason, in "Nature, Art, Reason, and Imagination in *Childe Harold*." Finally, the importance of the poet's companions and itinerary to the development of the early sections of that narrative is clearly illustrated in William Borst's *Lord Byron's First Pilgrimage* and Gordon K. Thomas's *Lord Byron's Iberian Pilgrimage*, both of which establish clearly for students the significance of Byron's reaction, here and in the rest of the canon, to "that which is immediate" (*Childe Harold* 3). (One should consult, of course, the extensive discussions of *Childe Harold* contained in the major studies cited throughout this essay.)

Since responses to the lyrics are chronicled in the section above on close readings—though I might add to the recommended sources L. C. Martin's Byron Foundation Lecture on that segment of the poet's works—I turn now to the Oriental tales that Byron composed primarily during his Years of Fame, from 1813 to 1816, and that were, until recently, regarded as sensationalistic and exotic outlets for the histrionics of the Byronic hero. Watkins's *Social Relations in Byron's Eastern Tales*, again, gives a solid program for viewing the narratives through the lens of the new historicism. Teachers may also consult Robert Hume's "*Island* and the Evolution of Byron's 'Tales' " for a general survey and, for a more limited and much too irascible monograph, Daniel P. Deneau's *Byron's Narrative Poems of 1813*. The first of the works analyzed by Deneau, *The Giaour*, has, unlike most of the tales, been a frequent subject of serious criticism in recent years. Its disjointed and fragmentary structure—"foolish fragments," in the poet's own estimate—has evoked many responses, from chapters in the major studies (especially, again, *Fiery Dust* and Gleckner's *Byron and the Ruins of Paradise*) to a number of articles, including Michael G. Sundell's "Development of *The Giaour*," William Marshall's "Accretive Structure of Byron's *The Giaour*," Shilstone's "Byron's *The Giaour*: Narrative Tradition and Romantic Cognitive Theory," and Marilyn Butler's "Orientalism of Byron's *Giaour*." Since Deneau's comments on this poem sharply contradict the views implicit in these essays that rank *The Giaour* a serious structural and, perhaps, philosophical experiment, that work and its critics provide a source for lively classroom debate. (For references to some further interpretations of *The Giaour*, consult Scott Simpkins's account in his essay on teaching the poem in the "Approaches" section.)

Manfred and its companions among the "exile" poems of 1816, especially *Childe Harold* 3 and *The Prisoner of Chillon*, have a rich critical tradition and are, next to *Don Juan*, among the most "eminently teachable" of Byron's works, in most estimates. Fine general overviews of this self-contained period in Byron's career, especially of the relationships between the public and private writings Byron produced during it, are Clubbe's " 'New Prometheus of New Men': Byron's 1816 Poems and *Manfred*"; Ridenour's "Byron in 1816: Four Poems from Diodati"; Ward Pafford's "Byron and the Mind of Man"; and relevant sections of Robinson's *Shelley and Byron*, whose focus dictates strong emphasis on the poets' summer together in Switzerland. Readings of *Manfred* alone are probing and legion. Among the best are Bertrand Evans's "Manfred's Remorse and Dramatic Tradition," which alerts us to the literary forebears of the most extreme of Byronic heroes, as well as the relevant sections of Bostetter's *Romantic Ventriloquists* (a convincing existential reading of the play) and, most recently, of Alan Richardson's *Mental Theater*, in which *Manfred* is, not surprisingly, a central document in defining the type of drama Richardson identifies and explores. Finally, no teacher should fail to consult Stuart M. Sperry's fine "Byron and the Meaning of *Manfred*," an exegesis that expands on Bostetter's view of the poem as catharsis, its writer's final confrontation with and banishment of the Byronic hero and all it represents to his mind and canon.

Teachers of the satires now have Beaty's work to guide them; the study supersedes while still acknowledging the previous work on those poems. The long-outdated *Lord Byron as a Satirist in Verse*, by Claude Moore Fuess, still contains useful material on the style and literary antecedents of the poet's invective voice. Three articles are helpful in preparing to teach the satires: Gleckner's "From Selfish Spleen to Equanimity: Byron's Satires," which traces the evolution of the poems from *English Bards* to *Don Juan*; Stuart Peterfreund's "Politics of 'Neutral Space' in Byron's *Vision of Judgement*"; and Truman Guy Steffan's "Devil a Bit of Our *Beppo*," in which the painstaking revisions behind the seeming casualness of Byron's ottava rima style provide the focus.

Survey respondents indicate a "regrettable tendency" to exclude Byron's late historical and religious dramas from their undergraduate syllabi, except in the most specialized courses, although *Cain* is occasionally worked into the already crowded agenda of the upper-level Romantics survey. Another reason for the reluctance to represent this facet of Byron's creativity, one he himself prized highly, may well be that no widely acknowledged, comprehensive study of those plays has yet appeared. Samuel Chew's *Dramas of Lord Byron* contains a generally sane account of the plays and their literary forebears, but it never attempts to evaluate the works in the context of Byron's entire literary achievement. Perhaps the best complements to Chew's book are two studies by John W. Ehrstine: "The Drama and Romantic Theory: The Cloudy Symbols of High Romance" and the monograph *The Metaphysics of Byron: A Reading of the Plays*. I remind those who do include *Cain* about the rich editorial materials included in Steffan's annotated edition. Further, those seeking a glimpse at the way current critical methodologies approach the plays should go to the relevant articles by Daniel Watkins cited earlier; the Byron chapter in John P. Farrell's *Revolution as Tragedy*; Thomas Ashton's "*Marino Faliero*: Byron's 'Poetry of Politics' ";and Jerome Christensen's "*Marino Faliero* and the Fault of Byron's Satire," which also relates that play to the broader arena of Byron's other works. Finally, a large number of monographs of varying quality on the plays appear in the Salzburg English Studies series; Clubbe's comments on these in the MLA *Review of Research* are a guide to their usefulness.

Don Juan has no close competitor as the most frequently included Byron work in courses at every level, and criticism focusing exclusively on that "epic" is, logically, voluminous. There is room here only to enumerate the most enthusiastically cited and pedagogically sound scholarship on that poem. All the major studies described earlier in this segment confront *Don Juan*, though Manning's *Byron and His Fictions* and Joseph's *Byron the Poet* devote the most attention to it, with laudable results. McGann has supplemented *Fiery Dust* with an entire volume, Don Juan *in Context*, which began the critical revaluation of the poem in the light of textual and historical considerations. Among other studies, teachers invariably point to Kernan's "Perspective of Satire," noted earlier, as a brilliant approach to the work's sprawling nature. Useful, too, in discussing the poem's vital relation to the epic tradition are Wilkie's "Byron and the Epic of Negation" and Reiman's probing response to McGann's *Don Juan* work, "*Don Juan* in Epic Context," part of an important forum of responses to McGann in *Studies in Romanticism*. As with *Cain*, teachers of *Don Juan* have the editorial materials in the *Variorum* to work with. Other highly reliable studies include Paul G. Trueblood's *Flowering of Byron's Genius*; Elizabeth Boyd's *Byron's* Don Juan, which includes an excellent survey of the poet's reading; Ridenour's *Style of* Don Juan, perhaps the beginning of contemporary criticism of the poem; Peter Vassallo's *Byron: The Italian Literary Influence*, a work that revises our sense of the literary origins of much of the tone and substance of the "epic"; and de Almeida's *Byron and Joyce through Homer*, an eloquent study that emphasizes the poem's modernity by juxtaposing it with *Ulysses*.

Teachers might also consult Manning's essay on the language of *Don Juan*, cited earlier, and Cecil Lang's fine "Narcissus Jilted: Byron, *Don Juan*, and the Biographical Imperative." In the mid-1980s Bernard Beatty issued his comprehensive study *Byron's* Don Juan, especially helpful in understanding the poem's articulation of the absurd. Finally, teachers may go to Bostetter's *Twentieth Century Interpretations* compilation, though, again, its abridgment of essays injures their usefulness.

I conclude this segment on specialized readings by recommending that teachers seeking a sense of the changing currents in Byron criticism consult the various collections of essays published on his verse, especially the most recent of them. There exist three general and widely available compilations of frequently cited criticism: for older essays, Paul West's *Byron*, in the Twentieth Century Views series; for newer ones, Harold Bloom's volumes in the Chelsea House *Modern Critical Views* and *Modern Critical Interpretations* issuings, *George Gordon, Lord Byron* and *Lord Byron's* Don Juan. Similar collections, though of original rather than reprinted materials, are Beatty and Newey's *Byron and the Limits of Fiction*; Jump's *Byron: A Symposium*; Charles Robinson's *Lord Byron and His Contemporaries*, with a thematic consistency, indicated in its title, that is helpful in teaching personal and literary relations in a survey; and Alan Bold's *Byron: Wrath and Rhyme*. Another thematically consistent collection is Stürzl and Hogg's *Byron: Poetry and Politics*, the result of an International Byron Symposium that was one of the opening chapters in the current historical-political reassessment of the poet and his age. A similarly useful collection is Trueblood's *Byron's Political and Cultural Influence in Nineteenth-Century Europe: A Symposium*. Perhaps the surest gauge of the directions in which the critical winds of Byron scholarship are blowing and will continue to blow is the two special issues of *Studies in Romanticism* devoted to Byron in recent years, the Fall 1985 and Winter 1988 numbers, the latter already described here in detail. The effect that such trends as feminism and the new historicism will have on our perception of Byron is apparent in these issues; these and future such collections will keep the debate on Byron going and our classroom presentations of that debate lively and fresh.

Teaching Aids

The cult of Byronism has left an enormous legacy of extraliterary materials, which I can describe only marginally in this section. Respondents report a wide range of opinions on the usefulness of such materials. Many find little or no time in the crowded surveys to digress from discussion of the poetry. However, a significant number use personally assembled collections of slides, maps, and portraits, while others would like to integrate more of these materials into their syllabi. Because the questionnaires reflect little use of professionally prepared audiovisual programs, I will mention them only briefly.

For those who do find a spot for prepared audiovisual aids, a number of programs exist in various media. Most frequently cited is "The Fallacies of Hope" episode in Kenneth Clark's *Civilisation* series, which includes a discussion of Byron and is available as both a slide presentation and a videocassette. Films for the Humanities distributes a more specifically focused video, *The Younger Romantics*, as well as a sound filmstrip, *Byron, Shelley, and Keats*, while NET offers a brief film entitled *The Portrait of George Gordon, Lord Byron*. Teachers wishing to introduce an artistic and musical dimension to their classrooms might consider Clark's *Romantic Rebellion* series (and accompanying book) or the sound filmstrip *Romanticism in Art and Music*. General overviews of the Romantic era that mention Byron in varying degrees include *English Romantic Poetry and Painting: A Series*; *The Romantic Age in English Literature*; *The Romantic Period*; *Romantic Poetry*; *The Romantic Age*; and *The Romantic Era*. A lengthy series, *The Romantic Spirit* (Andrews and Templeman), originally produced in France, was developed in England by Landseer Film and Television Productions in 1982. The episode "The Romantic Hero" focuses almost exclusively on Byron and Chateaubriand, and the entire series is occasionally broadcast in this country on the Arts and Entertainment cable network. Since the availability of many of the programs listed here is intermittent, I urge teachers to investigate the most current catalogs as they plan the audiovisual component of their courses.

Briefer and more specific programs include *Poems by George Gordon, Lord Byron*, "She Walks in Beauty," and *The Prisoner of Chillon* (two offerings). These works offer artistic and topographical illustrations much like those included in instructors' individual slide presentations and are perhaps most valuable as guides to assembling one's own complementary materials.

As mentioned above, those who employ audiovisual materials tend mostly to assemble—and recommend—individually produced ones. These fall into three categories: maps, paintings, and photographs related to Byron and his many habitations; art works based on or illustrating Byronic subjects and themes; and musical compositions bearing on or directly inspired by the poet's consuming presence in nineteenth-century culture and beyond. Since these materials are so numerous as to represent a major chapter in modern cultural history, I can list here only those most emphatically recommended by survey respondents.

Many teachers use maps of Byron's two major "pilgrimages" to emphasize the importance of travel and venue to his poetry; serviceable ones are printed in Borst's and Thomas's books on the first pilgrimage and in Page's *Byron Chronology*. More direct visual access to the poet's many environs is offered through slides and photographs, most commonly taken by instructors during tours of or residence in Europe, of key buildings and locales: Newstead Abbey, Byron's birthplace, the Alps, the Castle of Chillon, Venice, the Lido. The many contemporary portraits of Byron also prove fascinating to students, especially those intrigued by his reputation as "mad, bad, and dangerous to know"; most frequently utilized are the Westall portrait of 1813, Thomas Phillips's *Portrait of Byron in Albanian Costume*, and Sanders's rendering of the young poet disembarking in 1807. These and other portraits are often reproduced in the biographical studies discussed above. While, as John Clubbe notes in the MLA *Review of Research*, "no detailed iconography of Byron exists," his essay (587–88) lists several sources for portraits and provides hints on where to find frontispieces and other illustrations to the many editions of the poems. (McGann's edition of *The Complete Poetical Works* includes some of these illustrations—for instance, those to *The Giaour*—which help students understand how readers of Byron's day and after saw something quite different from the anthology formats in which we most often encounter his works today.) Works that convey Byron's impact and reputation are the cartoons and caricatures in George Cruikshank's illustrations to "George Clinton's" (Sir James Bacon's) *Memoirs* of Byron, especially the representation of the poet's "Fare Thee Well" to England, and in Max Beerbohm's "Lord Byron Shaking the Dusk of England from His Shoes," in his *Poet's Corner*. As images of a man whose personality frequently precluded serious consideration of his poetry, especially in his own century, these illustrations are perhaps more essential in portraying his reputation accurately than would be true of virtually any other English poet.

Nicholas Warner's essay in the "Approaches" section of this volume provides an excellent program for discussing Byron in relation to artists who were of kindred spirit or were inspired by his life and works. Most often cited as "atmospheric" complements to Byron's poems are the paintings of J. M. W. Turner and Caspar David Friedrich, especially when they are contrasted with the works of Constable and Gainsborough and their literary counterpart Wordsworth. Many of the relevant materials are reproduced in the catalog book *William Wordsworth and the Age of English Romanticism,* noted above—a valuable compilation of visual resources for teaching all the poets of Byron's era. Preeminent among artists inspired by Byron is Delacroix, who devoted numerous sketches and full canvases to subjects in the poems, including *The Execution of Marino Faliero, The Bride of Abydos, The Shipwreck of Don Juan,* and, most elaborate, The *Death of Sardanapalus.* Excellent plates and a discussion of Delacroix's Byronism appear in Frank Anderson Trapp's *Attainment of Delacroix;* the development of the *Sardanapalus* is painstakingly chronicled in Jack Spector's *Delacroix:* The Death of Sardanapalus. (Teachers might also consider using the excellent BBC videocassette *Delacroix: The Restless Eye.*) In connection with Delacroix, one might introduce his friend Géricault's *Raft of the Medusa,* as a counterpart to *The Shipwreck of Don Juan* and the corresponding segment of Byron's ottava rima poem, which the *Medusa* scandal may partially have inspired. (The entire sequence of shipwreck materials, as Nicholas Warner notes, provides a marvelous interdisciplinary opportunity when teaching *Don Juan;* those interested in pursuing it might consult "Shipwreck," a *New Yorker* essay by Julian Barnes, and "A Grandfather, a Raft, a Tradition: The Shipwreck Scene in Byron's *Don Juan*" by Shilstone, for details on the *Medusa* affair and its political and artistic aftermath.) Finally, teachers wishing to introduce an English artist inspired by Byron might look to the Pre-Raphaelites, especially Ford Madox Brown, whose many relevant canvases include *Byron's Dream* and *Manfred on the Jungfrau.* The latter, in fact, serves as the cover illustration for the 1988 Byron special issue of *Studies in Romanticism,* which also includes a fine essay by Martin Meisel on the relationship among Byron, Delacroix, and Brown.

Musical renderings of things Byronic are perhaps even more numerous than painterly ones. Clubbe counts "over forty operas . . . based on works by Byron" in his *Review of Research* essay (591); perhaps the best and most pedagogically useful of these are Verdi's *Il Corsaro* and *I Due Foscari* and Virgil Thomson's biographical *Lord Byron.* The musical counterpart to Delacroix in the Byron tradition is, however, assuredly Berlioz, whose *Harold in Italy* is the musical work most consistently mentioned on survey questionnaires. Berlioz also composed a number of overtures on Byronic subjects that can serve as lively introductions to discussion of their inspirations. The composer's fascination with Byron is one of many subjects brilliantly discussed in Jacques Barzun's *Berlioz and the Romantic Century,* whose general chapters on the Romantic spirit are among the best sources of information for anyone studying or teaching Byron and his age. In addition to Berlioz, survey respondents report playing, in whole or part, Tchaikovsky's *Manfred* tone poem, Liszt's *Mazeppa,* and Schumann's *Manfred* overture, and, for different reasons, Mozart's *Don Giovanni* (to compare versions of the Juan legend) and Gilbert and Sullivan's *Pirates of Penzance*, "which is pure Byron."

In the "Approaches" section, Brian Wilkie illustrates the importance of "hearing" Byron's verse. There are, however, few extant recordings of the poems: *Treasury of Lord Byron*; some selections on Bramwell Fletcher's *English Romantic Poets* tape and the Caedmon anthology *English Romantic Poetry*; and Padraic Colum's reading of "She Walks in Beauty." Most valuable, if of a somewhat different nature, is the audiocassette *A Selection of Hebrew Melodies*, which sets the poems to their proper airs. The tape was issued by the University of Alabama Press in conjunction with Burwick and Douglass's edition of the collaboration between Byron and the composer Isaac Nathan. As Wilkie notes, however, reading aloud can and should be a more informal classroom experiment, one that takes both his and David Erdman's hints in the ensuing pages to stimulate a debate over proper inflection and the relation between sound and sense.

The rich innovations reflected in the questionnaire responses surely obviate the need to employ packaged lecture materials, though two solid programs, one by Christopher Salvesen and William Walsh, the other by Graham Martin and Mark Storey, are still available. I might observe here, though, that, with so many other resources available to them, there is little wonder that few teachers of Byron have time for such programs. Interest in Byron and his circle remains so widespread that artistic representations appealing to students appear frequently. In recent years the films *Lady Caroline Lamb*, directed by Robert Bolt, and Ken Russell's *Gothic* have provided conversation pieces, the first for its "egregious" attempt, in one opinion, to portray the complexities of Byron's character in a hostile script and the casting of Richard Chamberlain in the role of the poet; the latter for the opportunities it affords for a discussion of what truly transpired during the *Frankenstein* summer, as teachers and students uncover the absurdities in Russell's rendering. And the continuing allure of the Byron-Shelley friendship has stimulated two even more recent creative renderings, the British playwright Howard Brenton's *Bloody Poetry*, staged in both London and New York in the mid-1980s, and director Ivan Passer's film *Haunted Summer*, which, like Russell's, confines itself to the poets' time together in Switzerland in 1816. In fiction, too, Byron's life has provided inspiration—for instance, in Doris Langley Moore's *My Caravaggio Style*, Frederic Prokosh's *Missolonghi Manuscript*, and, most current, Paul West's *Lord Byron's Doctor*. As measures of continuing fascination with Romantic figures and their tempestuous lives, these and future efforts will surely continue to provide us with a source of amusement and discussion.

Finally, I urge all readers to join and follow closely the activities of the American and International Byron Societies, whose programs, at the annual

Modern Language Association conventions and various locales abroad, are clear indications—as in the published proceedings noted above—of new directions in criticism and, thus, pedagogy. To join the American Society, write Marsha M. Manns, Executive Director, The American Committee, 259 New Jersey Avenue, Collingswood, NJ 08108.

Part Two

APPROACHES

INTRODUCTION

The essays in this section offer a rich and comprehensive set of reactions to teaching individual issues and works in Byron. Reflecting the consensus of the survey on which approaches and poems deserve primary emphasis in the classroom—a consensus that accounts, for instance, for the discrete and proportionally lengthy segment on *Don Juan*—the contributors describe programs for utilizing all the approaches stressed by survey participants, from biographical to textual, in all conceivable classroom settings, from the junior-college level, where one does not have the leisure to describe biographical and social background or to analyze longer works, to that of the senior seminar, where issues such as intertextuality and feminism can be explored. The essayists employ different strategies, ranging from narratives of actual classroom experiences to advice on textual elements and critical approaches that are most fruitful in arousing students' interest in and response to Byron. They all, however, mine extensive practical experience in the joys of and problems in Byron pedagogy and, together, give readers insights crucial in dealing with any classroom situation. Thus, while the organization I employ in the volume is roughly generic—moving from essays that discuss teaching the whole Byron, or at least widely cross-canonical issues, to those focused on individual poems or modes, and on to ones that discuss *Don Juan*, the poet's acknowledged masterpiece—I urge readers to cross those demarcations freely by thinking, for example, of how the social-historical approach outlined in Daniel Watkins's essay on the Turkish tales might also be applied to *Don Juan* and other texts. Taken as a group, the contributors have given us a terse yet comprehensive account of the past successes and future plans that will keep Byron alive and exciting in the classroom.

G. K. Blank inaugurates the "Approaches" section by addressing perhaps the largest and thorniest problem in Byron pedagogy, the poet's relation to his contemporaries and his age. Proposing that, contrary to received opinion, Byron should be regarded as the central figure in English Romanticism, Blank offers a compelling argument for a course that could conceivably begin with and pivot on the study of Byron. Nicholas Warner follows with a valuable interdisciplinary program for teaching the whole of Byron in relation to his painterly counterparts in England and on the Continent. Focusing rather more specifically, the remainder of the essays in the opening section look at relevant and topical branches of Byron criticism and pedagogy. Mark Reynolds concentrates on the use of pre- and post-reading exercises to enliven the teaching of selected lyrics in the junior-college literature survey. In a pair of related essays, Louis Crompton and Joanna Rapf explore the biographical and aesthetic implications of not censoring the evidence of Byron's bisexuality. Next, Mark Kipperman uses Shelley's *Julian and Maddalo* as the centerpiece for a discussion of the way in which that poet's idealism and Byron's worldly cynicism can be profitably taught against the background of "the historical facts of a Europe at war for two decades," thereby combining textual, psychological, and historical material. The opening segment concludes with two essays that effectively counter the traditional but now discredited denigration of Byron's poetic craftsmanship: sensitivity to poetics, David Erdman tells us, provides the clearest indicator of why the voice in *Don Juan* seems so much less forced than elsewhere; and Brian Wilkie observes how exercises in sounding Byron's verse represent a close-reading alternative to the New Critical techniques that generally have disregarded his compositional achievement.

Part 2 contains essays on teaching those poems that, in addition to *Don Juan*, are staples in undergraduate British and Romantics surveys. I have determined what to emphasize on the basis of how frequently the works appear on teachers' syllabi and how much course time is devoted to their discussion. The segment commences with Frederick Beaty's rich account of his experiences teaching two different yet related satires, the early, Popean *English Bards* and the late *Vision of Judgment*, a masterwork of ironic equanimity. Scott Simpkins next explores how the fragmentary nature of *The Giaour*, the most intriguing and fully discussed of the Oriental tales, provides an opportunity for analyzing the importance of fragmentation to the Romantic consciousness, as well as a source of fruitful reader-response exercises in the classroom. Daniel Watkins expands the perspective on the Turkish tales by offering a new historical program for discussing them, with special emphasis on *Parisina*, one of the final products of Byron's Years of Fame. We turn next to *Childe Harold's Pilgrimage*, surely one of the works most crucial to understanding the poet, yet also one of the most difficult to teach. Bernard

Hirsch first proposes a comprehensive approach to all four cantos of the Spenserian stanzas, one that uses their journalistic essence to reveal the poem's value as a running commentary on Byron's vision and character. Gordon Thomas confines his discussion to the opening cantos, the source of the poet's immediate and intense rise to fame after their publication in 1812; their basis in Byron's own travels on the Iberian peninsula, Thomas notes, alerts us to a recurring feature of Byron's verse, its grounding in the details of topography and circumstance.

The second part continues with three essays on works produced during the period in Byron's life following his self-imposed "exile" from England in 1816 (the source, too, of *Childe Harold* 3, touched on earlier by Hirsch). First, Ronald Schroeder confronts "Darkness," possibly the most popular of Byron's shorter poems. By concentrating on the poem's portrayal of nature, Schroeder is able to relate his teaching of the work to that of other writers, preeminently Wordsworth, for whom nature was a central measure of the Romantic vision. The almost universal sense of the importance of *Manfred* as a vehicle for presenting Byron's Romantic side is reflected in the two contributions that follow: Stephen Behrendt discusses the philosophical approach to teaching the work against the background of eighteenth-century skepticism, and Alan Richardson emphasizes Byron's description of *Manfred* as a "dramatic poem" in order to teach it as one of the many Romantic exercises in formal experimentation. Finally, Wolf Hirst's "Contexts of Eden in *Don Juan* and the Mysteries" acts as a transition between parts 2 and 3, exploring as it does the role of biblical allusion in Byron's works, especially in the mysteries *Cain* and *Heaven and Earth* but also in *Don Juan*, the exclusive focus of the final section of this volume.

The immense popularity and importance of that ottava rima masterpiece have elicited contributions as varied as the poem's own kaleidoscopic style and tone. Katherine Kernberger offers first a means to develop a unified approach to the massive "fragment" that concentrates on its hero, its narrator, and its view of the world outside the poem. Susan Wolfson's essay next examines how the issue of cross-dressing gives students insight into Byron's complex and sensitive understanding of sexual politics. Byron's self-representation in *Don Juan* can be taught, Peter Manning believes, by contrasting the improvisational and open-ended self Byron develops in the poem with the closural, end-driven autobiography Wordsworth constructs in *The Prelude*. Following John Clubbe's timely narrative of the uncharacteristically urban—for his time—muse Byron clearly heeds in vast sections of *Don Juan*, Paul Elledge looks at the dazzling intertextuality of the poem as an opportunity to teach a wealth of Western culture in one place. The section concludes with Hermione de Almeida's convincing argument for presenting *Don Juan* as a pivotal point in literary history, one that alerts students to the poem's—and Romanticism's—place as a transitional watershed that both reminds us of the continued presence of classical culture and hints at the visions of our own century. In writing a piece whose pedagogical implications encompass the literature of thirty centuries, de Almeida places an exclamation point at the end of a series of essays that illustrate the ingenuity and value that pervade the best teaching of Byron and his world.

A note on editions: Unless otherwise noted, references to Byron's letters and journals throughout this book are to the twelve-volume standard edition of Leslie A. Marchand. Quotations of Byron's poetry are from Jerome McGann's multivolume Oxford edition.

BACKGROUNDS, PEDAGOGICAL TRENDS, AND CONTEXTS

Teaching Byron in a Romantic Context

G. K. Blank

Teaching Byron in a literary or historical context is one thing; teaching Byron in a Romantic context is, of course, another thing—if, that is, one feels obliged to follow the thoroughly beaten path forged by those legions who have attempted to define Romanticism. It is, for many literary and intellectual historians, the "R" word. But the term and the problem of definition nonetheless persist, along with an unwieldy cluster of attributes and issues that swing with the critical fashions of the day. Romanticism as it applies to English literature remains useful inasmuch as we know more or less who—Blake, Wordsworth, Coleridge, Keats, Shelley, Byron—and roughly when—say, from 1798 (with the publication of Wordsworth and Coleridge's *Lyrical Ballads*) to 1824 (the death of Byron). So teaching Byron in a Romantic context, as part of a course on Romanticism, might be most simply viewed not so much as a problem of generating a definition and then plugging it into the poetry, but as a job requiring that Byron and his poetry be considered in the context of his time and his contemporaries.

One mistake, then, is to picture Byron as playing the game from the sidelines—that is, as writing from the periphery of mainline Romanticism. This view is explicit in that infamous moment in Romantic criticism when

M. H. Abrams leaves Byron out of (as he terms it in the subtitle of *Natural Supernaturalism*) the "tradition and revolution in Romantic literature": "Byron I omit altogether; not because I think him a lesser poet than the others but because in his greatest work he speaks with an ironic counter-voice and deliberately opens a satirical perspective on the vatic stance of his Romantic contemporaries" (13). Surprisingly, in this statement Abrams disacknowledges Romanticism as a dialectical process. But if we see Romanticism as such as process, we find the spirit of the age not so much changing as wearing itself out; and it is Byron's promiscuous wit that best articulates Romanticism's fatigue. Byron's voice comes from within, not from the margins; and as such he should not be squeezed in, squeezed out, or viewed as the Romantic black sheep. Byron's kind of apocalyptic poetry comes to be represented not by explosion but by collapse, and what is especially remarkable about the Byronic voice and posturing that presents us with this version of a fin de siècle is that there is a lamentation and nostalgia crossing over and through the more visible and dismissive "ironic counter-voice."

While contextualizing Byron is not the only way to teach his work, it is, I believe, the best way, and it is a way by which Byron's work profits as something eminently teachable and relevant to the very idea of a course that organizes itself around such a problematical term. It is simply true that, relative to the work of the other Romantics, more of Byron's poetry, all the way from *English Bards and Scotch Reviewers* (1809) to *The Vision of Judgment* (1822), is explicitly about the contemporary scene. And while much of this poetic commentary may appear detached and rather disaffected, much like the digressionary voice that rises out of *Don Juan*, this disaffection is an evolving and highly styled pose that represents a strong connection and commitment to the age. Shelley—who, of the other canonized Romantic poets, is the only one who can be considered both colleague of and friend to Byron—wrote in the preface to his *Prometheus Unbound* (1818–19) that "[p]oets, not otherwise than philosophers, painters, sculptors and musicians, are in one sense the creators and in another the creations of their age. From this subjection the loftiest do not escape" (135)—including Byron, despite his escape to southern Europe and his sometimes imperious stance. In teaching Byron, what we need to examine is how Byron is both creator and creation of his age—that is, to ask: Where does he fit in? How does he treat the Romantic subject material?

As suggested, if in teaching Romanticism we have to work out a perspective on Byron's place in it, we must put Byron's poetry beside that of his great contemporaries. Often courses on Romanticism are taught chronologically, beginning with Wordsworth and Coleridge (or sometimes Blake), and working through to Keats, Shelley, and Byron. There is obvious logic to this teaching plan. First, we can examine the history of the times and then follow the development of the poetry of the age, and within that the development of the individual poet. There is also the psychology of completion: now that we've done poet A, let's go to poet B. Likewise there is the comforting idea of respectfully beginning with the oldest poet (that is, the poet born first) and finally reaching the youngest. This is the order that anthologies normally lay out for instructors. Often, too, there is the tendency to begin with who we feel are the important figures—the founding father(s) rationale. Thus for English Romanticism Wordsworth is frequently not only given top billing but also presented as opening act. Most teachers of Romanticism in fact seem to hold that Byron is the least important poet in a Romantic context.[1] This, I believe, and as the present volume is likely to make clear, is a mistake, a mistake that can be righted if, instead of following the pattern of teaching I have just described, teachers employ other strategies.

The best way, then, to demarginalize Byron is to teach Romanticism synchronically—that is, the course can be organized around themes or issues or characteristics rather than around individual poets one at a time and in chronological order. Students might not then, for example, have to wait seven or eight months to figure out (often on their own) how Byron and Wordsworth treat the same subject. Students thrive on connections and comparisons. They are not, in other words, necessarily New Critics at heart. Let me demonstrate how, by means of this alternative pedagogical strategy, Byron's poetry can be seen not just to hold its own in a Romantic context but to be central to that context.

Take the example of the solitary poet-hero. The Romantic prototype for this figure evolves out of the characteristics of Wordsworth's protagonists and speakers: the sensitive, idealistic, and introspective outcast with imaginative and visionary capabilities, often unknowingly and paradoxically seeking acceptance, escape, and redemption. One of Wordsworth's earliest and strongest portrayals of this figure comes in "Lines Left upon a Seat in a Yew-Tree" (1798):

> He was one who owned
> No common soul. In youth, by genius nursed,
> And big with lofty views, he to the world
> Went forth, pure in his heart, against the taint
> Of dissolute tongues, 'gainst jealousy, and hate,
> And scorn, against all enemies prepared,
> All but neglect: and so, his spirit damped
> At once, with rash disdain he turned away,
> And with the food of pride sustained his soul
> In solitude.—Stranger! these gloomy boughs
> Had charms for him; and here he loved to sit,

> His only visitants a straggling sheep,
> The stone-chat, or the glancing sand-piper;
> And on these barren rocks, with juniper,
> And heath, and thistle, thinly sprinkled o'er,
> Fixing his downward eye, he many an hour
> A morbid pleasure nourished, tracing here
> An emblem of his own unfruitful life. . . .
> . . . .
>   . . . and so, lost man!
> On visionary views would fancy feed,
> Till his eye streamed with tears.
>   (12–29, 40–42)[2]

This figure with his issues (attitude toward self, others, nature, death) in various guises and voices continues to problemize Wordsworth's poetry, and the poetry is at its best when it attempts to render a positive formulation of the figure and those issues. By the time of *The Excursion* (1814), which is easily the most important bad poem of the age and which Byron in particular loved to hate, Wordsworth is still working on this figure, but he appears no longer to know quite what to do with him; he can no longer come up with the "tranquil restoration," "Abundant recompense," or "healing thoughts" of "Tintern Abbey" (1798; 31, 87, 145); nor can he answer the "obstinate questionings" with the "philosophic mind" as he does in the "Intimations" ode (1807; 144, 189). Despite the youthful promise and "intense and glowing mind" "received / From nature," *The Excursion*'s Solitary, with his sensitivity, is doomed; a "self-indulging spleen" leads to a "wandering course / Of discontent" and finally to a place "shut out from all the world" (2.164–332). Shelley worked at this Wordsworthian figure in his first mature poem, *Alastor* (1816), in which a wild-eyed, lovely, and lonely Poet, nurtured "[b]y solemn vision, and bright silver dream" (67), turns away from his home, and in his wanderings tragically conflates nature's secrets with his own solipsistic tendencies.

Shelley's *Alastor* Poet also crosses back to the Harold of cantos 1 and 2 of Byron's *Childe Harold's Pilgrimage* (1812), in which sorrow, world-weariness, and secret hopelessness lead the young hero to similar self-destructive travels. Harold in turn sounds much like Wordsworth's yew-tree figure with his "morbid pleasure" and "mournful joys" (28, 39). Of course, by canto 3 (1816) Byron admits there is no narrative distance between himself and his pilgrim; and canto 3 shows obvious signs of Byron soaking up some of Wordsworth's spontaneous overflowings because of Shelley's proddings (Blank, *Wordsworth's Influence* 118–20). Here, then, is an example of the kind of intercontextual issue that brings these poets and poems together.

This sets us and Romanticism up for *Don Juan*, a poem that, after a damning dedication to the older, balding poets of the age (and specific mention of Wordsworth's confusing *Excursion*), begins with a demand for a hero for the age—"I want a hero"—but this is an age that, as the poem goes on, and on, and still on, shows some signs of exhausting itself and its inherited conventions. And exhaustion translated into literary form specifically shows itself in two ways: bad art or good satire. Byron's poem is obviously the latter. The young hero, handsome and pensive, at the beginning of the poem does the Romantic thing: he deserts his home for "the lonely wood," plunges "in solitude," wanders by brooks, thinks "unutterable" thoughts, pursues "self-communion with his own high soul," and lies down in "leafy nooks":

> There poets find materials for their books,
>   And every now and then we read them through,
> So that their plan and prosody are eligible,
>   Unless, like Wordsworth, they prove unintelligible.
>   (1.90)

Thus, early on in *Don Juan*, not only do we have some satirical pokes at Wordsworth's verses but we also find Byron using that very material of the status quo Romantic hero (and setting) both to establish and to undermine his own hero. Byron's poetry wants to have its cake and eat it too.

Don Juan begins as a poem indeed full of its age, and with a hero following the style of the age, but by the time the poem begins to wind up (or perhaps, more appropriately, wind down), some thirteen years later in Byron's and Romanticism's time, Byron's voice begins to take over from the story and the character of Juan; moreover, the voice of light digression becomes, at moments, heavy despair—and it is a voice that can be seen as articulating the end of an age. In an important passage, Byron wonders where the age has gone and how it has passed so quickly (11.76–80). As a result, the Romantic hero and his experience become increasingly marginalized by Byron's own lament. Byron is having trouble keeping his unchanged hero Romantic in a changed world. The poem shows signs in the final cantos of tiring of the Romantic hero and even of the satirical perspective.

If we were to go even further with this suggestion for teaching Romanticism, it could be proposed that the course be taught backward: begin with Byron, and if we examine what *Don Juan* does best, it becomes difficult to read the Romantic poets in quite the same way. *Don Juan* taken in context comes to represent not just a critique of the Romantic hero but a demystification of Romanticism itself. Byron's natural peers, Shelley and Keats, died more or less half way through the composition of *Don Juan*. Wordsworth and Coleridge had ceased to write poetry that engaged the times. Byron thus finds himself as the final witness of the age, and he acknowledges as much in the extended "I have seen . . ." passage (11.82–85). Here Byron says he has witnessed in seven quick years "more changes . . . / Than might suffice a moderate century through" (st. 82). He has seen empires fall, monarchs flounder, governments squander, the poor get poorer, the rich get richer; he's seen violence, insanity, and oppression; he's seen the poets and writers (including himself) go on and on. For Byron, the Romantic trope of mutability, which once could be formulated and accepted as something inspirational, finally becomes too much: "Change grows too changeable" (st. 82). His world is gone, he writes, and gone in a flash:

> 'Twas there—
> I look for it—'tis gone, a Globe of Glass!
> Cracked, shivered, vanished, scarcely gazed on, ere
> A silent change dissolves the glittering mass.
> Statesmen, chiefs, orators, queens, patriots, kings,
> And dandies, all are gone on the wind's wings.
>   (St. 76)

Yes, "[a]nd dandies" too, like himself—all gone with the wind.

Don Juan does go on for a few more cantos, and certainly Byron could have continued indefinitely with this figure. But as his narrative voice takes over, Byron's interest in Juan himself seems to lose some romance, so that more and more Byron has to force his poem back to the story of a hero that at one time he wanted so badly.

The poet-hero is but one dimension of Romanticism that can be used to teach Byron in context. Other dimensions, such as treatment of nature, use of history, political concerns, the creative imagination, narcissistic themes, confessional poetry, and the meaning of secular experience, I've found equally useful in resituating Byron, so that he is not the Romantic exception but the Romantic exemplar.

NOTES

[1]In a survey I carried out of American, Canadian, and British university teachers of Romanticism, of the "Big Six" Romantic poets Wordsworth was ranked first by 80% of the 84 respondents. Byron was considered least important, being ranked fifth by 34% of the respondents and sixth by 46%. See Blank (*New Shelley* 245–46) for the complete results of this survey.

[2]Wordsworth quotations are from Stephen Gill, ed., *William Wordsworth*.

Teaching Byron in Relation to the Visual Arts

Nicholas O. Warner

Despite his notorious disparagements of painting and sculpture—"those two most artificial of the arts" (Marchand, *Letters* 5: 218)—Byron produced a body of work remarkably rich in its possibilities for interart teaching. In my classes on Byron, three basic areas of interart study stand out: Byron's affinities in attitude, subject matter, or mood with the work of certain Romantic artists; his "iconic" poems—poems that refer to or describe specific works of visual art; and illustrations to his poetry. While the following discussion of these three areas draws mainly on my interdisciplinary course in Romantic literature and art, the procedures outlined could be adapted to other courses and approaches to Byron—as they are in my more conventional course in British Romanticism.

I begin the Byron segment of my teaching with a traditional introduction to Byron's style and themes, focusing on some shorter poems. I then lecture on Byron's general attitudes toward painting and sculpture. Citing both his negative and positive assessments of visual art forms, I point out that many of Byron's comments reveal sufficient artistic knowledge and sensitivity to validate Stephen Larrabee's assertion, "Clearly Lord Byron protested too much his ignorance of the arts" (150).

Following this introduction, we begin the actual interart discussions with cantos 3 and 4 of *Childe Harold's Pilgrimage*, a poem rich both in iconic references and in affinities with the work of Romantic artists. After a brief lecture on the history, structure, and basic themes of *Childe Harold*, I ask students to consider what parallels the poem reveals with the works of art discussed in a companion text required in my class—William Vaughan's *Romantic Art*. Students generally note how the themes of political rebellion, freedom, war, the figure of Napoleon, individualism, and nature appear in Byron and in works by such artists as David, Ingres, Gros, Goya, Géricault, Delacroix, Turner, Caspar David Friedrich, and John Martin.

Chief among the parallels we examine, however, is the shared concern with the sublime, especially the sublime of nature, in Romantic art and *Childe Harold*. Already familiar with this theme from our earlier discussions of Burke, Blake, and Wordsworth, my students examine the ways Byron's aptly termed notion of the "pleasing fear" (*Childe Harold* 4.184) of untamed nature, especially the sea, relates to visual renderings of the sublime. Among the most interesting to discuss are landscapes by Salvator Rosa and Joseph Vernet—both mentioned among the painters whose work adorned Norman Abbey in *Don Juan* (13.71). Also helpful are scenes by such artists as de Loutherbourg, Martin, James Ward, Thomas Cole, Géricault, Delacroix, and, above all, Turner, who "seem[ed] to have perceived a literary equivalent of his own vision" in *Childe Harold* (Wilton 124). Of particular interest to students are Turner's famous shipwreck scenes, such as *Snowstorm, Wreck of a Transport Ship*, and *Slavers Throwing Overboard the Dead and Dying*, which elicit intriguing comparisons to Byron's celebration of the ocean's power to destroy mere human beings, while it rolls on "boundless, endless, and sublime" (*Childe Harold* 4.183). Included in our discussion is a comparison between the natural sublime in Byron and Turner and the treatment of nature in Wordsworth, Gainsborough, and Constable, studied earlier in the course.

I should add here that Turner's relevance to *Childe Harold* is evident not only in his work in the sublime mode, or in his illustrations to the poem (discussed in my later class sessions devoted to illustration), but in his Italian scenes, especially those set in Venice. Because of this city's importance to Byron and Turner, I approach the famous passages on Venice in *Childe Harold* 4 by way of some background comments on Venice's history and cultural significance for many writers and artists. I show students sample Venetian scenes not only from Turner (such as *The Grand Canal, Venice* and *Bridge of Sighs, Ducal Palace and Custom House*) but from Canaletto and Guardi as well. I then challenge students to argue for or against the general critical view that Turner's Venetian scenes evince a special rapport with Byron's descriptions of the city. For a number of students, subject matter is the only similarity between Byron and Turner. These students assert that Turner's "bright," "cheerful" colors in the Venetian scenes are markedly different in emotional effect from Byron's more wistful descriptions; that Byron's own verse, despite his often generalized vocabulary, is closer to the sharp clarity of Canaletto and Guardi than to his British contemporary's "soft-focus" paintings; that Guardi's and Canaletto's Venice is, like Byron's Venice of yore, *grand*, while Turner's is merely "dreamy" or "airy." Spirited discussions often ensue, since at least a few students believe, as I do, in the striking affinity between Byron's and Turner's treatments of the city. These students argue that both Byron and Turner evoke a nostalgic sense of Venice's past glory and that Byron's magical, unearthly "sea Cybele" rising from the waters finds a nearly perfect visual complement in Turner's shimmering canvases, with their suggestions of evanescent light and water, rather than in the lovely but more static-looking pictures of Guardi and Canaletto. Until the end of the discussion, I tend to keep my own opinions in the background, so as not to intimidate students from expressing opposing views. If necessary, however, I push the discussion along, usually by referring students to study questions that I have given them earlier, questions focusing on the characteristics of Venice in *Childe Harold* and in art.

In its later sections, *Childe Harold* 4 provides a natural transition to the topic of Byron's iconic descriptions. Students enjoy seeing slides and reproductions of actual works described by Byron, including the horses of St. Mark, *Venus de Medici, Apollo Belvedere, Laocoon, The Dying Gaul*. In connection with these works, I briefly describe Byron's attitude toward classical antiquity and his preference for sculpture over painting. I then urge students to probe the extent to which Byron's poetry actually interprets (rather than merely describes) the works in question, to consider the reasons Byron admires these works and the symbolic values he finds in or projects onto them. An example of such discussion centers on Byron's description of the *Venus de Medici*. Using Hugh Honour and John Fleming's *Visual Arts: A History* as a guide, we consider what Byron's admiration of the *Venus* might owe to the "more fleshly and malleable" rendering of the body, compared with other statues (Honour and Fleming 139); in this regard, we examine whether the greater fleshiness of the Venus distances it from what Byron would later mock as the "nonsense of their stone ideal" in *Don Juan* (2.118). We also discuss the ways in which the "hint of self-conscious coquetry in the turn of the head and almost alluringly defensive gesture" (Honour and Fleming 139) relates to Byron's attitudes toward women. Throughout, we seek to ground our comments in concrete evidence from Byron's life and work. This kind of textual anchoring encourages students to deal with visual-verbal relations in specific, responsible ways, to increase their awareness of the complexities of such relations, and, above all, to immerse themselves consciously in Byron's poetry.

After *Childe Harold* we generally study *Manfred*, a work that, with its supernatural characters and dramatic Alpine settings, again evokes comparison with the sublime in art. Referring to works by Turner (especially his mountain scenes), Martin, and Cole (both of whom produced paintings based on *Manfred*), I assign an in-class exercise, in which students write on the relation of visual sublimity to the verbal sublimity of *Manfred*. This assignment motivates students to analyze Byron's language more attentively and helps them gain a fuller understanding of the sublime, both as a theme in Byron and as a general literary and art-historical concept.

At this point, I often turn from the high tragedy of *Manfred* to the satire of *Beppo*. Here, interart issues appear most significantly in the iconic passages comparing Venetian women to portraits by Titian and Giorgione (stanzas 11–15). Venetian paintings, including the one thought by Byron to be by Giorgione and now correctly identified not as that painter's *La Tempesta* but as the *Triple Portrait* by a follower of Titian (Whittingham 55), provide concrete reference points for our discussion.

Iconic references appear again in the next and, usually, final work we study—*Don Juan*. Because most of these occur in the later sections of the poem and because time constraints and pedagogical preference limit me to the first six or seven cantos, we focus our interart analysis on the richly sublime shipwreck scene in canto 2 and on the theme of Orientalism.

I begin my teaching of the shipwreck scene by reminding students of our earlier discussions of the sublime and analyzing Byron's masterful shift from witty narration to the horrific pathos of the shipwreck. After viewing a dozen slides of shipwreck scenes in art, including those mentioned earlier in this essay, students, in small groups, discuss study questions that I have given them at the previous class meeting. One representative question asks students to compare the shipwreck scene in canto 2 with shipwreck scenes in art, especially Delacroix's *Shipwreck of Don Juan*, Turner's *Slavers*, and Géricault's *Raft of the Medusa*, the latter two reproduced and described in Vaughan. Which of these artists comes closest to Byron's mood and use of details? How so? The purpose of such a question, of course, is not to rank or evaluate artists in terms of their supposed closeness to Byron but rather to stimulate students to think in broader cultural terms and to reflect more precisely on Byron's text. Most students find Delacroix's scene a powerful, strongly "Byronic" work; it is also an obvious choice for discussion of illustrations to Byron. On the other two paintings, however, opinion is more sharply divided. Some sense a profound rapport between Turner and Byron, primarily in the ways that Turner's swirling vortices of stormy water, with hardly discernible human figures thrown about, recall Byron's ocean as it overwhelms puny humanity, not only in *Don Juan* 2 but in the apostrophe to the sea in *Childe Harold* 4 as well. Others argue that closer to Byron is Géricault's *Medusa*, with its hauntingly precise delineation of dead, dying, and desperate men. Géricault, these students maintain, emphasizes more than Turner does the personal agony of individual shipwreck victims; in this way the *Medusa* beautifully complements Byron's detailed narrative of the terror and suffering endured by Juan and his fellow passengers.

I have consistently found that the kind of interart approach just described, especially when centered on a specific passage in Byron, such as the shipwreck scene, has a double value. For one thing, it sparks animated class discussion. Even more important, it motivates students to closer, more considered readings and rereadings of Byron's text.

My students and I go on to note various other evocations of the visual arts in *Don Juan*—the comparison of Juan and Haidée to an antique sculpture (2.194), the references to classical statues (4.61), the tribute to the power of painting (6.109). But the bulk of our interart discussions centers on the theme of Orientalism, in connection with which we occasionally read *The Giaour*.

Fusing Edward Said's theoretical perspectives on Orientalism with the work of such scholars as Frederick Garber ("Beckford"), I point out how Byron's general fascination with exoticism, violent catastrophes, and sensuality found a congenial home in Oriental subjects. We then compare and contrast Byron's Orientalism with that in the countless canvases of colorful Arabs and voluptuous odalisques by such painters as Ingres, Delacroix, Bonington, and Gérôme. This study links Byron with a pervasive phenomenon in European art and vividly demonstrates some of the ways that literary-artistic study can be integrated into the broader framework of cultural interpretation.

The topic of Byronic Orientalism, with its ties to the work of painters like Delacroix, reminds one that Byron was among the most frequently illustrated of all writers. And indeed, illustrations to Byron's work constitute one of the richest areas for interart study, often leading students to look more closely at a text, to consider nuances of tone and implication that they had hitherto ignored. But because any intensive study of illustrations, as opposed to their occasional classroom use, requires a commitment to detailed literary and artistic analyses, I treat illustration as a separate topic only in my most advanced classes. Instructors can find numerous instances of illustrations to Byron—most notably, in my opinion, those by Turner, Delacroix, and George Cruikshank—in the sources listed in Clubbe ("Lord Byron"); also helpful on various aspects of illustration are Altick; the two essays by Hamilton; Gatton; Bathurst; and Meisel.

Since class discussion of illustrations can lead all too easily to the enumeration of student likes and dislikes, it is important that students think along more focused lines. I hand out worksheets, accompanied by photocopies of relevant illustrations, with questions to be answered by students in preparation for the next class meeting: What kinds of scenes do Byron's illustrators tend to select? What are the strengths and weaknesses of individual illustrations? What aspects of the Byronic text do particular illustrators emphasize, suppress, or distort? Do any illustrations enrich our understanding of the style, structure, or meaning of Byron's work? If so, how? If not, why not? And finally, how does the clash or complementarity between text and illustration illuminate the relation between verbal and visual modes of art? This question, which accommodates some of the other interdisciplinary issues described here, provides a logical point for concluding our segment on Byron.

In teaching Byron in relation to the visual arts, I am aware of how much more could be done, for example, with the Oriental tales taken as a whole, with iconic references throughout Byron's work, with Byron's affinity with caricature in such poems as *The Vision of Judgment*. With an exceptionally engaged class I can branch out into some of these areas. Still, even when we are limited to the basic issues addressed above, interart analysis of Byron has been a rewarding enterprise, resulting in lively classes and scholarly student papers. The complexity of the interart approach is always challenging, sometimes daunting. But if handled with tact, good humor, and a healthy dose of Byronic skepticism, it can be an exciting, effective means of placing Byron in a broader cultural context and of enriching our own experience of his poetic art.

Using a Reader's Journal to Teach Byron's Poetry

Mark Reynolds

The two-year college students I teach in the second part of an English literature survey take the course primarily to satisfy a sophomore literature requirement. Neither English majors nor literature lovers, they present a challenging audience, especially when asked to read poetry. To engage them more fully, I have developed text-specific prereading, reading, and post-reading exercises that students write in a journal. This informal, nongraded writing requires students to interact closely with texts and helps them understand what they read.

With Byron, these assignments have proved quite effective. I use as many different writing activities for each Byron poem as time allows. For every author in the course, I ask a volunteer to give a brief biographical report to the class, and for no author is a knowledge of biography more important than for Byron; no life is more interesting than that of this "mad, bad, and dangerous to know" poet. From the biographical report I lead easily into the first Byron poem we cover, "Written after Swimming from Sestos to Abydos."

Before assigning the poem, I may ask students to describe in their journals some physical activity they remember trying after reading about it. Responses have included solving some mystery in Hardy Boys or Nancy Drew fashion, building a tree house or race car, or swinging on a vine across a ravine or creek. Students also describe feats they have attempted "for glory," ranging from dares undertaken to efforts made to impress a girl- or boyfriend.

For additional background, I frequently ask students to read the Hero and Leander myth and write a response in their notebooks; to find the Dardanelles on a map and comment on its location; or to skim an encyclopedia account of events associated with that historic geographical area and briefly summarize them. I might even ask class members to list in their notebooks the extremes to which lovers will go to demonstrate their affection. These activities can be the focus of discussion among the whole class or in small study groups.

Another helpful prereading device is to have students look up all terms in the poem that cause them trouble: "wont," "tempest," "loath," "Venus," "degenerate," "wretch," "genial," "ague." Students' understanding of "ague" is essential because the poem's tongue-in-cheek humor depends on this single word, and it's one few students know. I also play the class a tape of the song "What I Did for Love" before assigning the poem and tell students the Hero and Leander story, since the contemporary song, like the ancient myth, relates to the poem.

Normally, one or more of these activities facilitates discussion of "Written after Swimming." Sometimes, before an analysis of the poem, I ask students to relate in writing how the prereading activities illuminate it; their responses lead naturally to open discussion. If students have taken the first part of the English literature survey and have read Marlowe's "Hero and Leander," they can also compare and contrast the two poems.

For Byron's "When We Two Parted," students write a journal description of how two lovers might feel several years after separating. Or they reflect on the plot of the movie *The Way We Were*, if they are familiar with the film, concentrating on the final scene, in which Robert Redford and Barbra Streisand meet by chance in New York many years after the end of their marriage. Additionally, students may suggest a biographical reading based on what they know about Byron's life. Because many students think Byron is writing about Augusta Leigh, teachers should explain that the work refers to Lady Frances Webster and her subsequent liaison with the duke of Wellington. Once they know about Lady Frances's role in Byron's life, they can focus on the idea of the poet's distress over a former lover now with a new paramour.

"Darkness" offers many possibilities to interest students. Most important, it provides an excellent opportunity to educate them about poetry itself, especially that it frequently deals with subjects other than nature and love and that, regardless of when it was written, it often has contemporary relevance.

As preparation for discussing "Darkness," students compile a list of the ways the world might come to an end, and then describe one list entry in some detail. After they share their lists and descriptions in small groups, each group reports to the class on its discussion. Students respond to this prereading assignment: "If the sun went out tomorrow, describe in your journal what would happen. What would be the physical consequences and how would human beings react?" As students read the poem, they can examine how one writer's description of the end of the world jibes with their own. It is sometimes amazing how similar their accounts are to the poet's.

Because "Darkness" purports to represent a dream, students may record a vivid dream they themselves had of some natural disaster or, after reading the poem, describe how its atmosphere resembles that of a dream. This activity usually results in lively comments on the nature of dreams and reality and the veracity of Byron's descriptions.

Byron's many vivid images in "Darkness" offer opportunities for discussion as well. Students catalog them and comment on their effectiveness, or they graphically illustrate the poem in their journals by picking out the most striking images and drawing them. Attempting to reproduce images from the poem forces students to analyze them closely and discover elements they overlooked when they read the work: birds fluttering on the ground, vipers twining among the multitude, dogs assailing their masters, lone survivors on whose brows "[f]amine had written Fiend"—all offer rich potential for students to use their artistic imaginations.[1] If class members are asked to explain their drawings, they are likely to read and think about the poem more carefully, to be sure that they have included appropriate details. Those who do not wish to draw may cut pictures from magazines to illustrate the poem. Students doing so have unearthed photographs of famine victims from Africa, earthquake rubble from the Soviet Union, and forest fires from California. One class observed how easy it was to locate pictures of disasters typical of those Byron describes in "Darkness." Students found it remarkable that the dreamlike horrors in the poem resemble present-day reality so closely. A realization of the impact of catastrophe provides a basis for examining Byron's treatment of the effects of the sun's demise both on the natural world and on human beings.

One additional prereading activity that works well with "Darkness" is to ask students to write a journal response to Robert Frost's poem "Fire and Ice." I find it profitable to have students compare "Fire and Ice" and "Darkness." Because Frost's lyric suggests that hostility among human beings could lead to the world's end, the class can explore the consequences of hate, especially as expressed in Byron's powerfully short assessment: "[n]o love was left" (41). The possibility that not only fire, ice, darkness, and nuclear holocaust but also human greed and wanton destruction of natural resources might destroy the planet gives students a subject for deeper reflection.

Another fruitful prereading activity is to give students a copy of the description in Genesis of the world's beginning and ask them to provide an appropriate end to a universe so created. The class first offers responses before seeing the poem; I later ask students why, given the "Let there be light" beginning of Genesis, Byron's work is in one sense a suitably biblical account of the world's end.

Since Byron's "Darkness" suggests a natural end to the world, a good postreading activity is to have students discuss or write about possible cataclysms *not* created by events in nature. Here again, Frost's "Fire and Ice" is an effective aid. Students with scientific interests also analyze Byron's work to determine the accuracy of his account: "If the sun did go out, would things actually occur in the way Byron presents them? Is the poet accurate scientifically in every detail?"

Finally, "Darkness" offers several possibilities for students to imitate specific lines because of their stylistic effectiveness. I often ask class members to mimic, in their own words, Byron's wonderful summation: "The world was void, / The populous and the powerful was a lump / Seasonless, herbless, treeless, manless, lifeless— / A lump of death—a chaos of hard clay."

Students particularly like Byron's "So We'll Go No More A-Roving," especially the idea that even its carousing author had to rest sometimes. That point is a good one to ask students to respond to in their journals: they might, for instance, have had the experience of partying or working so hard to have a good time that they had to call a halt to the fun from sheer exhaustion. Another thought-provoking topic is Byron's insight that too much of a good thing becomes not such a good thing after all, a novel idea for many young people.

When asked to write about the imagery of "So We'll Go," a surprising number of students discover its sexual nature, a few wanting confirmation that they are right about the sword and sheath symbolism and assurance that even for poets other than Byron, sex is a common and appropriate topic. Here again, Byron broadens students' sense of the range of poetic expression.

Writing exercises such as these help focus readers' attention on specific elements in Byron's poems. They force students to read closely and think carefully about what they have read. In addition, they help students examine their own experiences in relation to those Byron presents in his lyrics. As a result, class members appreciate Byron's poetry more fully and enliven the required sophomore course with their personal responses.

NOTE

[1]Quotations of Byron's poetry in this essay are from *The Norton Anthology of English Literature* (gen. ed. Abrams).

Byron's Bisexuality: The Biographical Evidence and the Poems

Louis Crompton

Until recently a strong taboo has attended the theme of homosexuality in English scholarship. One result has been that teachers have overlooked, or failed to appreciate fully, the homosexual side of Byron's temperament and its reflection in his poetry. G. Wilson Knight speculated in *Lord Byron's Marriage* in 1957, but Knight's views on Byron were often so eccentric that readers failed to understand that on this particular topic he had come near the truth. Leslie Marchand's definitive biography appeared a few months later. It published the crucial documents Knight lacked. But constraints imposed by their owners forced Marchand to such circumspection that few students of Byron grasped their real import.

In *Byron and Greek Love: Homophobia in Nineteenth-Century England* I treat Byron's homosexuality explicitly and try to place it in the context of English social history. One hopes that this information will eventually find its way into introductions to Byron's poetry. Since it has not yet done so, the teacher who wishes to explore the subject will have to present the essential facts to his or her class. The material relates primarily to four stages of Byron's career: his life in Cambridge, his first journey to the East, the genesis of the Byronic hero, and his final days in Greece.

Looking back at his adolescence when he was thirty-three, Byron wrote in his journal, "My School friendships were with *me passions*" (Marchand, *Letters* 9: 44). Byron was referring to the romantic attachments he formed at Harrow. Thomas Moore, in his 1830 *Life*, treated these relationships gingerly, leading Byron's intimate friend John Cam Hobhouse to note in his copy of Moore's biography: "M. knows nothing, or will tell nothing of the principal cause & motive of all these boyish friend[ships]" (Crompton 81). Shortly after Lady Byron had separated from her husband, Caroline Lamb told her that Byron had confessed to her that "from his boyhood on he had been in the practice of unnatural crime" (82), but Lady Caroline's testimony is not always trustworthy. Whatever happened at Harrow, there can be no doubt that Byron at Cambridge fell in love, at seventeen, with a fifteen-year-old choir boy named John Edleston. Later he was to call this "a violent, though *pure*, love and passion"—"the romance of the most romantic period of my life" (*Letters* 8: 24). Byron's feelings for Edleston were probably so intense because he had hitherto felt unloved. Acutely conscious of his club-foot, Byron had been devastated by Mary Chaworth's rejection; Edleston's love gave him the reassurance he desperately needed. In "Pignus Amoris" ("The Pledge of Love") he recorded an emotional scene. Edleston, who had given Byron a cornelian heart, feared his inexpensive gift would be scorned.

He burst into tears, and so did Byron when he discovered the depth of Edleston's feeling for him: "And still I view in Memory's eye / That teardrop sparkle through my own." When Edleston died, in 1811, Byron wrote the "Thyrza" elegies to mourn him, carefully disguising his identity by using a female name and pronouns. The most revealing lines are in "To Thyrza," which Byron appended to the volume that contained the first two cantos of *Childe Harold's Pilgrimage*:

> Ours too the glance none saw beside;
>   The smile none else might understand;
> The whisper'd thought of hearts allied,
>   The pressure of the thrilling hand;
> The kiss so guiltless and refin'd
> The Love each warmer wish forbore;
> Those eyes proclaim'd so pure a mind,
>   Ev'n passion blush'd to plead for more. . . .
> The pledge we wore—I wear it still. . . .
>   (29–41)

The Thyrza poems aroused immense interest in Byron's day, and guesses as to "her" identity abounded.

For more than a century the truth was obfuscated. To illustrate how this was done, I give the class photocopies of a note, supplied to E. H. Coleridge's 1900 edition of *The Works of Lord Byron* (3: 30–31), presumably by Byron's grandson, Lord Lovelace. Evidence from Byron's letters well known to Lovelace left little doubt whom Byron was writing about in the elegies. But Lovelace deliberately misleads the reader: he declares Thyrza's identity to be undiscoverable but at the same time implies that "she" was a "young girl." Students usually find this an interesting example of the extent to which Byron scholars were willing to go to hide the evidence of his bisexuality.

Byron's love for Edleston, though imbued with strong erotic feeling, remained chaste. We now know from his letters, however, that he looked forward with some enthusiasm to homosexual relations during his first visit to Greece (*Letters* 1: 206–07) and that he had extensive experience when he arrived there (2: 23). These facts were not perceived until 1957, when Marchand and Gilbert Highet deciphered the Latin code Byron used in his letters to Hobhouse. His most important love affair in Greece was with the fifteen-year-old Nicolo Giraud, whom he made his heir on returning to England.

Fear and apprehension attended Byron's homosexual amours from the start. In 1805, the year he met Edleston, Byron wrote to Augusta Leigh of his new "melancholy" with mysterious hints that it arose from a cause he could not reveal (*Letters* 1: 87–88). In his "Detached Thoughts" of 1821,

Byron dropped more hints about a secret side of his personality: "People have wondered at the Melancholy which runs through my writings. . . . If I could explain at length the *real* causes which have contributed to increase this perhaps *natural* temperament of mine—this Melancholy which hath made me a bye-word—nobody would wonder—but this is impossible without doing much mischief" (*Letters* 9: 38). These comments occur close to references to his emotional "excesses" at Cambridge. They suggest that the mixture of pride, guilt, and alienation that entered into the psychological makeup of the Byronic hero had its roots, in some significant degree, in Byron's realization of his bisexuality.

To help the class understand the extraordinary abhorrence Byron's English contemporaries felt for homosexuals, I distribute copies of his lines on William Beckford, originally intended for inclusion in *Childe Harold* 1. Beckford, the author of *Vathek*, the richest man in England, highly talented as a writer, musician, and connoisseur, had been ostracized by English society and forced into exile. Byron's stanza suggests that he saw in him a kind of alter ego:

> Unhappy Vathek! in an evil hour
> Gainst Nature's voice seduced to deed accurst,
> Once Fortune's minion, now thou feel'st her Power!
> Wrath's vials on thy lofty head have burst.
> In wit, in genius, as in wealth the first,
> How wondrous bright thy blooming morn arose[!]
> But thou wert smitten with unhallowed thirst
> Of nameless crime, and thy sad day must close
> To scorn, and Solitude unsought—the worst of woes.
> (McGann 2: 18n)

Students may at this point raise the question why Byron should here speak of homosexuality in such condemnatory language—"evil hour," "deed accurst," "unhallowed thirst." They may argue that it opens Byron to a charge of hypocrisy. Here the teacher may point to an important consideration: the taboo against even mentioning homosexuality in Byron's day was so intense that it could be broached only if the writer used strongly condemnatory language.

In Europe homosexuals had been regularly burned at the stake in earlier centuries. In Byron's day executions had all but ceased on the Continent, but male homosexuals were still hanged in England, on the average of two a year. Other men were sentenced to the pillory, where large and vicious crowds pelted them, sometimes to death. Jeremy Bentham, the most famous law reformer of Byron's era, wrote hundreds of manuscript pages of protest, which he did not dare publish, commenting on the extreme violence of English prejudice. In one note he describes a judge who had just sentenced two men to the gallows: "Delight and exultation glistened in his countenance; his looks called for applause and congratulations at the hands of the surrounding audience" (Crompton 21). In this persecution, Bentham charged, cruelty and intolerance wore the mask of virtue. The dark colors in which Byron paints Harold, Manfred, and Lara surely owe something to his awareness of the scorn he would have faced if his bisexual nature had been known. In *Don Juan* 1, the sardonic mockery with which Byron points to the homoerotic elements in the poems of Sappho, Catullus, and Vergil, which formed part of every public school boy's education, owes its edge to his consciousness of the strength of English homophobia. The rumors Lady Caroline spread about Byron's homosexuality were the major cause of the ostracism that finally drove him, like Beckford, from England. (The accusations of incest, made at the same time, would by contemporary standards have been somewhat less serious.)

Byron's last three poems dramatize the emotional turmoil of his final days in Greece. "On This Day I Complete My Thirty-Sixth Year" turns up as a signature piece in many anthologies. (It is not, however, in the *Norton*.) I reproduce it and the two less well known poems "Last Words on Greece" and "Love and Death" for class discussion. "On This Day" appeared shortly after Byron's death. The companion pieces were not published until 1887. To "Love and Death" Hobhouse attached a note, purportedly by Byron, to the effect that the lines "were addressed to no one in particular, and were a mere poetical Scherzo" (Crompton 331). All three poems are, in fact, autobiographical. We now know that they were inspired by Byron's obsessive, unhappy, and unrequited love for a young Greek boy, Lukas Chalandrutsanos.

After the bitter cynicism of *Harold* and *Manfred* and the laughing cynicism of *Don Juan*, it is startling to see Byron now emerging as an idealist—indeed, as two kinds of idealist at war with each other. "On This Day" begins with Byron's lament that he has fallen in love with someone who does not love him. He is determined to put this love behind him:

> Tread those reviving passions down
> Unworthy Manhood;—unto thee
> Indifferent should the smile or frown
> Of Beauty be.   (Crompton 323)

Finally, Byron pledges himself to the Greek cause, even to seeking death on the battlefield. For sixty years, Byron's readers assumed these were his last lines and, of course, assumed he had fallen in love with some woman. But Byron's passion was for Lukas.

The two later poems bear witness to a dramatic reversal in his feeling. "On This Day" puts duty above love; in "Last Words on Greece" Byron's resolution has collapsed. He is still willing to die for Hellas, but he now declares that this honor means nothing to him—he has become the "fool of passion," in thrall to a "maddening fascination." In his last poem, "Love and Death," Byron addresses Lukas directly and enumerates the proofs of his devotion: he had been willing to risk his life for him if the Turks had attacked the ship that bore them to Missolonghi or if it had sunk and they had had to swim; he had nursed him through a dangerous fever; he thought first of him when an earthquake struck and later when a convulsive fit nearly killed him. Far from being a "Scherzo," or mere literary exercise, the poem is an exact record of episodes in Byron's final days, minutely documentable from his letters and journals. Though hardly distinguished as poetry, these stanzas are a poignant versified journal in which Byron poured out his heart, ending with a painful cry of despair:

> Thus much and more—and yet thou lov'st me not,
> And never wilt—Love dwells not in our will,
> Nor can I blame thee—though it be my lot
> To strongly—wrongly—vainly—love thee still.
> (Crompton 329)

Classical literature and history provide innumerable instances of selfless devotion of older lovers (*erastai*) to their beloved youth (*eromenoi*) in ancient Greece. "Love and Death" appeals, by implication, to this tradition of Greek and Latin heroic love, the love of Achilles for Patroclus in the *Iliad*, Aristogiton for Harmodius in Athenian history, and Nisus for Euryalus in the *Aeneid*. It gives dignity to a now no longer "unworthy" passion. In "Love and Death" sacrificial valor and homosexual love are united in one encompassing ideal, though Lukas's indifference robs it of the joy of mutuality.

Poetic Performance: Byron and the Concept of a Male Muse

Joanna E. Rapf

In school I was taught that Byron was the most accessible of the Romantic poets, and I still believe there is a certain truth to this. Undergraduates enjoy the color and excitement of the Oriental tales, just as readers did in Byron's day. *Manfred* is dramatically impressive, and students respond sympathetically to those figures known as the Byronic hero and heroine. Poems such as "Darkness" are hauntingly prophetic of our knowledge of nuclear winter (Rudolf). Byron seems modern, his cynicism in tune with a generation that experiences political corruption, violence, and the devastation wrought by warfare on the nightly news and that has seen that the holocaust is not fiction but reality:

> No Love was left;
> All earth was but one thought—and that was Death,
> Immediate and inglorious; and the pang
> Of famine fed upon all entrails—men
> Died, and their bones were tombless as their flesh. . . .
> (41–45)

But despite this apparent accessibility, there are so many inconsistencies to Byron, such topicality, referentiality, and diversity of style, that he can be extremely difficult to teach without one's becoming mired in biography, lapsing into simplifications about his fondness for the eighteenth century or his contradictory struggles to assert and to annihilate himself.

If there were only the Oriental tales and works such as *Manfred* and "Darkness," we probably would not be teaching Byron as one of the canonized Romantic poets. It is the longer works, *Childe Harold* and *Don Juan*, that undergraduates must finally encounter, along with the paradox that these so-called great poems come from a man who himself wrote, "I by no means rank poetry or poets high in the scale of intellect. . . . This may look like affectation, but it is my real opinion. . . . I prefer the talents of action —of war—or the Senate—or even of Science—to all the speculations of those mere dreamers of another existence . . . and spectators of this" (Marchand, *Letters* 3: 179). With the other canonized Romantics, we have theories of poetry, and these, often in hazy and muddled form, are what most students bring to a course in Romanticism. These theories are also what have alienated many of them, for in an age of computers, MTV, and Star Wars, it is hard to believe in any art form as "the first and last of all knowledge . . . immortal as the heart of man" (Wordsworth 738, from Preface), bringing "the whole soul of man into activity," revealing a "balance or reconciliation of opposite or discordant qualities" (Coleridge 524, from *Biographia Literaria* 14), or as "the very image of life expressed in its eternal truth," strengthening "that faculty which is the organ of the moral nature of man" (Shelley 485, 488, from *Defence of Poetry*). These statements may well seem the product of "dreamers of another existence," or certainly *from* another existence, far removed from the realities of the second half of the twentieth century. With Byron, however, students see a man who deprecated the very art he and his fellow poets practiced so well. On what basis, I ask, can we label him a great poet, alongside his friend Shelley, who believed that poetry could create "anew the universe after it has been annihilated in our minds" (*Defence* 505–06)?

To elicit an answer to this question, I first have students think about the concept of the muse, the traditional inspiration of poetry. And traditionally, they see *her* as a beautiful woman with whom the poet is in love. He yearns for union with this female, and his poetry is a product of their love. They read "Stanzas to Augusta" and see clearly that Byron's muse here seems to be his half-sister. To many, the poem seems self-indulgent. It is the product of a sentimental worldview inherited from the eighteenth century that sees the self as passive and vulnerable, the victim of social and even cosmic forces beyond human control. This fictive self is "baffled" (a favorite Byron word), lost in a world where change is suddenly the only certainty and existence seems to precede meaning. Adrift, deracinated, and threatened with chaos, the self as poet turns to a woman, the female source from which he came, for solace, inspiration, truth, and stability in an uncertain world.

I explain that, early in its history, the term *muse* lost its specific reference to the ancient goddesses and was regularly used metaphorically to refer to whatever a poet imagined as a source of creative power. Traditionally, she was a mysterious female Other in relation to the creative man, the *anima* that must come together with the *animus*. Students soon come to see that for Byron this feminine ideal was problematic, in part because of his real-life idealization of his half-sister, Augusta, and the "deadliest sin" of incest (*Manfred* 2.4.123) and in part, perhaps, because of his homosexual tendencies. Where for Shelley the creative process involved "a going out of our nature, and an identification of ourselves with the beautiful which exists in thought, action, or person not our own" (*Defence* 487), for Byron the "not our own" was an obstacle.

But rather than linger on the lurid and sensational by reading from his journals and letters—although I do some of this and urge students to do so on their own—I use the narrative discrepancies of *Childe Harold* as a dramatic representation of these conflicts. On the one hand, we see a side of the victimized hero who claims to have reached a sort of philosophic calm by reluctantly exiling himself from the "normal" society of men and women and finding solace in nature: "Art, Glory, Freedom fail, but Nature still is fair" (2.87). On the other, we see this hero solipsistically relishing his own misery and instead of losing himself in some kind of eternal harmony represented by nature, isolating himself in a dark world of existential solitude: "To view each loved one blotted from life's page, / And he alone on earth, as I am now" (2.98).

I use two passages to illustrate this conflict between nature as "fair," the ideal "Other," a refuge, solace, or inspiration, and nature as a tormented image of self. The first is from *Manfred*, act 1, scene 2, in which there is an obvious difference between the way the Chamois Hunter views the morning mist and the way Manfred views exactly the same scene:

C. HUN. The mists begin to rise from up the valley. . . .

. . . .

MAN. The mists boil up around the glaciers. . . .

(82, 85)

The second is the famous description of the ravaged castles on the banks of the Rhine in canto 3 of *Childe Harold*:

And there they stand, *as stands a lofty mind*,
Worn, but unstooping to the baser crowd,
All tenantless, save to the crannying wind,
Or holding dark communion with the cloud.

(St. 47; italics mine)

Students pick up the italicized simile immediately. The poet turns toward the external world, but he sees only himself. It is clear that in spite of his sentimental eighteenth-century heritage, nature for Byron is not "fair," is not a feminine ideal nor a Shelleyan "epipsyche," but his own flesh and blood.

The problematic attempt to establish an Other, either as inspiration or as fictitious persona, is obvious in the whole structure of *Childe Harold*. Students have no trouble juxtaposing the preface, in which the poet insists that Harold is a "fictitious character . . . the child of imagination," and the letter to John Cam Hobhouse that begins the fourth canto: "The fact is, that I had become weary of drawing a line which everyone seemed determined not to perceive. . . . [I]t was in vain that I asserted, and imagined that I had drawn, a distinction between the author and the pilgrim." Harold vanishes, not in a creative gasp of ecstasy, a Shelleyan "annihilation," but in the gradual assimilation of his personality into Byron's own: the victory of selfhood.

Who or what is Byron's muse? Is it possible that Byron came to see his muse not as the traditional female "Other" but as self and therefore as male?

Since one usually does not write poetry to oneself, what might be the poetic outcome of this conscious—or more likely unconscious—discovery? It becomes clear that the inherited "Romantic formulas" that most students bring to the course will not fit a poet whose muse is himself rather than a female embodiment of an ideal Other or nature.

So we come to *Don Juan*, the dazzling offspring of this poetic discovery, in which a strong sense of self keeps Byron's fictive character, unlike his earlier Childe Harold, from dissolving into nothingness. In canto 6 he escapes Gulbayez—"self-love in man, too, beats all female art" (st. 19)—and in canto 9 he refuses Catherine as he falls "into that no less imperious passion, / Self-love" (st. 68). While Shelley's apocalyptic vision involves heterosexual activity, the creative union of male and female culminating in prophetic birth or rebirth, Byron's tends to be an introverted transaction with a male double. The biology is clear. Homosexual or autoerotic interplay cannot result in birth, the child who compels its parents to look toward the future, the Shelleyan idea of poetry as prophecy. As he wrote in the *Defence*: "Poets, according to the circumstances of the age and nation in which they appeared, were called in the earlier epochs of the world legislators or prophets: a poet essentially comprises and unites both these characters" (482). With Byron, however, the interaction with a self-identified male muse results not in an affirmation of the regeneration of humankind, a progressive vision, but in an affirmation of the *now*, a self-conscious display of artifice embodied in the art of performance, a poetic style that covets immediacy and delights in verbal virtuosity and the shock and attack of wit and satire. It strives to capture the intensity of a moment, relishing both dreams and follies. Because I also teach film, an art form that students respond to readily, I like to quote the great Spanish director Luis Buñuel to evoke what I think is at the heart of Byron's (and Buñuel's) performance art:

> I'm pessimistic; but I hope to be a good pessimist. In any society, the artist has a responsibility. His effectiveness is certainly limited and a writer or painter *cannot change the world*. But they can keep an essential margin of nonconformity alive. . . . Basically, I agree with Engels: An artist describes real social relationships with the purpose of destroying the conventional ideas about those relationships, undermining bourgeois optimism and forcing the public to doubt the tenets of the established order. The final sense of my films is this: to repeat, over and over again, in case anyone forgets it or believes the contrary, that we do not live in the best of all possible worlds.
>
> (Fuentes 71; italics mine)

This distinction between prophetic and performance poetry is new to most students. By its very nature, which is active and aggressive, performance poetry may be inspired by a male muse. Certainly it reflects a change of perspective from "art for humanity's sake" (prophecy and the female muse) to "art for art's sake" (performance and the male muse). With my film background and an emphasis on interdisciplinary approaches to teaching, I sometimes use a clip here from Donald Cammell and Nicholas Roeg's satanic *Performance* to visualize an oscillating, relativistic universe that students today know intimately from similar experiences with MTV. The film's stars, James Fox and Mick Jagger, serve as *animus* and *anima*, two halves of a whole that does not come together in a creative union. Rock music, drugs, sex, and crime stretch consciousness to its mortal limits and then beyond, into an inexplicable void. The only escape from this threatening madness is laughter: "And if I laugh at any mortal thing, / 'Tis that I may not weep" (*Don Juan* 4.4).

Don Juan is Byron's virtuoso "performance," a poem in which the word *muse* or one of its variants appears more often than anywhere else in his work and always, ironically, in refutation of its mythic and linguistic heritage. When Byron writes,

> Now, if my Pegasus should not be shod ill
> This poem will become a moral model,
> (5.2)

we know his Pegasus is deliberately "shod ill" and that we must turn upside down everything his narrator pronounces, including the lines in canto 12 in which he tells us he is finally going to begin the poem:

> These first twelve books are merely flourishes,
>   Preludios, trying just a string or two
> Upon my lyre, or making the pegs sure;
>   And when so, you shall have the overture.
>
> My Muses do not care a pinch of rosin
>   About what's call'd success, or not succeeding:
> Such thoughts are quite below the strain they have chosen;
>   'Tis a "great moral lesson" they're reading.   (12.54–55)

The "great moral lesson," of course, is that there is no moral lesson. So how can poetry strengthen "that faculty which is the organ of the moral nature of man" (Shelley)? In debunking generic, linguistic, and social conventions, Byron leaves us without a morality, without a reliable sense of tradition on which to fall back. In redefining the muse in his own image, he cuts himself off from established patterns of poetic thinking, especially psychosexual models that see inspiration and generation in the union of male and female opposites. For Byron, such prophetic activity leads to visions of doom, as it can for all of us who sense that in an unredeemably fallen world, the self is finally and desperately alone. Without a sense of a meaningful future, it is only the immediacy of the *now* that counts, a fact that in its grimmest embodiment can lead to a nihilistic indulgence in drugs and alcohol and other forms of self-destruction. Byron knew this, and so do our young students. But there is another side to the picture, reflected in the fact that we are still reading Byron today along with visionaries like Blake and Shelley. Again from film I bring in Woody Allen, a satirist of our own day as Byron was of his. There is a scene in *Hannah and Her Sisters* in which the Allen persona, Mickey, comes to the conclusion that "the only knowledge attainable by man is that life is meaningless." He recalls a botched suicide attempt (recall Manfred's in act 1): "In a godless universe, I didn't want to go on living." But then he asks, "But what if I were wrong?" This ambivalence, paradoxically, is Byronic. The assurance of prophecy is not the only road to "greatness"; performance can also make meaning. Although unregenerative, it helps to intensify experience, purging "from our inward sight the film of familiarity which obscures from us the wonder of our being" (Shelley, *Defence* 505), enabling us, as all art should, "to see anew." One hopes that Byron will also do this for our students.

Julian, Maddalo, and the Madman:
Byron on Civilization and Its Discontents

Mark Kipperman

Romantic poetry courses begin and end with revolutions. We like to begin with the triumph of the French Enlightenment's radical skepticism and faith in the secular progress of humankind; we end with Byron, the artist-hero, creating his skeptical narrator in *Don Juan* while leading the Greeks to liberation. It is a good story, and it argues for the victory of thought, imagination, and culture over repression and darkness. Byron is, of course, not so optimistic a figure as Shelley. Even so, concluding the course with *Don Juan* in the weeks after studying Shelley encourages us to leave our students with images (from Shelley's Prometheanism) of cultural progress and (from Byron's Prometheanism) of personal heroism. Nevertheless, the gloom of *Childe Harold* and the often bitter satire of *Don Juan* seem to make Byron a spoiler amid all this rejoicing. Byron's apparent despair over the fate of the very culture that produced him raises some new questions, at the course's end. How do we treat Romanticism's reputed idealism about culture, about the personally and perhaps socially transformative power of art and the artist? The fate of ideals in history becomes the theme of the last weeks of my course.

I also teach a seminar for seniors and graduate students on Byron and Shelley's literary and personal relations, and from this I have learned that the issue of cultural idealism or pessimism is not a simple matter of what would count as heroic victory over despair for Shelley or Byron. I have found that we cannot meaningfully discuss the apparently temperamental utopianism or cynicism of Shelley or Byron without defining their reactions to the historical facts of a Europe at war for two decades and of the disappointed optimism of republicans in the years after Napoleon. What I find important to stress is the context of felt crisis among Regency liberals, the fears and hopes generated by revolutions, emergent nationalisms, monarchist repression. How would poets whose notion of liberal culture is developed in a classical and aristocratic vocabulary find a way to articulate both this sense of a world in collapse and the value of their own aesthetic responses? Put another way, for both Byron and Shelley the question of the value of culture is often imaged as a struggle between madness and utopia.

Such a struggle, of course, is central to Shelley's poem à clef, *Julian and Maddalo*, a record of his talks with Byron in Venice in late August 1818. I teach this poem as embodying, to some degree, Shelley and Byron's debate over the saving power of poetry, of culture generally, in an era of growing violence, reaction, and soured hopes. Shelley's Julian is broadly idealist, arguing for the power of consciousness not only to determine individual experience but also through its created forms to embody and advance the

unrealized goals of civilization. Such aspirations suggest a social type of the
Romantic sublime, and indeed Julian characterizes himself as a lover of
vacant landscapes that—like the Mont Blanc of Shelley's lyric—urge the
mind to assert its power to make present: "I love all waste / And solitary
places; where we taste / The pleasure of believing what we see / Is boundless,
as we wish our souls to be" (14–17). He later argues that

> it is our will
> That thus enchains us to permitted ill—
> We might be otherwise—we might be all
> We dream of happy, high, majestical.
> Where is the love, beauty and truth we seek
> But in our mind?   (170–75)

Maddalo responds with Byronic archness: "You talk Utopia."

Maddalo had interrupted Julian's reverie on the Lido to turn his attention
from the glorious sunset, kindling the towers of Venice into a "fabric of
enchantment," toward the bell tower of a madhouse, ghastly, tolling "in
strong and black relief," the "emblem and the sign" of all lost souls called
to empty prayers (92, 106, 121). We might recall the opening of *Childe
Harold* 4: "I stood in Venice, on the Bridge of Sighs; / A palace and a prison
on each hand."[1] Students are quick to see the burden of such imagery; but
what they want to know is whether the madhouse in a wasteland demonstrates the hollow abstraction of Julian's optimism or only the bitterness of
Shelley's portrayal of Byron's darker side. Should we identify Maddalo as
the historical Byron anyway—with all that might imply for our students'
reading of his poetry—or is Maddalo no more than Shelley's Byron?

The alternatives are not mutually exclusive, yet both students and scholars
tend to see Byron as a critic of idealisms, perhaps even a nihilist, whose
satiric side is only the obverse of world-weariness. Some have even seen
the madman of Shelley's poem as Byron, or as a critique of the Byronic hero.
Charles Robinson (Shelley 94–101) sees elements of both here, while agree-
ing with most modern critics that Byron's Tasso, the poet maddened and
imprisoned for his forbidden love, is Shelley's source (see Baker, *Shelley's
Major Poetry* 127). Robinson sees Maddalo as implicitly defeated, the poem
a "judgment on Byron's errors" (103; compare the equally persuasive essay
by Hirsch, " 'A Want,' " which reaches the opposite conclusion). A more
broadly suggestive reading, however, is G. M. Matthews's suggestion that "the
Maniac in his heaven-illumined tower must typify the situation of *the poet*
. . . of poets generally" (75). Or, I would add, the situation of culture itself.

Maddalo has fitted the madman's cell—a peculiar detail not noted by
critics—with busts and books and a piano: "And those are his sweet strains

which charm the weight / From madman's chains" (259–60). There is a subtle irony in Julian's blithe wish to return to "sweet Venice" for *its* books, and busts, and paintings, where "one may write / Or read in gondolas by day or night, / . . . Unseen, uninterrupted" (551–54). The association is more unsettling if we recall Shelley's earlier gondola epithet, "that funereal bark" (88)—and Byron's: "like a coffin clapt in a canoe" (*Beppo* 151). Julian's urbanity seems a deluded defense against this world pervaded by horror. Indeed, Julian can do nothing for the Maniac and leaves Venice; it is Maddalo who cares for him with unspoken compassion. *Julian and Maddalo*, then, is no simple Shelleyan attack on Byronic cynicism. Neither Shelley nor Byron should be presented as embodying positions of universal optimism or pessimism. Rather, each man, in somewhat different terms, debates within himself a fundamental question about culture: does art advance civilization and regenerate and sublime human desire; or is civilization advanced at the cost of repressing those human energies that will always return to destabilize and perhaps destroy it?

My language here recalls Freud's great, gloomy 1930 essay *Civilization and Its Discontents*, whose terms uncannily resemble the sad ironies of Shelley's poem (consider the strange sexual violence of the Maniac's speech [420–38]). For Freud, art is among the illusions—along with religion and love—that are "not strong enough to make us forget real misery" (30); for "civilization is built up upon a renunciation of instinct" (49), instinct always threatening the economics of repression with violent aggression or neurotic anxiety (100–01). Some of the most dramatic moments in Byron's long poems seem to echo this dread. Freud begins his essay with the illusory "oceanic" feeling, "of limitlessness and of a bond with the universe" (16), like Julian's love of vastness, or Byron's address to the ocean at the end of *Childe Harold*. For Freud, our present self is only a "shrunken residue" of this bond, and what we face in the development of our mental life is the progressive accretion of ruin and fragmentation (his example is, in fact, the layers of Roman ruins). For Byron, too, the ocean seems to represent energies simultaneously maternal and erotic, a unity that contrasts with the ruins of actual civilizations in history (4.179–82). We might be tempted to read this image in similar terms, as reflecting an anxious fear of (personal and historical) disintegration coupled with a slightly weary childhood nostalgia (as Peter Manning implies [*Byron and His Fictions* 96–97]). But on one point, Byron's sense of ruin, of destructive energy, is unlike Freud's, and the contrast is instructive: Byron is a Romantic ironist, for whom there is a saving affirmation in art, in the power of articulation itself. And here I think there is even a residue of idealism in Byron, so that it becomes less accurate to speak of Byron as a simple pessimist than as a particular kind of ironist.

By idealism I mean that for Byron the ego counters the opacity of the given world with self-creative mobility: in *Childe Harold*, the mobility of a self able to abandon its early strivings after fixed ideals and accept tentative orderings. In this sense, the narrator of *Childe Harold* 4 comes to accept the order of art—represented by the vast dome of St. Peter's, for example—not as illusion but as a way of tempering and harmonizing the conflicting currents of the developing self. In *Don Juan* the world seems always in excess of the ordering mind, and the mobility is that of a detached storyteller whose infinite capacity for reflection and re-creation both satirizes the world and meets its vast, often destructive energies and lets them show forth.

At the same time, Byron does, in the course of his career, accept the tragic depletion inevitable to all civilized orderings, such that, as Alvin Kernan has said of *Don Juan*, "all things, man, society, civilization, and nature, are swept forward by their own pressure into new conditions of being and ultimately to oblivion" (205). To some degree, this reflects what Marilyn Butler calls the "mood of grim stoicism" of postwar English writers (*Romantics* 127). And, too, Byron was attracted to the devolutionism of Cuvier and other pessimistic cosmologies. Shelley had argued against what he often saw as a fashionable aristocratic grudge that denied progressive historical evolution, but he also understood the force of Byron's pessimism on this point. Shelley hoped that the cyclical destructions of history swept away only imperialism and its ponderous ideologies, allowing liberal culture to progress on its own anarchic way. Might it not be madness alone that is self-consuming? Yet there is something abstract about the madness of his tyrants Jupiter and Mahmud and Cenci: they seem to any civilized mind always already defeated. Byron saw destruction as both more general and more concrete than Shelley, a power within history that sweeps away culture like Chaos in *The Dunciad*.

And yet, what is remarkable is how this initial pessimism (which at some times Shelley shared, and which had been a fashionable Enlightenment view of empires, as in Volney and Gibbon) becomes energizing for Byron as a satirist and an ironist. For the power of reconstitution will belong not to the impersonal forces of history or culture but to the individual artist, as observer, maker, storyteller, wit. This is a pose Byron takes, in part, from Pope, but he adds a broader irony and a sense of paradoxical joy at the opportunities chaos presents. Nor is this a matter of uncorking champagne on the deck of the *Titanic*. It is a question of psychic wholeness, a struggle for integration in a sense utopian, but in a radically different sense from that in Shelley. This wholeness is always a-making, always in the future; and although it is a largely personal, rather than social, ideal, Byron's creation of the poised, skeptical ironist in *Don Juan* does provide a model of what "civilized" man might be.

The urbane artist creates order while allowing a bit of chaos in across the threshold. In absolute order—death or marriage—storytelling, after all, stops short. In building supreme fictions, the author builds without being taken in. In this sense, I teach the author of *Childe Harold* and *Don Juan* as redefining sanity in a world of crisis.

Not all Byron's hero-creators are so successful: but that Byron created Tasso, Bonnivard, the bound Prometheus, does not prove that these are for him types of the human condition. They may also witness Byron's tendency to associate madness with stasis, enclosure; or, as in the case of Manfred or the Giaour, with the self-imprisonment of too passionate a pursuit of a lost ideal. Both the suspicion of excessive idealism and the fascination with lost paradises are certainly typical obsessions in eras of social upheaval, and both Byron and Shelley created heroes afflicted with such longings. But in Byron, particularly, we see a developing fear of enclosure and a rejection of para- lyzing nostalgia. I tend to agree with Edward Bostetter that Byron's career progresses, after *Manfred*, not to disillusionment but to an "existential" redefinition of autonomy. This freedom is not the so-called Byronic self- assertion that is really a kind of "absorption" of experience into the self (or, what is the same thing, the search in experience for the self's double). It is, rather, freedom from disabling illusion:

> Manfred's desire for oblivion is Byron's desire for the comforting il- lusion, the escape from self-responsibility. . . . [But Manfred discov- ers] that he can look for no aid or comfort beyond himself. . . . For Byron, Manfred's discovery meant not death but release. He could now emancipate himself from his hero and from his fear and despair. He was free to develop the larger view of himself and the world in which the defiant hero became increasingly unnecessary and even a little silly.   (*Romantic Ventriloquists* 281)

I do not, then, teach the concluding address to the sublime, destructive ocean in *Childe Harold* 4 as undercut by a lingering regressive hope to recover feelings of maternal unity. Unity—indeed sanity—is at this point in Byron's career defined not as nostalgia for a lost coherence but rather as the ironist defines it, as increasing openness to the currents of change, and continuous aesthetic rearticulation of the boundaries of self and world. In his recent study of Byron as ironist, Frederick Garber puts it this way: "Whatever genuine wholeness [the] self comes to have will not be an ancient unity recovered (it never really had one) but that sort which comes into being as the self moves along in the world, seeking to possess the world" (*Self* 50). This (quite un-Freudian) sense of the civilized self places Byron, historically, between a Romantic, exuberant faith in the artist's power to order and reorder and an existentialist acceptance of the provisional nature of all human orderings in the face of the concrete, the ineluctable strangeness of being.

NOTE

[1]Quotations of Byron's poetry in this essay are from McGann's one-volume Oxford Authors edition.

Teaching Byron's Poetic Techniques by Game Playing

David V. Erdman

An important factor that any teacher of Byron must first gauge is the spirit of the class as a whole. Any approach that contributes to the understanding of literature depends on this spirit, the numbness or liveliness of class members. Sometimes students can readily grasp how to read poetry visually and aurally. To help the members of my class discover the rhythms of Byron's poetry and his manipulation of them, I ask students to brush up on definitions of the various verse forms Byron used: sonnets, heroic couplets, Spenserian stanzas, blank verse, ottava rima. I hand out scanned examples of Byron's Spenserians and his octaves, and we play games with random examples of the "poesie." From this point it is easier to discuss scansion and the way games can be played Byronically by making the "tune" contradict the "message."

After this preparation I lecture on the role of opposition in Byron's poetic art. In other words, what did ottava rima do for Byron? When Byron wrote, "I was born for opposition," he meant opposition to "tyranny of all kinds" (*Don Juan* 15.22), prosodical as well as political. Politically he considered himself a permanent revolutionary: he was against the Tories and the Holy Alliance, but if a revolution should place the underdogs in power, his natural spirit of opposition might incline him to

> turn the other way.
> And wax an ultra-royalist in loyalty,
> Because I hate even democratic royalty.
> (*Don Juan* 15.23)

His was the natural dilemma of the aristocratic rebel. And opposition got him into many a scrape—his word for revolutions political, amatory, or pugilistic. It was, he claimed, the tyrannous censure of the critics that forced him, through opposition, to keep on writing verse. Yet when he wrote, he found himself up against the tyrannies of rhyme, Aristotle, Alexander Pope, and reality. Whatever he did, the impact of reality drove him to further rebellion:

> I think I should have made a decent spouse,
> If I had never proved the soft condition:
> I think I should have made monastic vows,
> But for my own peculiar superstition:
> 'Gainst rhyme I never should have knock'd my brows,
> Nor broken my own head, nor that of Priscian,
> Nor worn the motley mantle of a poet,
> If some one had not told me to forego it.
> (*Don Juan* 15.24)

Byron's technical dilemma as a poet was resolved only when he found a verse form in which he could keep, as he desired, "more than one Muse at a push" (*Don Juan* 10.5) each in opposition to the others—a form in which he could break loose with wild Byronic jam sessions and yet make music and keep time.

As a versifier he was no more patient than he was as a husband. He knocked his brows against one traditional verse form after another, and yet he persisted in wooing the Muses. And in one rhyme, ottava rima, he succeeded excellently, not only on first acquaintance but for many years. Why? Byron quarreled with the Muse of the heroic couplet and misused her violently; he played fast and loose with the short couplet in his Turkish tales in a spree of experimentation, without much reason and with too much rhyme, as reckless and fatal as that experiment of Phaeton's. He took blank verse and tried conscientiously to break it down essentially to mimic prose, only to succeed too well. Why did this poet who broke his head against every venerable verse tradition of English poetry, the venerability of which he insisted on and the corruption of which he hastened, why did Byron find so completely to his taste the Italian octave stanza of the medley tradition? How did ottava rima accommodate his spirit of opposition?

The psychology of Byron's behavior is a little more complex than mere "opposition," or a simple love of liberty because his mother had deprived him of that birthright in his youth. This is Byron's account. But his was a rebellion frightfully unsure of itself. Shelley thought that all Byron needed to do was to follow the instincts grounded in his natural poetic genius, but Byron did not know how to trust his genius. He needed both freedom *and* a good road map.

We can observe his pattern of behavior at its simplest in his childhood. If he disobeyed the authority of "Mrs. Byron furiosa," she might slap him or she might fondle his pretty hair. If he did just what she told him to do, he might receive a smile or he might receive a bit of crockery in the side of the head. A timid soul might have crept into itself and hidden. Fiery George Gordon Byron developed an elaborate system of defensive bluff, so that the world could never know just where to have him. What he did might or might not win approval; he could never understand why. There was no way of guessing the fate of it—so he always chose courses that were ambiguous, or impossible tests, the impossibility of which could always be his defense: his own ego always escaped. If his heroic couplets were imperfect, how could anyone be expected to do better than imperfect Alexander Pope? If he failed in marriage, who could succeed without love? If he failed in love, it was not Byron's fault that society condemned incest. Critics are still arguing whether Byron did or did not write his plays for the stage. But

Byron had been careful to arrange that whatever fate befell his plays, that fate was the one he had intended. So too of *Childe Harold*.

He obeyed authority or tradition with defiance—and defied it with a sense of insecurity. As a boy he was never able to learn to read music, but he could get a tune by rote. In the same way, he began to learn to read books—by memorizing, not by intelligently following the prescribed method. As a poet he would mimic a traditional verse form closely and then run amuck as he got familiar with it. He aped the Popean couplet well at first and then increased the tempo until the paired rhymes clanked with monotony. His blank verse, as he wrote on, got more and more blank and lineless. Even in the Spenserian stanza, once he found the trick of enjambment, he ran on recklessly. But here a complex rhyme scheme kept him from monotony on the one hand and blankness on the other, and he did well.

Childe Harold was Byron's training ground. There was room in the nine-line stanza to develop his cadences and a framework to hold them in shape. He perfected a line sense not dependent on "stopping." He learned the intricate tune of a stanza. He learned to do almost anything with it in a theatrical way. But the ornate line scheme and rhyme scheme of the Spenserian stanza were, no matter how managed, still a bit too ornate, a bit too much in need of being wielded. Even more important was the tradition of mind and tone that clings to each form of verse. And Byron would write more naturally when he did not feel the need of holding one pose, one theatrical attitude, throughout a poem. Discovery of the most beneficial verse form is of supreme importance to such a poet. Byron is particularly prone to follow the strict dictates of the poetic form he has chosen in a given work, and he knows no other way but to get his tunes from tradition. Yet the tunes are equally at his mercy, and he will work havoc with any form if it is not both "pliable as Pindar" and orderly as Pope.

The discovery of ottava rima, then, was a happy accident, if it can be called an accident. Byron had been a reader and enjoyer of Italian poetry for many years. Even at the time he was composing the romantic *Manfred*, he was reading the merry, coarse tales of Casti in ottava rima. But perhaps the use of the merry octave in English might not have occurred to him if he had not seen John Hookham Frere's *Whistlecraft* (1817–18). Here was a verse form venerable with tradition. Yet its tradition was one of complete license: there was no pretense to unity of construction; no limit to scenes, or length, or subject; no structural restraint but the order of the rhymes. Digressions by the author were allowable at any point desired, as was any medley of tone, from solemn wit to sudden bathos. Here Byron could be good while being bad! Nobody could know just where to have him, so he could let his genius take its natural direction. He could dispense with the strain of "designed irregularity" (as he called his experiments in short couplets); with the strain of imitated regularity, as in his heroics; with the strain of making blank verse blank. He could do away with all benighted straining and "rattle on exactly as I'd talk" (*Don Juan* 15.19) yet easily leave his "conversational facility" (15.20) and "pass the equinoctial line" (13.34) at any appearance of something "Gothic" or "sublime," jumping back before anyone might laugh.

Byron's evasion of criticism is a perfect job. Technically it is impossible to find flaws in his octave poems *Don Juan, Beppo,* and *The Vision of Judgment.* We can turn to the least melodic stanza and yet not smugly criticize its ugliness, since plainly it is meant to tease us—and then at the end the couplet strikes up a catchy tune after all.

As for the art of sinking in burlesque poetry, the efforts of Frere and the Italians appear quite puerile alongside the Byronic. Their shifts of tone are simple. Frere generally uses mere bathetic drop. Byron's psychological need of evasion has developed into the skillful variation of a thousand fine shades of tone, with shifts from one to the other of greatly varying abruptness. Without the stanzaic framework, the flights of Byron's wanton muse end often in an awkward crash or uncertain collapse of rhythm. With the octave for assistance, she always manages to right herself and begin again.

I am not thinking merely of the implicit variation demanded by the rhyme scheme—a sestet of alternating lines giving two rhymes three times, calling forth skill in the research and the display of rhymes and holding them apart for breadth and full exploitation, similar to the discourse of two themes in polyphonic music; and then a couplet, final and clinching, putting two rhymes close for virtuosity and salience. I am thinking also of what I call the sin-and-repentance formula, developed on the Italian tradition of digression. As he begins *Don Juan,* the poet announces that "[t]he regularity of my design / Forbids all wandering as the worst of sinning" (1.7). And soon we find him, with great show of reluctance, committing this congenial sin. The octave, indeed, provides both the opportunity to wander and the means to repent.[1]

NOTE

[1]This essay is a shortened version of material in my book *Byron's Poetic Technique,* published in 1991 by Locust Hill Press, West Cornwall, CT.

Byron's Poetry: Sound Effects

Brian Wilkie

The proliferation of critical approaches to literature since the 1970s has, by and large, worked to the advantage of Byron's poetry, including the teaching of it. Structuralism, deconstructionism, psychoanalytical criticism, the new historicism, feminist criticism—all these approaches can be fruitful avenues to an understanding and appreciation of Byron. The only widely employed critical approach that may do a disservice to his poetry is the one that, a generation ago, critics and teachers used almost exclusively in interpreting literature. I refer, of course, to the New Critical close explication aimed at detecting systematic, unifying patterns of diction and symbolic imagery.

That generalization is, I suppose, not absolutely true; a few of Byron's poems have been amenable to close explication—*The Prisoner of Chillon*, for example, with its insistent, and consistent, strategy of fusing physical with mental or spiritual phenomena. ("Our voices took a dreary tone, / An echo of the dungeon stone" [63–64].)[1] For the most part, though, the quixotic attempts at New Critical explication of Byron merely went to support his detractors' charges that his poetry was mere—and dated—verbal fireworks, superficially lively but empty of substance. By almost all the New Critical criteria, Byron fared badly, deficient as he was in ironic or aesthetic detachment, in structural architectonics, and in verbal and imagistic density. The more recent critical approaches, especially those that tolerate anomalies of form and those that scrutinize the relation of poetic statement to culture in general, reveal a much more interesting and important Byron. It is easy, for example—in the classroom and elsewhere—to provoke heated and meaningful debate about the societal implications of Byron's paradoxical attitude toward women, combining as it does deep respect with condescension and perhaps even, at times, contempt.

The troubling limitation—as it seems to some of us—of the recent approaches to Byron is that they implicitly surrender on the question of his artistry, as a lost cause. To treat Byron chiefly as a revealing specimen in the history of culture is surely, one feels, to omit something crucially important, an omission felt with special keenness in the classroom. Since few undergraduates have had the opportunity to become adepts in cultural history, discussions can easily turn into airings of half-digested commonplaces or of personal biases that, even though they may be inherently important in the process of reading, do not make for useful classroom communication. For the instructor (presumably better informed) to lecture to students is a dispiriting alternative; there is, moreover, the problem of controlling the instructor's own biases. One needs to discover what Byron's poetic art is and how it works and to have the students participate in the discovery. But the only method that most teachers feel is available to them, however emancipated they may feel from the New Criticism, is that of New Critical analysis, a method that even when it was in vogue did not get very far with Byron.

My purpose in this essay is to suggest a way of understanding and teaching the art of Byron's poetry that does not depend on New Critical definitions of what constitutes artistry or on the concomitant New Critical method of "systematic" close explication.

My main premise about Byron, which I have argued at greater length ("Byron: Artistry and Style"), is that his verse belongs in the long tradition of rhetorical poetry that, ultimately traceable to ancient classical models of compliment and oratory, has as its twin keynotes the private voice of sophisticated, worldly gallantry and the public voice of parliamentary oratory. In the two centuries before Byron, the tradition is evident in passages such as these:

> The thirst that from the soul doth rise
> Doth ask a drink divine:
> But might I of Jove's nectar sup,
> I would not change for thine.
> > (Jonson, "To Celia" 5–8)

> Where'er you walk, cool gales shall fan the glade;
> Trees, where you sit, shall crowd into a shade;
> Where'er you tread, the blushing flowers shall rise,
> And all things flourish where you turn your eyes.
> > (Pope, *Pastorals*, "Summer" 73–76)

> The applause of listening senates to command,
> > The threats of pain and ruin to despise,
> To scatter plenty o'er a smiling land,
> > And read their history in a nation's eyes,
> Their lot forbade. . . .
> > (Gray, "Elegy Written in a Country
> > Churchyard" 61–65)

The hallmarks of this rhetorical style include deliberate pleonasm and a reliance on commonplaces, aimed at achieving a swelling orotundity and nobility of expression too lofty to be preoccupied with fussy originality or with fine-tooled ingenuity.

This style was second nature to Byron; he used it, for example, in his youthful speech to the House of Lords arguing against the death penalty for frame breaking:

How will you carry [the death penalty] into effect? Can you commit a whole country to their own prisons? Will you erect a gibbet in every field . . . ? or will you proceed . . . by decimation? place the country under martial law? depopulate and lay waste all around you? . . . Are these the remedies for a starving and desperate populace? Will the famished wretch who has braved your bayonets be appalled by your gibbets? . . . Will that which could not be effected by your grenadiers be accomplished by your executioners? (27 Feb. 1812; Prothero 2: 429, 1898–1901 ed.)

The entire controversy about Pope that Byron waged with William Lisle Bowles, the sonneteer and editor, makes it clear that Byron considered this rhetorical tradition a conservative one, a mode directly opposed to the new Romantic mode characterized—as Shelley put it in the preface to *Prometheus Unbound*—by its "peculiar style of intense and comprehensive imagery." (The New Critics could scarcely have stated their own ideal more neatly.) Students should be reminded, however, that the rhetorical style has not simply disappeared, even in the twentieth century:

> I know that I shall meet my fate
> Somewhere among the clouds above;
> Those that I fight I do not hate,
> Those that I guard I do not love. . . .
> (Yeats, "An Irish Airman
> Foresees His Death" 1–4)

> These, in the day when heaven was falling,
> The hour when earth's foundations fled,
> Followed their mercenary calling
> And took their wages and are dead.
> (Houseman, "Epitaph on an Army
> of Mercenaries" 1–4)

One effective way to energize, or at least help define, this rhetorical poetic tradition for students is to send them on exploratory missions (scavenger hunts, the New Critics might have called them) through the realm of Romantic poetry or of English poetry in general. If the course is Romantic poetry, students can be asked to ransack their textbooks—the David Perkins anthology, for example, if they are using it—for other specimens of the rhetorical style. They can be left to an unguided search or else (which is more expeditious) given a list of poems by the instructor and asked to cull out from among the poems listed those that fit the bill. The results will be instructive (and not just to the students). For example, in exploring the major poets, they are certain to find the pickings slim, though not quite nonexistent: the *Experience* version of Blake's "Holy Thursday" ("And their sun does never shine, / And their fields are bleak & bare"), parts of Wordsworth's "Extempore Effusion upon the Death of James Hogg" ("The mighty Minstrel breathes no longer, / 'Mid mouldering ruins low he lies"), Coleridge's "Sonnet to the River Otter" ("Visions of Childhood! oft have ye beguil'd / Lone manhood's cares, yet waking fondest sighs"), and Shelley's "Song to the Men of England" ("The seed ye sow, another reaps; / The wealth ye find, another keeps") will fit the specifications. But these are lonely exceptions. It is doubtful that students will find anything at all to the purpose in Keats, or almost anything to the purpose, by anyone, that was written in blank verse, which (especially in the hands of the Romantics) tends to convey sentiments too inwardly meditative or too cerebrally ambitious for rhetorical poetry.

On the other hand, students will find—predictably, from the instructor's point of view—myriad examples among the alternative poets, as it were, of the period: in Scott's "Lochinvar" ("He stayed not for brake and he stopped not for stone") and "Coronach" ("Like the bubble on the fountain, / Thou art gone, and forever"); in Thomas Campbell's "Poland" ("Where barbarous hordes on Scythian mountains roam, / Truth, Mercy, Freedom, yet shall find a home" [339–40]) and "Ye Mariners of England" ("Your glorious standard launch again / To match another foe!"); in Thomas Moore's "The Harp That Once through Tara's Halls" ("No more to chiefs and ladies bright / The harp of Tara swells") and "Let Erin Remember" ("Ere the emerald gem of the western world / Was set in the crown of a stranger").

If students extend their search into the twentieth century, they had better be directed toward particular poems. Sometimes these will be problematical to classify. If, for example, they are asked to look at (and listen to) Yeats's "To a Friend Whose Work Has Come to Nothing" and "Easter 1916," they may find that the poems belong generally to the rhetorical tradition but they will probably note also that the rather eerie reference in the former to "a laughing string / Whereon mad fingers play" and, in the latter, the tortured third section, about hearts enchanted to a stone, are too eccentrically crafted, too gnarled, to be at home in the tradition.

More than academic learning is involved in such discriminations; instructors are likely to find that students enjoy these rhetorical poems very much. In the New Critical heyday, such enjoyment would have marked students as jejune in their tastes, or mentally lazy, or emotionally immature. No longer need we jump to those conclusions, nor, I think, should we. The reader-response movement (when it truly is that and not a mere rationalization for the instructor's own form of revisionist bias) should encourage more open-minded evaluation and receptivity to the rhetorical tradition's keynotes: nobility and sonority.

For teaching purposes, we can best locate Byron in this tradition by sensitizing students to the sound of his verse. Byron should be heard in the classroom—through recordings perhaps but especially through recitals—or declamations—by student and teacher. To put this in practice requires some work; as in any dramatic or oral performance, one must prepare and rehearse. The ocean stanzas (179–84) near the end of *Childe Harold* 4, once a favorite anthology piece, will suffer, in silence, if we merely scrutinize them analytically in the New Critical way, ignoring the effect of their swelling rhythms and cadences: "Roll on, thou deep and dark blue Ocean—roll! / Ten thousand fleets sweep over thee in vain" (st. 179) and

> The armaments which thunderstrike the walls
> Of rock-built cities, bidding nations quake,
> And monarchs tremble in their capitals,
> The oak leviathans, whose huge ribs make
> Their clay creator the vain title take
> Of lord of thee, and arbiter of war—
> These are thy toys, and, as the snowy flake,
> They melt into thy yeast of waves, which mar
> Alike the Armada's pride or spoils of Trafalgar.
>
> (St. 181)

It is not beneath our pedagogical dignity to recognize the sheer fun of performing Byron, as people liked to do in the nineteenth century. "The Destruction of Sennacherib" was on the declamation program in Tom Sawyer's schoolroom, as Northrop Frye once reminded us (*Fables of Identity* 175). But the exercise pays several other, more intellectual, dividends in addition to its aforementioned value in defining Byron's poetic lineage. Take, for example, one of the passages in Byron that I especially like to read with my students, the stanzas (69–117) of the first canto of *Don Juan* in which the narrator relates the bumbling progress of Juan and Julia toward their love affair. We can learn a great deal about Byron's versification from this section, as from almost any passage in Byron's best poetry. I am not thinking of the elusive pleasures of scansion (although students ought to be aware, at least, of Byron's obsessive concern with metrical discipline) but rather of certain other aspects of tone, sonority, and rhythm that are not obvious but are nevertheless palpable. Students need to understand that such lines as "Love, then, but love within its proper limits / Was Julia's innocent determination / In young Don Juan's favor" (st. 81) are expert poetry, especially in their management, within a matter-of-fact conversational mode, of polysyllabic words. Byron might well have learned such management from such masters of the trick as Andrew Marvell: "It was begotten by Despair / Upon impossibility" ("The Definition of Love").

The rendering of Byron's verse aloud is also the readiest way to understand the "mobility" that Byron attributed to himself, which amounts to opalescence not only of thought but of narrative or discursive movement. This mobility has something in common with the strategy of constantly shifting, transitionless alterations of stance and viewpoint that gives *Gulliver's Travels* its distinctive artistic brilliance. The narrating persona in the passage cited from *Don Juan* is sometimes a half-bored worldling, sometimes a leering lecher, sometimes a disingenuous innocent embarrassed by his own material. Moreover, this material itself and the characters are sometimes inherently innocent, sometimes charmingly culpable, sometimes suspectly so. Detached analysis could, possibly, do justice to these multiple variables in the Byron passage, but a quicker way, which has the additional advantage of not pouring the cold water of analysis on comedy, is simply to recite particular passages, like stanzas 79 and 84, registering the poem's gearshifts through one's oral timing and varying tones of voice. How to track, and orally capture, the rapid-fire shifts of tone in these stanzas will be less than obvious, but one set of directions might run as follows, with the point of view specified and the numbers keyed to the words of the poem that immediately follow the numbers: 1: Julia, in exalted fervor; 2: the narrator, with jaundiced skepticism; 3: Julia, with gleeful delight at so wonderful an inspiration; 4: the narrator, wickedly leering; 5: Julia, musingly; 6: Julia, with pious abhorrence (within limits; after all, the loss is "common"); 7: the narrator or Julia, wistfully or perhaps languishingly; 8: Julia, irritably (why must people take her so literally at her word?); 9: the narrator, in sotto voce confidence.

[1] And then there are such things as love divine,
    Bright and immaculate, unmixed and pure,
[2] Such as the angels think so very fine,
    And matrons, who would be no less secure,
[1] Platonic, perfect, [3] "just such love as mine":
[2] Thus Julia said—and thought so, to be sure;
[4] And so I'd have her think, were I the man
    On whom her reveries celestial ran.   (St. 79)

[5] And if in the mean time her husband died,
[6] But Heaven forbid that such a thought should cross
    Her brain, though in a dream! [7] (and then she sighed)
[6] Never could she survive that common loss;
[5] But just suppose that moment should betide,
[8] I only say suppose it—*inter nos.*
[9] (This should be *entre nous*, for Julia thought
    In French, but then the rhyme would go for nought.)
                                        (St. 84)

Admittedly, rendering these tonal changes calls for pretty advanced theatrical skills, but students enjoy making the attempt. Even if they fail, they can be asked to explain (as in the set of directions just outlined here) what tone they were aiming at.

It may be apparent by now that I tend to whipsaw my students with two complementary aspects of Byron's work: his aggressive old-fashionedness and his anticipations of twentieth-century absurdism. Both of these contradictory tendencies are reflected, in different ways, in Byron's handling of language, not just as a notional medium but as an affective one. The nostalgic side of him emerges in the swelling periods of his rhetorical style; the modernist side emerges in the kaleidoscopic, fragmented, "mobile" aspects of his work. Both sides are most readily accessible in the classroom through the direct experience of the sound of Byron's verse.

Partly because critics today are increasingly interested in the capacity of literature to propagate and reflect values, rhetorical poetry is making at least a modest comeback, after decades of New Critical condescension. Minds are now open to this mode of verse as they have not been for a long time. This development blends, though sometimes ironically and indirectly, with recent attempts to redefine the literary canon. The desire to elevate the status of women writers and of representatives of disadvantaged groups to parity with the quondam masters has led to a generalized suspicion of the elitist indirection once prized by New Critics, along with certain other once-established criteria of literary value, including aesthetic self-sufficiency and philosophical and social detachment. By current revisionist standards, Byron slips back into the academic mainstream, along with other released political prisoners of the sometime literary establishment. To the extent that this is happening, there are huge ironies: in the first place, because Byron himself, several generations ago, was the very prototype of the canonized titan and, in the second place, because Byron's style and attitude are essentially patrician, despite the liberal stances he struck. The ironies would, doubtless, have bemused if not necessarily pleased him.

Such considerations, which may seem to be the stuff of trendiness, mere passing skirmishes in the ever-shifting war games of the house of intellect, do nevertheless have quotidian implications for classroom teaching: to the extent that students, through and alongside their teachers, become acclimated to a literature of forthright statement rather than of half-concealed indirection and implication; to the extent that the directly affective qualities of literature assume priority over, or at least parity with, more detached and cerebral qualities; and to the extent that the literature of the local and particular (as in *Don Juan* and much of *Childe Harold*) comes to be valued as highly as the literature of noncircumstantial insight, to just such an extent will Byron's poetry—*heard*, in more than one sense—be more cordially encountered and highly valued.

NOTE

[1]Quotations of Byron's poetry in this essay are from *English Romantic Writers* (ed. Perkins). Quotations of Jonson's and Gray's poetry are from Kermode and Hollander, vol. 1; the Pope quotation is from Bredvold et al.; and the Housman lines are from Abrams, *Norton Anthology*, vol. 2.

THE SATIRES, "ROMANTIC" POEMS, AND PLAYS

Teaching Satire in *English Bards* and *The Vision of Judgment*

Frederick L. Beaty

The popularity of present-day cartoonists and columnists, as well as of television ironists such as Mark Russell, gives ample proof that modern readers and audiences are responsive to the satiric spirit. Clearly the art of ridiculing topical events, issues, and personalities flourishes among a populace able to grasp its implications with ease. Contemporary satire can be instantly comprehended and enjoyed because its practitioners and their fans share the same environment, are familiar with the same news, and are accustomed to the same modes of expression. But those of us who attempt to revive for students the pleasures of earlier satire face a crucial knowledge gap. We must bridge it by re-creating some sense of immediacy about the entire matrix—both historical and biographical—that generated the works we teach. In doing so, we must supply just enough background material to illuminate topical allusions and literary forms that are no longer current. Through judicious delvings into the literary, social, and political circumstances of Byron's time, we can show it to be as exciting and vulnerable to derision as our own. To illustrate the diversity and effectiveness of Byron's satiric voice within his milieu, I suggest the widely differing *English Bards and Scotch Reviewers* and *The Vision of Judgment*.

The Augustan tradition of formal satire, from which *English Bards* springs, is one that Byron very much admired and used as a model for several of his early compositions. One of its well-established conventions was the reworking of inherited material in order to bring it up to date. An ingenious readaptation of generally accepted truths could play off the degenerate present against a superior past to show lapses in taste, rational judgment, and social behavior. By offering a diagnosis of what ailed the stricken patient (to use the healer's metaphor that Byron applies to himself in the preface to *English Bards*), formal satire strove to improve social and literary health, whether or not it simultaneously prescribed the appropriate medicine.

Although many Romantic writers considered the tradition outmoded, Byron regarded it as still viable in his day; but he also wisely recognized the need to accommodate it to social conditions and author-reader relationships that had changed radically since Pope's day. The Augustans had been able to write satire with the assurance that their literary standards and codes of ethics were unimpugnable, that transgressions from them would be unanimously condemned, and that reader endorsement was guaranteed. But amid the cultural diversity of the early nineteenth century, such certainties were impossible because there no longer existed a single set of absolute values or a single group of like-minded readers. While verbal tribute might still be rendered to Christian morality and to the classical tradition of literature, the cherished norms had lost their dominion over actual practice. Hence it became imperative for Byron to develop a compelling voice with which to enunciate his *own* normative values so persuasively that, by contrast, antithetical assumptions would appear ridiculous. Indeed, there is such forcefulness in Byron's thought and phraseology—the passionate intensity ascribed to him by Matthew Arnold in "Memorial Verses"—that students can immediately recognize its vitality even though they may initially view its authoritarian, didactic approach, embodied in a seemingly fossilized medium, with some skepticism.

In addition to pointing out Byron's objectives in writing *English Bards*, we must give adequate attention to the circumstances that galvanized him into poetic action. This approach is all the more essential because anthologists often excerpt only those passages in which Byron skewers famous contemporaries. Such selectivity results in a limited, slanted perspective on the poem as a whole and, in view of posterity's kindlier judgment on the early Romantics, calls Byron's critical acumen into question. It is helpful, therefore, to emphasize Byron's allegiance to the classical tradition and consequent antagonism toward those who would subvert it, the arrogance of anonymous *Edinburgh* reviewers who condemned all productions deviating from what Byron derided as "Scottish taste," the sheepish English writers whose preoccupation with inanities made them easy prey for the *Edinburgh's* wolves, and Byron's Promethean determination to resist any form of tyranny. Nor should we forget that Byron's critical stance on the early Romantics was sanctioned by the prevailing conservative opinion of the day or that Shelley, in *Adonais*, praised Byron as the poet who had given the critics what they deserved.

Although students who come to *English Bards* after some acquaintance with Pope may have enough background to appreciate Byron's stylistic achievements, it is never amiss to offer a brief analysis of his attempts to imitate Pope—through conciseness of language, balance of phrase, antithesis, parallelism, verbal polish, and epigrammatic wit. Some mention should also be made of the techniques commonly employed by satirists to disparage their targets—caricature, burlesque, parody, mock encomium, and irony—for Byron often uses these subtleties, instead of derogatory labels, to undercut his adversaries. Byron's prowess in *English Bards* is perhaps most successfully demonstrated by the attack on Francis Jeffrey, which is cast as two mock encomiums apostrophizing his greatness. In praise that likens the achievements of the *Edinburgh*'s editor to those of George Jeffreys, the infamous "hanging judge," students readily perceive the ironic tone and are gratified that poetic justice will be done, since those who live by the noose will ultimately perish by it. The mock-heroic burlesque of the aborted duel between Jeffrey and Thomas Moore also shows how, by elevating the absurd to heights of mythic grandeur that are unsustainable even with divine intervention and a prophecy of Jeffrey's imperium, the satirist indirectly undermines his victim through inappropriate praise, pompous diction, and fantastic personifications.

Often students need to be reminded that Byron does not intend to present a balanced view of what he is satirizing. Like a caricaturist, he singles out vulnerable features for exaggeration; and like a journalist, he acts on the principle that clever, barbed assertions attract more attention than colorless statements of fact. Although he is careful not to alter reality so much as to prevent our recognition of it, the mirror he holds up to nature inevitably produces a distorted image. In *English Bards* he emphasizes the simpleness and prosiness of Wordsworth's verse, citing "precept and example" to verify his charge, since what concerns him are idiosyncrasies and excesses rather than merits or the whole truth. Consequently he feels no compunction about claiming that Wordsworth is himself the hero of "The Idiot Boy" or that Coleridge shows a natural affinity for the subject of his poem "To a Young Ass." Such charges cannot be taken literally but must be seen as part of the satirist's rhetoric. By overstating the case, he assumes that readers will put some credence in his belief that Wordsworth and Coleridge, in violation of decorum, have identified themselves with subjects unworthy of poetry.

Perhaps the most challenging pedagogical task in making *English Bards* come alive is calling up the entire literary scene from the perspective of a poet who believes his country's literature has taken a wrong turn. Most of the writers, critics, and fictive characters whom the author parades before us deserve to be restored to their original vitality in the context of their historical setting, especially since *English Bards* postulates a correlation between the state of society and the condition of its literature. But so many of the specific references that Byron employs to give his satire its punch— and that were well understood by readers in 1809—are now recoverable only through elaborate footnoting. We must reach a sensible balance between overwhelming the student with facts and furnishing so little background information that the satiric jibes remain incomprehensible.

The Vision of Judgment, in contrast, generally elicits greater approval from undergraduates, who find its satiric irony more compatible than the head-on confrontations of *English Bards*. *The Vision*, usually uncut by editors, also has the benefit of an amusing fable that ensures artistic unity, propels the action, and provides a clothesline on which the narrator can hang his casual reflections. British courtroom scenes are so familiar to modern readers and viewers that there is nothing strange about trial procedures except the novelty of judging a man's soul to determine his habitat throughout eternity. The style, as well as the content, is immediately appealing because of its more relaxed conversational mode. The loose construction of the ottava rima stanza liberates Byron's exuberance and enhances the sophistication of his satiric technique. The concluding couplet especially facilitates the presentation of irony, for it permits incompatible rhymes and digressive comments to wrench the tone or the thought established in the preceding six lines. Students may need some elucidation of the many ironies stemming from incongruity, juxtaposition, unfulfilled expectations, and the art of conveying an idea without ever expressing it. Some mention should be made of the ironic detachment of the narrator, who pretends to be emotionally uninvolved in reporting his "true dream" as seen through a telescope.[1]

The poem can be enjoyed as a colossal joke—not only on the fools involved but also on the institutions they represent. Its fantastic humor should evoke sufficient laughter to bring down royal, judicial, and religious roofs; and students ought to feel that they have front-row seats at a highly dramatic, wildly comical performance. Flip, often irreverent, diction throughout the poem allows the narrator to make fun of his characters without appearing venomous, while the characters themselves often inadvertently expose their own shortcomings through actions or comments. A nodding gatekeeper, Saint Peter (addressed as "Saint porter") bumbles around heaven with angels who have nothing to do but fulfill prosaic chores. An urbane Satan and a temporizing Michael oppose each other with the hypocritical politeness demanded by courtroom protocol. And even the radical Whig politician John Wilkes, whom Satan expects to give incriminating testimony against his sovereign, reveals himself more concerned with political advancement than truth. Further invalidating the solemnity of this august convocation is that, in the midst of confusion, its original purpose drops out of sight. The trial of George III (whereby, according to Byron's theology, good works rather than faith should determine admission to heaven) turns into a political roast. Although Satan's arraignment of the king is more impressive than Michael's defense, the tumult created by the laureate, Robert Southey, enables the king to steal into heaven without due process. Instead, it is the conceited laureate who is tried and unanimously condemned for his poetic transgressions and lack of principle after the reading of his *Vision* offends the entire assemblage.

It is debatable how much time should be devoted to an intertextual study with Southey's antecedent funeral ode, *A Vision of Judgement*, since Byron's poem can be understood independently with a minimum of annotation. Without some comparison, however, we cannot appreciate Byron's travesty as a rejoinder or understand how it was designed to subvert, from a Whig perspective, Southey's fable of the king tried before heaven's bar. Without Byron's prose preface it is impossible to comprehend the intensity of his hatred for the laureate, who had charged him with being leader of a "Satanic School" of poetry, or the delicious irony of having Satan utter the worst indictments against George III and claim Southey as well. It is easy to deduce from Byron's text his conviction that Southey was a sycophant, a spineless turncoat, and a mediocre poet unaware of his own limitations; it is more difficult to assess Byron's ambivalence toward a king who had died blind and insane after long suffering. But Byron's animus toward George III's reactionary political stance and his perverse virtues (such as abstinence from wine and women), as well as Southey's absurd apotheosis of him, offered too good a target to pass up. Moreover, Southey's adulation necessitated Byron's undermining, just as Southey's presumption in granting the king eternal salvation prevented Byron from making any definitive judgment on that score. Since American students, lacking a conditioned respect for royalty and having already acquired some notion of George III as the enemy of American liberty, usually revel more in his debasement than in Southey's, it is often necessary to emphasize the case against the laureate, whom Byron intended as the prime target of the satire.

Nor can we overlook the poem's less obvious implications on monarchy, politics, and religion. Strongly republican, even rebellious, sentiments are detectable in the narrator's deflation of George III to the level of common men, in Satan's assertion about the insufferable wickedness of kings, and in angelic observations on the arrogance of royalty. The hypocrisy, opportunism, and amorality of political life are well illustrated by Wilkes's response to Satan. Even doubts concerning Christian dogma are raised by the narrator's remarks on eternal damnation, the Atonement, and the awarding of grace. From his perspective, conformity to the dictates of a power elite may seem to spell salvation, much as rebelliousness appears to invite damnation, or the judgment of heaven, which permits an unwitting tool of evil such as George III to gain celestial bliss, may be as capricious and unjust as that of humanity's highest tribunals.

Inherent in these unsettling speculations is the philosophical irony now generally termed Romantic, for serious, unanswered questions about divine justice and humanity's fate lie incongruously beneath the poem's surface buffoonery. Moreover, the antitheses, or binary oppositions, that abound in Byron's *Vision*—good and evil, bright and dark, realistic and fantastic, solemn and ludicrous, sacred and profane—are never resolved. As representations of the paradoxical nature of existence, their inconclusive conflicts, carried out through all time and space, must remain forever indeterminate. Appropriately, therefore, the ironically detached poet stands apart from his subject, allowing it the unrestricted scope of his imagination and sublimating the righteous indignation that inspired the poem. By expanding the dimensions and changing the character of the satire, Byron transcends the nineteenth-century English roots of his *Vision* to give it universal significance.

NOTE

[1]Quotations of Byron's *Vision of Judgment* in this essay are from McGann's one-volume Oxford Authors edition.

The Giaour: The Infidelity of the Romantic Fragment

Scott Simpkins

Because, unlike most works that students encounter, *The Giaour* requires a type of final assembly, it poses a considerable teaching challenge. Resistant to easy interpretation, it discourages readers content with the processed works that seem to presuppose an acquiescent response. In fact, the poem's infrequent appearance in Romantic literature anthologies is undoubtedly related to the difficulties it presents.

Yet discussion of the historical context of fragmented works and the textual mechanics involved can enable students to engage poems such as *The Giaour* on a more satisfying level. Readers during Byron's time would be surprised to learn of our modern resistance to *The Giaour*, for it was a great commercial success that went through editions so quickly that critics sometimes complained of the appearance of a new version before they had had a chance to finish reviewing the previous one.

Offering a fragmented text was a common—though still radical—practice during the Romantic period, and because Byron consciously designed *The Giaour* as a flamboyant work in this mode, it can serve as an exemplary model of this facet of the Romantic project. With its studied engagement of an outlaw genre, it epitomizes the widespread use and favorable reception of the fragment during the early part of the nineteenth century. And, as a medium-size fragment (at 1,334 lines), it is better suited for demonstrating the genre's range of possibilities than some of the shorter well-known fragments (such as Coleridge's "Kubla Khan"). Even if editions or anthologies that do not contain this poem are used, the relative brevity of *The Giaour* makes it easily reproducible for classroom use.

As an infidelic genre, the fragment offered the Romantics a seductive outlet for lawless projects. It allowed for considerable latitude in creating the perimeters of a work by essentially placing the notion of textual agreement into question. Faced with the task of conveying the significance of this form during the Romantic period to a group of potentially unexposed and possibly indifferent students, I have found it beneficial to discuss *The Giaour* in relation to other famous fragments, such as Wordsworth's "Nutting," Coleridge's *Christabel* and "Kubla Khan," Keats's Hyperion poems, and Shelley's *Triumph of Life*, although there are so many Romantic fragments that the possible combinations are endless. Comparison of *The Giaour* with other fragments from this period demonstrates the Romantics' shared interests in revaluating our conceptions of textual completion and acceptable literary genres. Regardless of whether Romantic fragments were intentional (many simply were not finished), their existence points to a definite trend toward the antigenre that allowed a wide-open literary form to develop.

Furthermore, the then-popular attitude toward ruins encouraged writers to adopt the genre that so powerfully mimicked this condition. Byron in particular takes advantage of this vogue in *The Giaour* by indulging in extensive commentary on the ruins of modern Greece. The Giaour himself is depicted as a human form of decay. Accordingly, the reader is presented with a ruined text, as well as a ruined symbolic landscape and a ruined main character. The fragmented state of the poem is intensified as Byron claims in the advertisement that the text was whole at one time but now exists only in pieces. A discussion of the importance of ruins in Romantic works— Wordsworth's "Michael," Byron's *Manfred*, Shelley's "Sensitive-Plant" and *Alastor*, and "Kubla Khan," among others—sheds light on *The Giaour* in this respect. Fortunately, a number of influential critical works exist that I have drawn on in exploring this genre, including Edward Bostetter's *Romantic Ventriloquists*, Robert F. Gleckner's *Byron and the Ruins of Paradise*, Marjorie Levinson's *Romantic Fragment Poem*, Thomas McFarland's *Romanticism and the Forms of Ruin*, Philippe Lacoue-Labarthe and Jean-Luc Nancy's *Literary Absolute*, and Balachandra Rajan's *Form of the Unfinished*. I encourage undergraduates (and require graduate students) to refer to these and other secondary works to deepen their exposure to modern perspectives on the fragment; most students convey a genuine sense of insight from the research that has grown steadily in recent years with the continued interest in the implications of nonstandard textual forms.

I develop an overview of fragmentation in Byron's works as an essential tool for placing *The Giaour* in context. Since the fragmented text and ruination are so important in works such as *Childe Harold's Pilgrimage* and *Don Juan*, for instance, as well as *The Giaour*, it is useful—especially for those students who are not familiar with Byron's oeuvre—to focus on this particular work, which takes the broken form to the extreme. Moreover, I link the rather consistent pose that Byron's proud characters assume with his use of the fragment, which, like his characters as a whole, announces a nonconformist ideology that perilously resists the trappings of most generic confines.

Like many Byronic heroes, to adopt Peter Thorslev's term, the fragment stands as a loner among all others, steadfastly maintaining a careful distance between itself and genres that adhere to rules imposed by strict convention. As a rebel genre, the fragment—like the Giaour in retirement—refuses the comfort of institutionalized values, retaining its individual identity to the end regardless of the consequences. And, if we consider the consequences for *The Giaour* in terms of coherence and readability, Byron's decision to employ this form can be explored more knowledgeably as a consciously risky proposition. Again, like the Giaour himself, Byron's fragmented work runs the risk of being misunderstood because it defies membership within a group of confining genres. Thus, the various misreadings of the Giaour's character throughout most of the poem are no different from the insufficient readings that usually result from initial exposure to the poem itself. This comparison is further suggested when the Giaour himself, near the end of his story, remarks, "Such is my name, and such my tale" (1319).

If this poem causes so many difficulties, many might question the wisdom of dealing with it at all. But *The Giaour* is an extremely lively example for demonstrating Romantic fragmentation, with its radical dislocation amid killings, dismemberment, vampirism, and chase scenes. Because it presents itself as a work that requires assembly, it offers a stimulating hermeneutic challenge for those willing and able to tackle it. To lessen some of the exegetical problems and to assist students in their own construction of the poem, I prepare a handout that outlines and identifies the major fragment units. Many have written in response essays that this supplement was an essential aid, particularly for students who are quick to abandon works that frustrate them on initial reading.

Through experience I have found that, to illustrate the poem's fragmented condition, it is useful to compare *The Giaour* to common cultural examples, such as a jigsaw puzzle with some pieces missing; yet I stress that the incomplete picture that a careful assemblage yields is by no means unappealing in the case of *The Giaour*. In fact—and this is a realization that the Romantics clearly made—the fragment can be far more satisfying than other forms precisely because of its lack of completion. It allows for a range of interpretive practices, none of which will necessarily be canceled by a final reading. The fragment offers no final or complete text to refer to for an authoritative reading (as, again, is often the case in Romantic literature), and thus the reader is presented with a deliciously open set of interpretations limited only by the individual's imagination—something students appreciate, since it encourages their input and reduces the perceived gulf between canonized works and their own.

This, of course, is exactly the result the Romantics sought through fragmentation. By questioning the validity of textual boundaries and completion, they attempted to rewrite the concept of acceptable forms through the one form that ruled out such norms.

Conveying the sense of novelty and sheer impact that the fragment had for early-nineteenth-century audiences can be difficult. Most students express disbelief that the fourteen editions of *The Giaour* were wildly popular as they appeared in succession from 1813 through 1815. One technique I have employed to establish a sense of the reception of the poem is to discuss the critical reviews of the time (readily available in Donald H. Reiman's *Romantics Reviewed*), which were emphatically favorable while at the same time sensitive to the potential negative reactions to this incomplete genre. But perhaps the most successful way to contextualize *The Giaour* is to point out parallels between social concerns in Byron's day and those in our own time—an approach that also allows students to see that poems of this nature are by no means lifeless artifacts lacking contemporary relevance. By demonstrating the influence of cultural trends on artistic expression, we can show how such factors play a crucial role in the selection of themes or forms within a certain period. I compare the fear of acquiring AIDS, for example, with the awareness of mortality during the Romantic period created by the specter of tuberculosis. Or I offer the example of the international stardom of a figure such as Michael Jackson and the subsequent public adulation of his work, and liken it to the mania for anything Byron published following the appearance of *Childe Harold's Pilgrimage*. Judging from students' responses to these illustrations in class and in their essays, I have found that the awareness of historical connections can assist students' comprehension of Byron's strategy in fragmenting *The Giaour* and the audience's eager acceptance of an intentionally disjointed and incomplete poem.

Because numerous examples of the fragmenteer's technique can be drawn from *The Giaour*, it literally becomes a textbook illustration of the Romantics' use of this form. Its narrative presentation is subdivided, for instance, so that the reader has no consistent—and therefore comfortably stable—point of view. Classroom discussion can be generated by exploring the effects of multiple perspective on the conveyance of a story. This is especially important here because the narrators throughout the bulk of the poem hate, or are at least wary of, the Giaour, and consequently their impressions of him are, not surprisingly, biased. I solicit examples from students of the phenomenon of differing "sides" of the same story (such as several witnesses' versions of a crime) to demonstrate the effect Byron creates by employing several narrative viewpoints.

The temporal rupture in *The Giaour* also promotes confusion by thrusting the reader into rapid shifts in time that serve, on the surface, to disorient rather than enlighten. Byron races back and forth in time, discussing characters early in the poem who have long since died, only to present them fighting a battle later on. Students frequently say that the time dislocation significantly contributes to the reader's disorientation, but I compare the poetic method with film techniques that employ the same device. After all, students are likely to be familiar with sudden temporal leaps in film and television, and a consideration of flashbacks and flash-forwards from these media leads to an easily recognized similarity with *The Giaour*.

In addition to introducing time shifts, Byron hampers the linear reading process by inserting sections of text that seem only remotely connected with the main line of the story. Perhaps the best example is the section on the butterfly and the scorpion. Every semester when I ask my students what they make of this part, I receive the same looks of baffled incomprehension.

Yet this fragment offers useful illustration of Byron's approach in *The Giaour* as the butterfly and the scorpion are described in terms loaded with metaphorical potential. The narrator, referring to the butterfly as a desired object destroyed in the act of capture, links the process with the pursuit of a beautiful woman, thereby creating a distinct parallel to the Giaour's pursuit of Leila that ends in her death and his ruin. The self-extinguishing scorpion is likewise presented as related metaphorically to "[t]he Mind, that broods o'er guilty woes" (422). Because the Giaour spends a great deal of time doing exactly that, another analogy clearly emerges. From this example, I show that Byron places his readers in the active role of writers (as all fragmenteers do) by forcing them to assemble the final connections and associations of the poem for themselves. Faced with commentary on butterflies and scorpions, they have no alternative but to construct a reading that can eventually accommodate this initially puzzling information.

Fragmentation, as many scholars have suggested, is an important technique and theme for the Romantics. Because it is an extensive yet manageable text, *The Giaour* is an excellent work for teachers who want to address this issue in Romanticism. With its battles, mutilations, a drowning, mysterious anger, and eerie hallucinations, it remains a vital and exciting reading experience for those willing to roll up their sleeves and participate in its production.

A Historical Approach to the Eastern Tales: The Case of *Parisina*

Daniel P. Watkins

It is a curious irony of literary history that the poems on which Byron's initial fame rested are seldom taught today in undergraduate English courses. One reason for this omission is that the Eastern tales (*The Giaour*, *The Bride of Abydos*, *The Corsair*, *Lara*, *The Siege of Corinth*, and *Parisina*) seem to represent Byronism less effectively than do *Childe Harold* 3 and *Manfred*, the poems most often used to demonstrate this venerable Romantic phenomenon, or that as poetry they are inferior to *Don Juan*. Another reason is that these early tales resist interpretation more successfully than any other body of poems Byron ever produced, with the possible exception of the dramas. They appear to be mere stories of adventure—as Byron cynically put it, they were written "to interest the women" (Marchand, *Letters* 9: 125)—and lack the aesthetic merit or intellectual seriousness that would make them worthy of study in the classroom.

Deciding to teach the Eastern tales thus poses a special challenge, for instructors must show students not only that these poems warrant serious scrutiny in themselves but also that they throw light on the history and literature of Romanticism. Sending students on a journey through the hastily written poems of Byron's turbulent years as a Regency dandy must somehow lead to literary and intellectual insight and not simply to the cheap thrills that customarily accompany melodramatic adventure narrative.

One way to help students glimpse the importance of the tales is by bracketing out, at least initially, questions of their aesthetic merit and biographical details and focusing instead on such matters as personal life, law, and gender. These issues not only offer students a familiar reference point but also help situate the tales among the most important social and historical crosscurrents of the Romantic period. While these elements are not always present on the surface of Romantic literature, they often appear at its deeper levels, and in Byron's tales they can effectively be explained not so much as products of Romanticism (or Byronism) as underlying structures and relations that produced Romanticism. In the tales, the categories and issues around which the narratives are constructed serve as bases for the many expressions of beauty, desire, and need for harmony—just as marital, familial, and legal conflicts today often stimulate nostalgia, fantasy, and escapism. Approaching the tales from this social-historical direction, then, demonstrates some of the concerns behind the Romantic imagination, and at the same time helps students conceptualize important issues that define their own situation.

In the following pages I discuss one of the tales, *Parisina*, in the terms I am suggesting to show how its historical explanation makes the poem eminently teachable, providing insight into the workings of Byron's imagination, into some of the social and historical problems of Romanticism generally, and into the relations between past literature and our contemporary history.[1] To understand *Parisina* historically, students must be led past conventional considerations of plot, theme, and character, and past easy black-and-white moral judgments that may tempt a student reading this tale for the first time. For *Parisina*, while at the level of plot portraying the taboo issue of incest, illustrates on a larger level the complexity of individual desires and belief systems, and the ineluctable authority of social relations in forming those desires and beliefs.

In *Parisina*, Byron depicts the inner workings of family life, a subject omitted in the earlier tales but that reappears in *Cain* and *Don Juan* some years later and that is central to other literature produced during the Regency—for example, Shelley's *Cenci*. Byron's handling of the family is significant in at least two ways. First, he draws attention to the social dimension of domestic life and even of domestic turmoil, not to deny the personal quality of life but to emphasize the larger circumstances that necessarily help condition it and give it meaning. The internal workings of the family are directly associated with, and made to answer to, the larger network of relations governing society, to the extent that the very survival of the family is shown to depend on the proper alignment of personal and public values. The incest relation between Hugo and Parisina, for instance, is not portrayed as a purely private crisis, but rather as a crisis of sweeping social proportions, as exemplified in the public trial and punishment of the transgressors. While the burden of the crime falls only on a few individuals, the crime itself is not viewed, finally, as a violation of family relationships alone but of social relations as well.

Second, Byron's portrayal of the family makes a specific political statement by exposing the close connection between family life and public power. One ingredient of Azo's political strength is the family unity that he has created around him: the tranquil domestic life that is implied to have been securely in place before the incest ordeal reflects the supposedly solid values being disseminated through society under his authority. When Hugo and Parisina are caught in their illicit love affair, and it becomes clear that everyone except Azo has been in on the secret, the damage is not only emotional but political as well—an insult to and a denial of Azo's authority. This is why he acts swiftly and publicly to punish the offenders. Fully exercising the power at his disposal, he has his own son executed in public, and he banishes his wife, replacing them with a new and more submissive family, from which "goodly sons grew by his side" (531), effectively reasserting his authority at the most fundamental level. To explain the action in these terms is not to question Azo's moral earnestness—when he passes judgment on his wife and son, he believes he is carrying out the demands of justice (see, for example, lines 575–76)—nor to say that the incest affair is handled with such extremity because it poses a direct threat to his political position. Rather, it is to suggest that political power is sustained, among other ways, by its absolute penetration into every facet of human experience, down to the most personal.

To contextualize the narrative action in this way encourages students to move beyond their own immediate experiences of family life, beyond the quick moral judgments that all of us so often bring to bear on certain kinds of personal activity, and to conceptualize personal life in terms of its public social determinations. When students realize that Hugo's personal situation and Azo's political authority are intricately connected with structures of public life, they begin to understand that a character's needs, desires, and actions are not simply the result of individual choices but are often determined by material and ideological forces. This emphasis has an added payoff: once students see in poetry the grid of demands and beliefs within which the lives of characters play themselves out, they gain insight into their own family life and its entanglement in networks of social relations not readily visible from within the family itself.

Beyond the issue of family life, the tale demonstrates the way legal structures can be used to maintain the social order by imposing ideological as well as judicial controls on individuals. Again, the portrayal of this element provides students with a familiar point of reference—the institution of law —while at the same time presenting the social function of law in such a way as to question commonplace assumptions about it.

The subjection of the narrative hero, Hugo, to the state's legal power illustrates the law's function of preserving the existing structures of authority. When Azo ascends "his throne of judgment" (135), he does so to fulfill his social responsibility, not from blind love of power (see lines 198–204). But if his actions are sincere, they are not entirely innocent, for they serve to maintain a social arrangement in which Azo has a vested interest. By assuming unquestioningly that the state is beyond reproach, and by deflecting the incest issue entirely away from the state to those on trial, Azo hides ruling-class interests beneath abstract legal and moral considerations, effectively demonstrating state authority and, by implication, legitimizing his position as part of that authority.

By approaching the institutions of family and law in this way, students can better account for the hero in the tale. Hugo is unlike earlier and later Byronic heroes in that he submits without resistance to the controlling codes of his world. Rather than standing moodily outside the culture that has alienated him, he is from the first a loyal citizen and son in every way (except in his love for Parisina), and he never attempts to deny this. Unlike the

Giaour, Selim, Lara, and Alp—heroes of the earlier tales—he never seeks
to overthrow a state leader, attempting instead to overcome his alienation
without challenging the existing power structure. The authority of a father,
the decision of the law, his own subordinate role and final punishment—
these are readily accepted as the inescapable facts of his situation.

This explanation would see Hugo's conduct as a last, desperate attempt
to overcome alienation by acknowledging the claims of society on him, much
as Arnold, in *The Deformed Transformed* (written much later), attempts to
combat alienation by embodying fully the values of his world. Moreover,
Hugo's submission may be regarded as one sign of the unavoidable power
of prevailing social authority. Certainly his long speech preceding his execution suggests this (see lines 234–317). Without questioning the authority
of social institutions per se, this speech attacks deeply rooted values that
undergird those institutions governing the world of the poem, focusing the
vital connection between the subjective and objective conditions of social
life. So deeply submerged beneath plot-level concerns as to go virtually
unnoticed, this critique nonetheless elucidates deep contradictions between
human value and social authority in Hugo's world and, further, suggests the
debilitating impact of these contradictions.

One way the narrative effects the exposure of social contradiction is by
focusing directly on the social dimensions of criminal conduct, rather than,
say, on the mysterious and often mystifying allure of the outlaw (as Byron
had done in earlier tales). While never denying the authority of the instru-
ments of law, Hugo's speech before his father provides a context for eval-
uating the interests and suppositions of this authority. And what becomes
clear in the light of his remarks is that the crime of incest exists only because
Azo's political power overrides the basic human commitment of Hugo and
Parisina to one another—Azo's personal claims have state authority behind
them; the claims of Parisina and Hugo do not. This difference alone establishes the legal and moral right of Azo to punish the transgressors. The
emphasis on the particular conditions surrounding the crime not only suggests the role of social relations in criminal conduct; more important, it
illustrates that social authority rather than individual conduct is in this case
guilty. In the larger context of social life, in fact, the crime tells more about
the kind of world that individuals are forced to live in than about personal
malice or integrity.

An additional point made in Hugo's speech should be seen by students
as of pressing contemporary importance—namely, that social authority, in
Byron's day as in our own, most often discriminates along gender lines.
While Hugo, having been sentenced to death, valiantly addresses his father
on the subjects of injustice and inhumanity, Parisina not only remains silent
but goes through a series of stereotypically feminine responses to extreme

pressure: she first weeps (173–82), then faints (348), and then suffers an attack of amnesia (360–85). Like the heroines of the earlier tales, she seems to be all beauty and no substance. Although students may fault Byron for such a predictably masculine view of women, they should be encouraged, again, to consider these events within the larger social context of the narrative action, for this context disrupts the narrative surface of the poem to expose the power relations that typically oppress women.

Beginning from social relations rather than from individualist or biographical details, students can dislodge Parisina from stereotypical interpretations of women, learning how she is a victim of an oppressive, exploitative world. Although Hugo is consistently vocal, and although the central conflict in the narrative is ostensibly between him and Azo, the real victims in the poem, from the beginning, are women, as power is arbitrarily exercised against them, effectively silencing them and relegating them to the fringes of society. Hugo's own "heritage of shame," the tale stresses, results from Azo's irresponsible use of his power against a woman (243–51). Further, Azo's marriage to Parisina is a blatant compromise of a woman who does not care for him. Even if he dotes on her, it is the dotage on a thing possessed. Despite his affection for her, he never allows her equal (or even human) status. He uses her, for instance, to taunt Hugo (whom she loves) for being illegitimate and powerless (253–63). After Parisina is banished, too, Azo again exercises the privileges of patriarchy, finding "another bride" (530), one who presumably will be submissive.

In such a patriarchal world as this, where institutions and codes are believed to constitute a fixed and permanent reality, where history is elided and replaced by abstract principles, and where extreme conflict defines everyday life, incest becomes more than a psychological issue. It becomes symbolic, in various ways, of the complex dimensions of the world being portrayed. As we saw before, this particular case of incest is a product of a specific social situation that evolved over time; it is mediated both by personal struggles and injustices (that is, the father's usurpation of the son in sexual matters) and by public history: the power in Azo's hands is built into and has been passed down by culture itself. Further, as becomes apparent in Hugo's speech, the entire incest issue is to a large extent fabricated; the mother-son attachment is originally an innocent, emotional, mutual commitment made by two individuals to each other, and it becomes incest only when Azo abuses his political power, marrying Parisina to taunt Hugo. The structures of everyday life in the world of the narrative are isolating and oppressive, as individuals are denied access to social and thus individual power and rights. Hugo as a bastard son and Parisina as a woman have nowhere to turn to satisfy basic human (social) needs; both can serve the state as military or emotional subordinates, but neither can enter into the unalienated stream of social productivity and fulfillment.

In describing the workings of personal life, law, and gender, *Parisina* provides students with an excellent opportunity to consider how individual actions, needs, and desires arise within, and are shaped by, specific social situations. Further, by focusing on these and other social matters (such as war and religion), students are exposed to the social contradictions that lie beneath all Romantic literature, serious and popular alike, and beneath the personal and public experiences of their own lives. While the approach sketched here assumes rather than discovers history and society as determining forces, and can be faulted for this assumption, it nevertheless shows students a way past conventional assumptions about plot, character, and theme, gives them conceptual tools for studying Romantic literature as a historical (and literary) phenomenon, and (one hopes) vitalizes the study of literature by bringing it into the crosscurrents of past and present history.

NOTE

[1]Some of the ideas in this essay are taken from Watkins, *Social Relations* 124–37.

Byron's Poetic Journal:
Teaching *Childe Harold's Pilgrimage*

Bernard A. Hirsch

Childe Harold's Pilgrimage is a poetic journal. Written over an eight-year period, it marks the major stages of Byron's life and art. By treating the poem as a journal, I provide students a comprehensive framework within which to understand both the poem's textural diversity and the sense of immediacy, of life being lived, that Byron is at such pains to convey. Byron creates textural diversity by mixing and juxtaposing, often surprisingly, cosmic commentary and the mood of a moment, careful reflection and gut reaction, autobiography and fictive narration; such a mix, expected in a journal, often baffles students who confront it in a poem. The sense of immediacy for which Byron strives is also characteristic of journal writing and conveyed in *Childe Harold* through the rapid shifts in tone and point of view, the sudden mood changes, the contradictions in thought and word. Once the students have come to terms with the poem's journal-like character, we can consider the appropriateness of Byron's method to his larger purpose: to express and keep a faithful record of his emotional, psychological, intellectual, and imaginative development. The poem is no less than the story of how, in Byron's own view, he became what he was.

I teach the whole of *Childe Harold* in a course on Byron, Shelley, and Keats for advanced undergraduates, both English majors and nonmajors, and graduate students. Rather than devote a section of the course to each poet, I mix the three so that patterns of response and influence can be more readily discerned. Such a structure is especially useful in treating Byron and Shelley, and *Childe Harold*, given its chronology and journal-like character, provides an apt basis for it.

Most of my students have been required to keep a journal in their introductory English courses, and a surprising number continue the practice. But even those who have never kept one seem to grasp the process—the fits and starts, with the resulting discontinuities of mood and narrative, the silences (empty pages) that persist for days, weeks, months sometimes. Thus it makes sense to them when I stress the essential unity of all four cantos of *Childe Harold* while insisting on a piecemeal approach to the poem along chronological lines. I find such an approach necessary because the poem in its entirety is simply too much for most undergraduates to swallow whole, and desirable because it enables me to prepare for cantos 3 and 4 in several ways. Much happened to Byron between the publication of cantos 1 and 2, in 1812, and the writing of canto 3, in 1816, and while I cannot effectively consider all that occurred, I can highlight those events that most significantly affect his poetry.

I use Jerome J. McGann's Oxford Authors *Byron* for my course, and the first assignment is cantos 1 and 2 along with Byron's letter to his mother of 12 November 1809. This letter works well in setting up my particular approach to the poem—first, because it is in some ways a more polished public performance than the poem itself and, second, because the letter writer's self-assurance and command of detail contrast markedly with what for my students is the muddled, somewhat confusing narrative voice in cantos 1 and 2. Though my students rightly regard a personal letter as more intimate and thus more unconsciously revelatory of a writer than a poem intended for publication, they invariably sense how deliberate Byron's construction of his persona is in this letter. His reinforcement in his reader's mind of the exoticism and dangers of Albania is not lost on them, nor are his efforts to present himself as a man of consequence and in control of circumstances. My students, however, do not find this persona in cantos 1 and 2. Indeed, they are not sure exactly who the narrator is and how, in spots, his thoughts can be distinguished from Harold's. And where is Byron in all this? Is he present in the character of Harold, as many of his contemporary readers believed but which Byron was quick to deny? Surely, Byron isn't the pompous, judgmental narrator who opens the first canto—but what about the obvious biographical links between the narrator and Byron?

When assigning cantos 1 and 2 and Byron's letter, I ask students to read the preface and its "addition" closely, to pay special attention to Byron's emphasis on the poem's "experimental" nature (McGann 19) and to his rationale for using "the stanza of Spenser" (20). These assertions alert us to an essential quality of these cantos; they are a testing out of sorts, and he decides to use Spenserian stanzas because this "measure . . . admits equally of all . . . kinds of composition" (20).

This flexibility is also inherent in the process of keeping a journal. My students know that journal writing involves more than describing places, people, and experiences. It is a means of recording their responses to their environment and the effects, singly and accretively, of those responses on the development of their thought and being. A journal forms an account of what one was and is in the process of becoming, and it is in the context of such a record that *Childe Harold* is most accessible to my students. In that context they are more willing to surrender their insistence on a singly discernible and determinate voice in the poem.

I have elsewhere discussed the identity of the narrator in cantos 1 and 2 and the erosion over the course of the poem of his system of values ("Erosion"), so I won't repeat myself here. But few of my students like the narrator at first; they find him narrow, overbearing, and judgmental. "He seems to have an answer for everything," one student said, "and contempt for most of it." When I pushed for specifics, she cited his rigidity toward Harold and his bigotry toward the Portuguese. I then asked the class if, in their view, this attitude characterized the narrator throughout the two cantos. Another student said, "No, and that's kind of the problem." I asked her to explain; she pointed to the narrator's early criticism of Harold's lack of "virtue" (1.2) and his frankly sexual admiration of Spanish women later in the first canto (stanzas 57–59). This last, she said, sounded more like the Byron she had heard of. Others admired his stand on the Elgin marbles and sympathized with his loss of friends at the end of each canto. My students' gut reactions to the narrator helped me make three important points. (1) The poem, like a journal, is very much about gut reactions, and gut reactions directly reflect the inconsistencies that often exist between what we feel and what we think we think. (2) The narrator becomes a progressively more sympathetic character over the course of cantos 1 and 2. As the poem opens, his perspective is governed by certain absolutes that lend a false coherence to experience. These erode unceasingly throughout his journey, and the severity of that erosion is best measured by the very inconsistencies in tone and point of view my students initially find so baffling. The narrator becomes increasingly vulnerable as his journey continues and thus, for most of my students, more human and more humane. (3) Harold, aimless and rudderless, is representative of what for my students is a seductive and uncomfortably common response to a world seemingly resistant to meaning—and the solipsism and defensiveness that characterize the narrator at the end of canto 2 define that response.

The narrator's defensive posture is for Byron at this point in his career a natural response to his profound sense of loss. Cantos 1 and 2, my students come to recognize, proceed in large part on the basis of a painful series of separations: Harold from his father's hall and native land, from his beloved, and, he hopes, from himself; and the narrator from his England, from the faith and patriotism that inform his values, from his Enlightenment beliefs in the educability and progress of humankind, and from dear friends. Ironically, the only movement in the poem toward unity involves the merging of the narrator and Harold, conveyed through the narrator's increasing sympathy for Harold as their journey proceeds, and his adoption of Harold's stance toward the end of it.

This movement begins to reverse itself in canto 3. McGann has argued that "the direction of the poem changes at the beginning of Canto III from an educational pilgrimage to a therapeutic one" (*Fiery Dust* 77); I agree—and, ironically, Shelley is central to Byron's therapy.

By the time I assign canto 3, the class has read and discussed *Alastor*, "Hymn to Intellectual Beauty," *Mont Blanc*, and "On Love." In introducing canto 3 in this context, however, I've learned to be careful. For most of my students, the notion of influence is limited. If they can find passages in canto 3 that contain Shelleyan language or imagery, or express a thought they have come to associate with Shelley, they feel that they have discerned "influence" and that's the end of it. And such passages abound in canto 3. I try to make them see that "influence" is a dynamic rather than a static concept, that it involves not merely a poet's reproducing in his work language or thought similar to that of another poet, but rather the poet's active engagement with that language and thought. Here again is where I find the "journal" concept helpful.

I assign, along with canto 3, Byron's "Alpine Journal," written during the same year (McGann 981–90). My students' pleasure in reading this journal derives from the various aspects of Byron revealed through his engagement with the landscape and people he encounters. The passage that ends the journal is an especially apt entry into *Childe Harold* 3, for it suggests, as does the poem itself, that Shelleyan idealism will not provide a satisfying end to Byron's search for meaning in the world and in himself (McGann 990). It also suggests, however, that it is part of that search, that it is a potential answer that, like the narrator's beliefs in cantos 1 and 2, demands trial in the arena of experience.

When I introduce Byron at the beginning of the course, I mention that he differs from Shelley and Keats in his lack of an overt commitment to poetry as a calling. Throughout most of his life he draws a distinction between a life of action and the writing of poetry. Thus when Shelley urges him to pursue his grand destiny, to be the enlightener of humankind (Jones 1: 507–08), Byron does not rush to heed the call. He cannot pretend to Shelley's faith in the power of poetry to change the world.

"The world," as one of my students dramatically but nonetheless accurately put it, "seems to triumph over the power of poetry" in the opening stanza of *Childe Harold* 3, in which another painful separation intensifies Byron's despair. "But doesn't poetry," I counter, "reverse things in stanza 6?" "Perhaps, briefly," my student concedes, "but what about stanza 14?" Of course, neither of us, nor Byron, is yet ready to declare a winner. Still, approaching the poem as a journal has helped wean my undergraduates from their expectations of thematic and structural consistency.

The self-referential character of a journal also helps my students come to terms with Byron's use of historical events and individuals in canto 3. These are important not in their own right but for what they teach Byron about himself—and what he learns provides the basis for his challenge to Shelley. Napoleon, for example, was imbued with the fervor and genius to redeem his nation, but his very aspirations turned him tyrant. And Byron sees that what drove Napoleon drives him.

The "Rousseau" stanzas, however, present for my students the clearest challenge to Shelley. Napoleon, after all, seen even in terms of Byron's balanced depiction of him, was ultimately a tyrant bent on conquest. Rousseau was a writer, an artist, a being "[k]indled" "with ethereal flame" whose "love was passion's essence" (3.78). More, he was a primary inspirational force for the French Revolution, the great theme on which Shelley urged Byron to write. The revolution was, though, to Byron, "a fearful monument" (3.82) that seemed only to perpetuate the cycle of violence Byron condemned in Spain (canto 1). In fact, as Byron conceived of it, the revolution was the expression in the world of events of Rousseau's "phrenzied" interior life (3.77–80).

The "Lake Leman" stanzas follow the section on Rousseau. This landscape is beautiful and seductive and seems to affirm within Byron himself Shelley's profound sense of the harmonizing power of universal love—the very power by which the poet might change the world. But the quiescent harmony expressed in these stanzas is shattered by a fierce storm, emblematic of the control-less passion within the poet that will not let him rest within the bosom of a landscape or a philosophy that, however comforting, is contradicted at every turn by life lived.

Even though the compelling beauty of Clarens reawakens in Byron a hope in his own revivified and expanded capacity for love (4.99–109), canto 3 ends with the sense of loss with which it began. Byron's active engagement with the world of experience, and in canto 3 with the world of ideas, continues, and only in the very act of engagement itself, as Byron will come to learn, is salvation possible. Such salvation, however, will depend on Byron's ability to see the writing of poetry as a means of engagement.

For Byron, Shelley's poetry has little to do with life in this world. Shelley's highest conceptions, in Byron's estimation, derive from Shelley's belief in the poet's capacity to direct humanity toward an idealized future. Byron, in canto 4, firmly commits himself to the present. Salvation, and I follow McGann in this, insofar as it is possible at all, is a consequence of the present moment. "There woos no home, nor hope, nor life, save what is here," Byron tells us at a pivotal point (4.105) and reiterates toward the end of the poem (4.176). It is this disparity in Byron's and Shelley's views of the poet's calling and art's potential that leads me to begin class discussion of canto 4 with Shelley's comments in a letter to his friend, Peacock, of 17 or 18 December 1818.

Peacock had earlier criticized what he perceived as the misanthropy of *Childe Harold* 4, and Shelley agreed with him: "The spirit in which it is written is, if insane, the most wicked & mischievous insanity that ever was given forth" (Jones 2: 57–58). Shelley's comments disturb my students because most of them find canto 4 to be considerably more optimistic than the preceding cantos. "It certainly ends on a more positive note," they tell me, and they are glad to learn that at least Shelley feels as they do about the "Ocean" stanzas: "that he is a great poet, I think the address to Ocean proves" (Jones 2: 58). In any case, Shelley's distaste for canto 4 as a whole, coupled with his praise of the "Ocean" stanzas, provides a useful context for the class's consideration of canto 4 and a means of refining their own perceptions of the poem.

One especially perceptive student called attention to the "Egeria fountain" section and the pessimistic view of the human creative potential that seems to emerge from it: "It's a direct hit on Shelley's conception of love, especially where Byron says, 'Of its own beauty is the mind diseased, / And fevers into false creation' " (4.122), he maintained, and proceeded at my urging to effectively summarize Shelley's conception of love as he understood it from the Shelley he had read. Another student, who had read all of Shelley's letter to Peacock, wondered if Shelley's criticism wasn't more of a response to the dissolute life he felt Byron was leading in Venice than to canto 4 itself. By referring the class to Shelley's literal complaint—against the "spirit in which it is written"—I was able to take advantage of my student's fortuitous shift in focus. For Shelley's letter does make a precise connection between the poetry written and the life lived; and despite his uncongenial view of this connection, it is the very thing that Byron, and we as readers, discover over the course of *Childe Harold* and that Byron finally affirms in canto 4.

To pursue this idea, I direct my students to the dedication to Hobhouse, in particular to Byron's agreement with Alfieri that "[i]n Italy man is a plant that grows stronger than in any other country" (McGann 147, 1032). However much Byron may later modify his view of the Italians, his perception of them here suggests a basis for the optimism my students discern in canto 4. The sense of history that emerges from the poem may initially resemble, on a grander scale, the cycles of outrage and vengeance that, in canto 1, define Spanish history. Tyranny's inevitable triumph and the futility of human creativity appear to be the primary lessons taught by experience at various points throughout canto 4, and Byron's despair at learning them is palpable. What mitigates this despair, however, is apparent in the creative persistence of a people whose genius is expressive in proportion to their sufferings. This persistence, moreover, is what Italy enables Byron to recognize in himself, that "there is that within me which shall tire / Torture and Time, and breathe when I expire" (4.137).

There are fits and starts throughout canto 4, as in the preceding cantos, but, as a student noted, "the depressing parts don't seem to dominate like they did before." They are qualified structurally as well. The movement throughout cantos 1 and 2 is from certainty to uncertainty, from belief in an ordered if often intractable world to a deep awareness of the chaos of human events, a chaos reflective of that within the individual. In canto 3, Shelleyan idealism seems at times to provide a way of seeing and knowing capable of restoring harmony to the world and within the self, but the moments of contentment or revelation it occasionally yields soon give way to renewed and intensified despair as its insufficiency becomes apparent. In canto 4, however, this movement is reversed. Periods of depression over what seems the inexorable flow of history toward violence and dissolution give way to renewed hope in the power of human creativity, if not to wholly transform experience, to endure and illuminate it, and by so doing endow it with dignity and worth. Thus the persistent dream of freedom, of which Byron writes in the dedication, reclaims the poet from despair at the failure of the French Revolution (stanzas 93–98), and his remembrance of Cicero, Trajan, and Rienzi, of the recurrence through time of such individuals, renews his commitment to his pilgrimage through time. This movement from depression to self-renewal is repeated at several points in canto 4, most dramatically through a succession of powerfully inspiring moments over the final thirty-three stanzas: Saint Peter's, the Vatican Gallery, the death of Princess Charlotte, and Ocean.

As Shelley symbolically converts time into space in *Lines Written among the Euganean Hills*, Shelley's poetic response to canto 4, so Byron converts time into people and events. This is not to say that Petrarch, Tasso, Dante, Ariosto, the Caritas Romana, the dying gladiator, and others lose their character as individuals. Indeed, it is precisely in that character that their redemptive potential exists. But that potential is equally reliant on their identity as moments in the flow of time, moments that endow human history with its true significance. Byron, in canto 4, comes to identify with such moments, to see himself as one of them.

Byron openly declares himself a poet in stanza 9, and he is sustained in that role by both the poetry and the lives of the Italian poets he considers. My students sometimes wonder, though, why he didn't stick to poets and poetry if his goal is to affirm their power. Why mingle poets with others, with statesmen, philosophers, prisoners, and gladiators? Because poetry, as Byron conceives of it, derives its power from the flux and variety of experience. That is what the "Ocean" stanzas express. The Ocean, in the literal sense, is the constant by which that flux and variety are thrown into relief. Symbolically, however, it is experience itself, immutable and familiar, destructive and sustaining, violent and gentle, a terror and a delight. As a child Byron had "loved thee, Ocean!" (4.184) and has learned through arduous pilgrimage to love Ocean again. Fortunately, we can understand how he has come to do so. He kept a journal.

Pilgrimage to Creation: Byron in Iberia

Gordon K. Thomas

> Was it for this you took your sudden journey,
> Under the pretence of business indispensible . . . ?
> —Byron, *Don Juan*

If students understand why Byron went to Portugal and Spain in 1809, what conditions and experiences he encountered there, and what effects that first journey had on his life and writing, they can examine the very heart of Byron's poetic character and achievement. Students who think of their educational process as a voyage find a roughly comforting familiarity in Byron's repeated uses of the same metaphor; but they can find much more—an unfolding of complex historical backgrounds of the early nineteenth century, a revelation of Byron's rich poetic personality, a key to his artistic methods and stance and his manner of linking and often confusing life and art—in discovering and sharing Byron's Iberian travels. His journey provides a structure for teaching students about the poet's development and his increasingly varied compositions.

Why did Byron, in a mood that many of our students today can recognize, leave home at age twenty-one for an uncertain destination? To John Hanson, his financial adviser, who cautioned him against such extravagant plans, he insisted simply, "There are circumstances which render it absolutely indispensible, and quit the country I must" (Marchand, *Letters* 1: 200–01). The reasons for the journey of Childe Harold are no clearer, for he "e'en for change of scene would seek the shades below" (*Childe Harold* 1.6). Like many scholars, students may enjoy speculating about such mysteries, but they may have to conclude, with Leslie Marchand, that "there is no solid evidence" to explain Byron's, or even Harold's, motives for undertaking the journey (*Letters* 1: 232n). Proposed destinations mentioned in the poet's very vague plans for the trip included Sicily, the Greek Isles, Persia, Calcutta. Yet it was not the whim of a moment. Almost three and a half years before his departure from England, he wrote his mother that he was dissatisfied with university life at Cambridge and wanted to travel for real education, "to pass a couple of Years abroad, where I am certain of employing my Time to far more advantage and at much less expence, than at our English Seminaries" (*Letters* 1: 89). Students may be interested to discover that Byron was right—his travels had far greater educational value than his studies at the university did.

Byron, like Harold, "from his native land resolv'd to go" (*Childe Harold* 1.6). In the initial plans for the journey his desire to depart seemed to matter more than his destination did. It was England that he fled, a fact that explains many of the opinions he took with him and clarifies some of his experiences in Iberia. Childe Harold, watching the English coast fade away, "of his wish to roam / Repented" (1.12). He seizes his harp and sings the famous "Good Night" to his native land. Perhaps Byron, as he waited to leave the harbor at Falmouth, felt some similar pang: "The world is all before me," he wrote in a letter to his mother, echoing many a young student setting off on a geographical or literary adventure and echoing also Milton's description of Adam and Eve on their expulsion from paradise. Perhaps he felt a bit of anxiety at the start of a new adventure—and perhaps not, for Byron immediately added, "I leave England without regret, and without a wish to revisit any thing it contains, except yourself" (*Letters* 1: 206).

How does a writer—a budding young poet or even a budding young student burdened with an assignment—get started in writing? The question, I find, always interests my students. They also enjoy the wonderful combination of Byron's polished (sometimes *too* polished and not altogether convincing) poetry, like parts of *Childe Harold*, studied in tandem with his slapdash journals and letters, which make up some of the most readable and immediate prose in our language. As Byron set sail from England on the only boat he could find, bound for Lisbon (a long way from the Persia and Calcutta he had once expected to visit), he claimed to have no serious plans for a travel poem: "I have laid down my pen" (*Letters* 1: 208). But the exuberance, a crucial element in his greatest poetry, that he began to feel as he set sail enabled him to make discoveries beyond his expectations. To persuade himself, as he wrote in a letter to Francis Hodgson while waiting for the boat to sail, to "Laugh at all things / Great & small things, / Sick or well, at sea or shore" (*Letters* 1: 213), was to serve his own creative purposes.

On the fifth day out from England, Byron and his companions had their first view of Iberia; they saw "Cintra's mountain" (*Childe Harold* 1.14) offering its dramatic greeting, with convent and castle standing on adjoining peaks. To understand the poet's writings on the lands he was about to visit, students need some awareness of events of the time; they also need a better source of information than Byron himself provides, for he more than once displays an amazing ignorance and insensitivity. Portugal endured three invasions from Napoleon's troops, the second of which had occurred only four months before the poet's arrival, bringing with it much destruction and demoralization. England had joined with the Iberian peoples in an anti-French alliance in 1808, but the behavior of these newly allied English forces in the months immediately preceding Byron's arrival in Lisbon had only deepened a prevalent mood of despair and cynicism. The British betrayal of freedom—as the notorious Convention of Cintra was popularly viewed throughout Portugal, Spain, and even England—surely had to undermine trust. When the Portuguese saw the French flag lowered over Lisbon and then replaced by the English banner, they felt, as the *Times* of London reported, that they "had not recovered their liberty, but had been consigned over to new masters" (26 Sept. 1808: 2). Lisboans, feeling trapped by their dependence on British aid against Napoleon and now keenly alert to signs of disdain and unreliability in their allies, exhibited understandable ambivalence toward Britons in their midst after the Convention of Cintra. Surprisingly, Byron did not at first understand this attitude. He expected to be greeted in Lisbon as a liberating hero; instead, though struck by the spectacular beauty of the city's setting, he resented the mood of its inhabitants: "A nation swoln with ignorance and pride, / Which lick yet loathe the hand that waves the sword / To save them from the wrath of Gaul's unsparing lord" (*Childe Harold* 1.16).

The source of Byron's negative appraisal of the Portuguese was probably a combination of the people's demoralization after recent events and the poet's state of mind. Certainly students should realize that the world-weariness and the sense of futility attributed to Childe Harold at the beginning of his journey also characterized Byron's life in those days: "Oft-times in his maddest mirthful mood / Strange pangs would flash along Childe Harold's brow" (1.8). An effect of Byron's Iberian pilgrimage, one well worth demonstrating to students, was that it lightened his mood—but not at first and not in Lisbon.

We need to take our students on a little tour of Portugal (a field trip would be most effective of course, but slides or even a good map will do) so that they may begin to appreciate Sintra as Byron appreciated it. Lisbon seemed quite unpleasant to Byron, but "Lo! Cintra's glorious Eden intervenes" (*Childe Harold* 1.18). Byron describes Sintra, with its ancient mountaintop castle, its palaces, and its astonishing natural beauty, in considerable detail in *Childe Harold*, and the setting remained permanently in the poet's mind as a special paradise—his own lotusland. He glowingly wrote his mother that it "is perhaps in every respect the most delightful [village] in Europe, it contains beauties of every description natural & artificial, Palaces and gardens rising in the midst of rocks, cataracts, and precipices, convents on stupendous heights a distant view of the sea and the Tagus," and "it unites in itself all the wildness of the Western Highlands," which he had known as a boy, "with the verdure of the south of France," which he had never seen (*Letters* 1: 218). Childe Harold shares his creator's enthusiasm for this "variegated maze of mount and glen," which he finds "more dazzling unto mortal ken" and more impossible to describe adequately, he said, than poetic visions of heaven itself (*Childe Harold* 1.18). Byron's appreciation, however, did not include getting all the facts straight in his poetic rapturizing, as, for example, when he quite erroneously calls the Hieronymite monastery on a hill above the town a "house of woe" set amid a scene of lawlessness and "murderous wrath" (1.20, 21).

Above all, Sintra held two particular attractions for Byron that are significant for students of literature. One was the spirit of William Beckford, which still seemed to Byron to linger in the hills, although Beckford had left Sintra and Portugal for good in 1796. The other was the infamous Convention of Cintra, which the poet mistakenly believed had taken place in the town. Politics, warfare, and the study of literature can profitably merge here: Byron would certainly have read the two installments of Wordsworth's great tract of protest *Concerning . . . the Convention of Cintra*, which had appeared very prominently in the London *Courier* in December 1808 and January 1809, and students of Byron's sojourn in Iberia should consult that work too. Sintra, wrote Byron to his mother, "is remarkable as the scene of Sir H[ew] D[alrymple]'s convention" (*Letters* 1: 218), and John Hobhouse, a traveling companion, recorded in his diary, "We entered the very room in which the famous Convention was signed" (qtd. in *Letters* 1: 218n). In *Childe Harold*, Byron describes not only the room in which he thought the convention was signed, and not only the effects of the treaty, but also, to demonstrate the power of pure imagination, the physical and mental anguish experienced by the sensitive traveler who visits the site of the treaty signing: "Behold the hall where chiefs were late conven'd! / Oh! dome displeasing unto British eye!" (1.24), and, further, "Ever since that martial synod met, / Britannia sickens, Cintra! at thy name" (1.26). Teachers should tell students outright, but humbly (for we all make mistakes), that the convention was actually negotiated at Torres Vedras and ratified at Lisbon; the name "Convention of Cintra" is a misnomer, one that Byron helped to perpetuate.

The visit to Sintra changed the poet's mood, and teachers can encourage students to find evidence of this shift in *Childe Harold* and the letters. Back in Lisbon, where he and three companions were to begin their ride on horseback across Portugal and southwestern Spain, Byron summed up his adventures in much more cheerful language than he had used earlier:

> I am very happy here, because I loves oranges, and talk bad Latin to the monks, who understand it, as it is like their own,—and I goes into society (with my pocket-pistols), and I swims in the Tagus all across at once, and I rides on an ass or a mule, and swears Portugese, and have got a diarrhoea and bites from the mosquitoes. But what of that? Comfort must not be expected by folks that go a pleasuring. . . . I am infinitely amused with my pilgrimage as far as it has gone.
>
> (*Letters* 1: 215)

As his mood changed, he was getting ready to write great poetry.

In this positive state of mind, Byron was also getting ready for Spain. His enthusiasm now became unbounded as he passed through countryside rich in history and in scenes of the recent war. "Oh, lovely Spain! renown'd, romantic land!" he exults (*Childe Harold* 1.35). His letters were similarly animated; Spanish men, he wrote, were "far superior" and so were the roads, the women, the food, and the horses; the cities were beautiful, "only exceeded by the loveliness of [the] inhabitants" (*Letters* 1: 216–20). While he approved wholeheartedly of the Spanish guerrillas' valiant struggle for freedom in 1809 ("Awake, ye sons of Spain! awake! advance! / Lo! Chivalry, your ancient goddess, cries" [*Childe Harold* 1.37]), he had growing doubts about the English intervention in the peninsula ("the fond ally / That fights for all, but ever fights in vain" [*Childe Harold* 1.41]. Both these beliefs, students need to know, became increasingly important in his later poetry and life.

As the poet and his companions traveled south toward Seville, they reached the rugged, heavily fortified terrain of the Sierra Morena, "passing over ground every inch of which had recently been fought over by French and Spaniards," as Hobhouse wrote (1: 10). "The barbarities on both sides are shocking," said Byron (*Letters* 1: 217). Near the town of Monesterio they met "two French prisoners and a Spanish spy on their way to Seville to be hanged" (Hobhouse 1: 10). In this exotic, dangerous, and beautiful setting, Byron appears to have conceived the masterpiece of his later career, *Don Juan*. His preface to that poem, a preface never published until the twentieth century but certainly not to be omitted in our teaching, asks readers of *Don Juan* "to suppose . . . that the following epic Narrative is told by a Spanish Gentleman in a village in the Sierra Morena in the road between Monasterio and Seville, sitting at the door of a Posada with the Curate of the hamlet on his right hand a Segar in his mouth . . ." (Steffan and Pratt, *Variorum* 2: 5). If the Iberian journey had produced nothing more than this moment and scene of inspiration it would have been fully justified. Every odyssey should bring forth an epic.

The poet's mood became increasingly light as he continued across Spain. He thought that the women of Spain were more friendly and candid than those of England, and even the churches were superior: "I prefer the Gothic Cathedral of Seville to St. P[aul's], St. Sophia's and any religious building I have ever seen" (*Letters* 1: 251). He made repeated comparisons at the expense of things English, both in his prose ("Cadiz, sweet Cadiz! is the most delightful town I ever beheld, very different from our English cities" [*Letters* 1: 220]) and in his poetry: "Oh never talk again to me / Of Northern charms and British ladies; / It has not been your lot to see, / Like me, the lovely Girl of Cadiz" ("Girl of Cadiz" 1–4).

From Cadiz, Byron and his friends sailed to Gibraltar. It could hardly have been the spectacular setting of that British colony that depressed the poet; indeed, it seems to have been simply his return to British soil. Whatever the cause, the high spirits he had shown in Spain were suddenly gone. He wrote, "Cadiz is the prettiest town in Europe, Seville a large & fine city, Gibraltar the dirtiest most detestable spot in existence" (*Letters* 1: 217–18). Students who wonder why Byron almost omitted Gibraltar from *Childe Harold* may wonder even more at the explanation offered by an early biographer, John Galt, who first met the poet in Gibraltar and who saw his behavior as a combination of a "voluntary power of forgetfulness" and "vindictive spite" against his compatriots (74). Actually, Byron's stay in the colony, a miniature England at the tip of Iberia, furthered the sense of alienation from his native land that he had carried with him from the beginning of his journey and that he would carry with him to the grave.

The Iberian pilgrimage began with desperation in England and ended with frustration and anticlimax in Gibraltar. But, in between, as our study of Byron's journey reveals, the poet found new hope and new insights and a new and jovial spirit, discoveries that served him well in later years. Especially in his most mature poetry, written a decade and more after he left Gibraltar, Byron returned to Iberian scenes and peoples in his memory. For *Don Juan*, his most penetrating study of human nature, he chose Iberia as his opening setting, skillfully weaving Spanish legends and customs into his treatment of modern, universal life. Iberia was an afterthought in the poet's travel plans. He missed much that any tourist today would expect to see. He always said he wanted to go back, but he never did. Yet, in the course of his often hurried journey, he gathered undying impressions, and he used those impressions to create unique and great poetry. His Iberian pilgrimage is a journey no student of the poet should miss.

Byron's "Darkness" and the
Romantic Dis-Spiriting of Nature

Ronald A. Schroeder

Although some critics of "Darkness" suggest the poem is "un-Byronic" (Adams 200; Gleckner, *Byron* 199), "Darkness" shows up consistently in anthologies that include literature from the Romantic period (for example, Perkins, *English Romantic Writers*; Mahoney; Noyes; Heath; Woods; Abrams, *Norton Anthology*, vol. 2; Kermode). The poem's availability, moderate length, general directness of language, and subject matter (something close to science fiction) make "Darkness" an inviting poem to use in classes in Romantic literature, but through my years of teaching, I have sometimes encountered problems with it. First, the poem appears almost too direct and even obvious. When students finish reading it, they occasionally seem confused, as if to them the poem speaks for itself and they have nothing to add to it. The published scholarship helps little here; it tends to bring with it a wagonload of abstractions, whose sense of finality chills students' interests in further discovery. Critics, for example, speak of "Darkness" as a "terrifying" (Gleckner, *Byron* 199; Bostetter, "Masses" 266; Marchand, *Byron: A Portrait* 246) "nightmare" (Cooke, *Blind Man* 116) of "uncompromising bleakness" (Dingley 21), "nothingness" (Bostetter 259), "absolute loss and desolation" (Pafford 125), and "void" (Gleckner 199). Now "nothingness" and "void" are powerful abstractions that are apt to be a bit remote from the real experience of college undergraduates. At their ages, after all, their lives are still pretty much filled with possibilities and with things. When they hear these interpretations, the more skeptical students almost seem to mutter, "So big deal—he's written a poem about nothing." Finally, even the most scientifically naive students know too much to be "terrified" by the prospect of the sun's suddenly burning out. Whatever they may fear from a nuclear holocaust, the greenhouse effect, genetic engineering, an epidemic of AIDS, or some other potential world-ending disaster, they are understandably confident that the light of the sun will not be extinguished in their lifetime.

When we talk about "Darkness" in class, I try to cover a broad range of topics and approaches. For example, we discuss the puzzlement of the opening line, the behavior of humankind in Byron's vision, and the possibilities for allegorical interpretations.

I have found, though, that the class seems to make the most progress with "Darkness" when we focus on Byron's portrayal of nature. This, I recognize, is not necessarily the central issue of "Darkness," but it offers a way to create a context for the poem. Byron's vision of nature in "Darkness" is radical, but students' consideration of it with an eye toward other treatments of nature in Romantic literature helps clarify some critical issues in the poem and helps students see why "Darkness" is both terrifying and courageous.

In brief, Byron's vision in "Darkness" represents a nature wholly emptied of spirit. It utterly lacks whatever there might be of intangible reality that could give material nature order and meaning. In discussions of the poem, it is this view of the dis-spirited universe that I encourage my classes to discover—or at least to admit as an interpretive possibility. If they will see it, they are in a better position to understand the poem's place in and contribution to a larger Romantic dialogue about nature and human consciousness.

I start with the initiating event. In line 2 of the poem, Byron reports, "The bright sun was extinguish'd." His abruptly matter-of-fact statement suggests the action was both sudden and arbitrary. In fact, it is well to point out (if students do not pick up on it for themselves first) that Byron (with the logic of a dream) reports the event without reference at all to any cause, either distant or immediate. It simply occurs.

Critics disagree as to whether Byron meant to imply an explanation for this remarkable event. Dingley (25–26) and Adams (201), for instance, suggest that Byron may be referring to current and credible scientific theories. Students see, though, that in the poem itself Byron offers no overt accounting for what happened. He does not hint that the darkness follows causally from some human action; nor does he indicate that it is the consequence of any causally ordered sequence of events in nature. Occasionally in other poems (like *Don Juan* 4.72) Byron suggests a kind of entropic decay in the natural world, but the suddenness of this darkness argues against the hypothesis of a gradual but steady natural decline in the sun's vitality. Finally, while "Darkness" contains references to prayers (though "selfish" [9]) and to an altarplace (turned to an unholy use [58–60]), it does not convey a compelling sense of the presence of any God in this universe. The vision offers no substantial evidence that the sun's going out is the consequence of divine intervention or providence. Dingley argues that there is "more than a hint that world-ending constitutes a judgement" (26), but his evidence notwithstanding, George M. Ridenour's comment seems more accurate: "There is no feeling of divine purpose being worked out" ("Byron" 458; see also Kroeber, *Romantic Narrative* 55). Sudden, arbitrary, causeless, purposeless, planless—the very fact that such an occurrence could take place in the cosmos suggests the absence of any inherent order in the universe, and without such informing order, there is no discoverable innate meaning, only an utter emptiness of "eternal space" (line 3).

The first consequence of the sun's going out follows immediately: randomness. If this is a universe in which there is no God and no inherent moral order (see Adams 200), it also becomes a nightmare for science. The random, dis-spirited nature in "Darkness" is unpredictable and therefore unreliable and undependable. Once the sun's light goes out, the stars "wander . . . pathless" (3–4); the earth swings "blind" (5); matter becomes no more than an inert "lump," which is simultaneously a lifeless "chaos" (72); ultimately that matter is reduced to stasis (73–81). From this evidence not even science can extrapolate a meaningful order. There is nothing to observe because nothing is observable ("Darkness . . . was the universe" [81–82]); there is nothing to predict, and no reliable principle for testing that prediction.

The inversions and disorder that occur in the moral sphere of human action parallel the deepening chaos of the material universe when the light of the sun goes out. Humankind regresses from enervation ("men forgot their passions" [7]) to "mad disquietude" (29), war, famine, cannibalism, and ultimately extinction. The arc of this narrative is a steadily declining spiral, a regressive curve to savagery, bestiality, and a "hideousness" (67) that is moral as well as physical.

In a universe uninformed by some spirit or ordering principle, nature proves to be finite and consumable. Before the end of the poem, everything in nature that can be burned has been, and conservation-minded students today may see in this a prophecy of civilization's reckless disregard for natural resources. The fact in "Darkness" is that the extinction of the sun has brought about the end of nature's power to replenish itself; when the sun goes out, there are no renewable resources. Nature's own life principle (the sun's light) is finite and vulnerable. Morning comes and comes again, but there is no day (6); the year is "seasonless" (71). Cyclical (renewable) time and history thus have ended, and the universe has moved into an entirely different order of temporal (or nontemporal) existence (as it has entered an entirely different order of causation—or causelessness), which leaves both organic nature and human life behind. (Blackstone's opinion on this point differs [150].) What soon remains in "Darkness" is not nature in any formerly recognizable form; it is mere matter—only a "lump," "A lump of death— a chaos of hard clay" (70, 72). Some students (especially if they have read book 2 of *Paradise Lost*) might want to consider the paradox of that last phrase as an index of the transformation nature undergoes in "Darkness."

To help students clarify their thinking about the significance of the radical dis-spiriting of nature in "Darkness," I encourage them to examine Byron's vision in this poem in relation to other Romantic treatments of nature. Romantic poetry at large offers numerous views of nature, but among them the norm tends to be a nature that is animated and inspirited rather than the opposite. Sweeping generalizations typically create problems, but for purposes of illustration, I suggest two broad types or representatives as a way of giving some coordinates and lines of reference to Byron's vision in "Darkness."

First, some parts of Wordsworth's poetry express a powerfully optimistic

conviction that nature is an active, benevolent, enduring power and presence. It is a "sense sublime," "a motion and a spirit" that can "so inform /
The mind" that nothing may disturb "Our cheerful faith, that all which we
behold / Is full of blessings" ("Tintern Abbey"). Humankind and nature are
"essentially adapted to each other" (Preface to *Lyrical Ballads*); mutually
"fitted" to one another, they act together "with blended might" (prospectus
to *The Recluse*). Human consciousness contributes to the inspiriting of nature. The creative spirit of the mind works "in alliance with the works /
Which it beholds," and human beings can experience "an ennobling interchange / Of action from without and from within" (*Prelude* 2.259–60,
13.375–76). This is a nature of which one might well proclaim confidently,
it "never did betray / The heart that loved her" ("Tintern Abbey").

A spirit-filled or spiritually active nature, however, need not always be a
benevolent one, and Romantic poetry includes its share of anxiety about the
discontinuity between humankind and the natural world. In *The Rime of
the Ancient Mariner*, for example, Coleridge poses an alternative possibility
for a more problematic nature. The Mariner moves eerily and fearfully
through a landscape inhabited by invisible spirits, who exact a terrible vengeance on him. Their relentless pursuit indicates that they may not be
altogether benevolent. Even worse, the actions of some spiritual beings
suggest that the inherent order of their world defies rational explanation.
Coleridgean spirits operate in ways that are mysterious and unintelligible
to human understanding (like casting dice to see which mortals die and
which live). Nevertheless, what Coleridge's disturbing possibilities for nature
in *Ancient Mariner* share with Wordsworth's optimism is the conviction of
a nature permeated, penetrated, and informed by spirit.

I do not suggest to my students that Byron's vision of nature in "Darkness"
is definitive or even necessarily typical of his attitude toward the natural
world. But in "Darkness" Byron assuredly introduces a distinct and articulate
third voice to that dialogue, which I have outlined with the examples of
Wordsworth and Coleridge. The vision of "Darkness" posits a true alternative: benevolence, malevolence, intelligibility, inscrutability have all become irrelevant; this nature is simply, finally, and unequivocally without
spirit of any sort.

Juxtaposing "Darkness" against other Romantic versions of the inspirited
universe helps students see, I believe, the radicalness of Byron's vision, and
I have found that that discovery may be charged with more than usual
emotional force. Once, for example, when we discussed this poem in a
general survey of Romantic literature, one student confronted vividly and
chillingly the idea of nihilism without ever mentioning the word itself and
without getting lost in abstractions about nullity or nil. Profoundly (and even
visibly) moved by the poem's sense of hopelessness and futility, by its pow-

erful impulsion toward emptiness, and by its antipathy to theological con-
solations of salvation, redemption, and moral meaningfulness in the universe,
this student said with an unmistakable note of awe in her voice, "I think
this is a *very* pessimistic poem. I think Byron is saying, 'That's *all* there is.
Period.' " It was a tense but rewarding moment in the class, for the young
woman's nervous, emphatic comment revealed two things: first, her own
fortitude in admitting the disturbing implications of "Darkness" that chal-
lenged her personal view of the universe and, second, her deep respect for
Byron's unflinching commitment to represent without compromise the full
extremity of those implications.

A second incident may perhaps also illustrate how this approach has encouraged students in my classes to make discoveries about "Darkness" that
connect to larger (and sometimes more personal) contexts of experience and
belief. After we had talked briefly about the place of "Darkness" amid contrasting visions of nature in Romantic poetry, one student suggested reading
"Darkness" as a parody of Genesis: to her the poem adumbrated a powerful
myth of decreation that culminated in a negative (that is, reversed) image
of Eden—nature on its way back to becoming void or chaos, and two individuals who destroy each other by the recognition of their own hideousness
rather than beauty (created in God's image?). To be sure, the process of
destruction and collapse in "Darkness" does not precisely trace in reverse
order the chronology of creation in Genesis, but as this student elaborated
on her initial comment to the class, she found another way of articulating a
useful and intelligent point about the poem: that it conveys the sense of a
universe steadily and inexorably being depleted of its vitality and spirit; that
it creates an image for the paradox of a universe infinite in matter, space,
and time, yet contracting (and ultimately disappearing) in spiritual presence.

In the dis-spirited universe of "Darkness," human consciousness cannot
supply what nature lacks inherently; human imagination cannot animate or
inspirit this matter. "This vision of human weakness in the face of unman-
ageable forces lies behind all of Byron's work. No power of imagination can
change this, no vision can make much difference" (Ridenour, "Byron" 459).
The fact is that in "Darkness" before too long there simply is no human
presence to supply an inspiriting consciousness. Editors and critics frequently refer "Darkness" to the Last Man theme, a popular one in Romantic
literature, but "Darkness" is an odd rendition of that theme because it
contains no one last man (see Dingley 20). In the end there is only the
consciousness of the narrator, disillusioned and estranged from the human-
less, spiritless world of his own vision, which he has just graphically represented. Yet as the "author" or envisioner of it, he assumes a place at the
center of that dis-spirited universe. This approach to the poem, then, ultimately directs students' attention back onto the envisioning self, and it helps

them understand one reason that "Darkness" is a courageous poem. To live in a universe, the implications of which are projected in the nightmarish vision of "Darkness," is an awesome responsibility.

In the cryptic opening line of the poem, the narrator of "Darkness" seems to question the authority of his own vision: "I had a dream, which was not all a dream." Which part was not, and how do dream and consciousness interpenetrate? In general, after discussing "Darkness" along the lines I have proposed, students are better prepared to grapple with this question than they were before, when the issue was premature. Byron's exploration of the connection between vision and perception, and even of the indeterminacy of his own vision, aligns his poetic speculations somewhat curiously with the like speculations of Wordsworth ("Tintern Abbey's" "blessed mood" [37–49] and the Lucy poems) and Keats ("Sleep and Poetry," "Ode to a Nightingale," "The Fall of Hyperion"). "Darkness," then, is not only a vision of nature but an active part of the whole epistemological and cognitive exploration of the age (see Wasserman).

It is ironic that some critics see "Darkness" as "un-Byronic," for the poem certainly relates to other works from the period of Byron's exile in 1816 (see Ridenour and Gleckner). From a biographical perspective, for one, the poem can be seen as another barometer of Byron's personal desolation at the collapse of his marriage and his relation to his half-sister. In this regard the poem bears comparison with his poems to Augusta, to his autobiographical poem "The Dream," and to the poem "When We Two Parted." It also suggests some linkage with *The Prisoner of Chillon*. Only with difficulty can one find the similarities in theme and treatment to be purely coincidental: both examine the agonizing retrogression of a mind under stress, caused by isolation and by utter alienation from the immediate presence of a spiritually informed nature.

Second, the Byronic narrator's questioning of the authenticity of his own vision relates "Darkness" to Byron's concern for creativity and the creative process in other poems of 1816—notably "The Dream," but also parts of *Childe Harold's Pilgrimage* 3 (for instance, stanzas 6 and 14). In each poem Byron questions, in fundamental ways, the relation between "mind" and "nature," between "consciousness" and the reality or illusion of a spiritual presence in material phenomena.

Finally, Byron's treatment of nature in "Darkness" stands as another example of his irresistible attraction to the theme of humanity's paradoxically mixed essence, a theme that begins to be insistent in this period. In *Manfred* Byron refers to humankind as "[h]alf dust, half deity" (1.2.40); in "Prometheus" he speaks of man as "in part divine, / A troubled stream from a pure source" (47–48); and in *Childe Harold* he laments that he "can see / Nothing to loathe in nature, save to be / A link reluctant in a fleshly chain, / Class'd among creatures, when the soul can flee" (3.72). The configuration of this paradox is complicated somewhat in "Darkness," where the informing consciousness of the narrator is alienated from the dis-spirited nature of his vision. A contrast may illustrate the connection better than a comparison. In *Manfred*, like the Abbot, we are left asking where a masterful spirit goes after death has separated that "Promethean spark" (1.1.154) from the mere matter of his body's "atoms" (1.2.109); we are left to wonder what a universe of infinite time and space and of purely spiritual existence might be like. In "Darkness," on the other hand, we are left (like the narrator) to contemplate the world that spirit has left behind.

As I have said, there are other ways to approach "Darkness," but discussions focused on Byron's radical dis-spiriting of nature and on the relation of that vision to other treatments of nature in the Romantic period and to other poems in this phase of Byron's career enable students to discover what is unique and powerful about "Darkness." It helps them locate Byron's dark disillusionment in the context of his poetic preoccupations in other works of his exile. And perhaps most important, the approach helps them see how Byron and "Darkness" are critically engaged in the great dialogue of his time, the dialogue of Romanticism itself.

Manfred and Skepticism

Stephen C. Behrendt

Manfred offers a splendid opportunity to introduce and explore the function of skepticism in Byron's art. Particularly in a course in Romantic poetry (but also in more broadly based courses in Romanticism generally, or in courses that examine the hero and heroine in Western culture), *Manfred* generally proves an eminently teachable work, in part because its dramatic situation is inherently compelling and in part because, like the familiar childhood tale of the Lady and the Tiger, it resists conventional expectations of closure. Consisting wholly of dramatic dialogue, *Manfred* denies its readers the reassuring presence of any authoritative narrator who might at least provide some clear internal guidance for assessing the tale as moral or philosophical fable. Without such a narrator, readers are forced to evaluate on their own the characters, their beliefs and arguments, and the events, and to participate actively in the processes of questioning and judging that lie at the heart of skepticism, individually formulating intellectual positions that, even if they synthesize elements of several characters' views, are finally identical with none of them.

I have found that relating Byron's text to several aspects of skepticism helps elucidate *Manfred* at the same time it familiarizes students with one of the philosophical systems of the Enlightenment the Romantics (the second generation in particular) explored. Manfred supplies an immediate indication of the work's skeptical foundation when he remarks on "our mixed essence": that we are precisely "[h]alf dust, half deity" (1.2.41, 40; my emphases) ensures that, in keeping with the skeptical tradition—in which absolute truth does not exist and all hypotheses must be tested rigorously—the two sides of Manfred's view of humanity (and of himself) are equally strong. Set against Manfred's own character, as he reveals it through words and actions alike, are the indwelling Wordsworthian naturalism of the Chamois Hunter and, more compelling because intellectually more nearly equal to Manfred, the philosophical humanism of the Abbot, who echoes Manfred's own self-assessment in his recognition of the "awful chaos" of discordant elements— significantly expressed in dualistic fashion: light and darkness, mind and dust—that shapes and governs Manfred's character (3.1.160–67).

In teaching *Manfred*, particularly at the undergraduate level, I briefly outline the premises of eighteenth-century skepticism and point out that by the time he wrote *Manfred*, Byron had read widely in the works of French skeptics like Voltaire and English ones like Hume, whom he reportedly considered the most profound thinker of the eighteenth century (Marchand, *Byron: A Biography* 1108). I suggest that we therefore have good reason to investigate the consequences of this philosophical underpinning in the drama, where it activates a number of dualisms both within the text and, by extension, within the consciousness of the reader. In fact, I encourage students to compile a list of these embedded dualisms, in language and in character or incident, to help them discover how pervasive the dualistic framework is. Once they recognize the presence of that framework, they can better appreciate its function in the work.

Especially important is the primacy that skeptical philosophy attributes to experience: if nothing is inherently "true" (or "false") and all premises must be tested, then only personal experience can provide the appropriately rigorous testing, and the personal experience in question is not just that of the characters in *Manfred* but also that of its readers. Therefore I call attention to *Manfred*'s form and to what Byron had to say about it. For instance, I point out that while Byron's scattered comments on this work are often characteristically deprecating, he nevertheless pointedly instructed his publisher, John Murray, to call it "a poem" and, in fact, "a 'poem in dialogue' " (Marchand, *Letters* 5: 209). I also like to distribute the first half of his letter to Murray of 17 June 1817, in which, in discussing *Manfred* in more candid detail, Byron remarks that "although it is not a drama properly—but a dialogue—still it contains poetry and passion" (5: 239). Byron's conspicuous alteration of terminology here—that the poem is not "a play in dialogue," as he had written earlier, but rather "a *dialogue*"—is another indicator that we may profitably see in this "metaphysical dramatic poem" (11: 164) an internal dialogue in which Manfred is the first speaker and all the other voices, taken collectively, the second. It is, in fact, a "dialogue" whose rhetorical model is that of the skeptical debate.

The prototypical skeptical debate imposes a considerable burden on the reader or auditor, for in this rhetorical exercise the two sides perform so well that each subverts (or entirely demolishes) the other, leaving it for the reader or auditor to construct a third position that both subsumes and transcends the now bankrupt original arguments. Once the students learn how this model works, they see it everywhere in *Manfred*. For instance, Manfred's move from relative impotence and the desire for "[f]orgetfulness" and "self-oblivion" (1.1.136, 144) to relative power (or authority) and knowledge (particularly self-knowledge) at the conclusion marks what can be perceived as progress on his part, as the acquisition of experience and, presumably, wisdom. But that supposed "progress" is at the same time called into question by the presence and the comments of the Abbot, who is in many ways Manfred's equal in the implied skeptical debate. Manfred and the Abbot each recognize the visible indications of mixed elements in the former's character (and even talk about them in similar terms), but they interpret those signs differently. That the Abbot wishes to preserve what seems to concern Manfred so little—his own mortal existence—underscores their dualistic opinions not just about Manfred himself but, more important, about the nature and dignity of life, experience, and knowledge generally.

The Abbot's high regard for Manfred demonstrates the latter's essential worthiness and also that of the Abbot himself, whom Manfred for his part respects and takes seriously. Thus each side in this skeptical framework is lent validity and authority, and in virtually equal measure. It is helpful to distribute copies of Byron's original version of act 3 (McGann 4: 467–71), so that students can see how Byron's substantial revisions elevated the Abbot to an intellectual and dramatic stature that made him a worthy adversary (or counterpart) to Manfred. When one appreciates the extent to which Byron made them relative equals in his revision of act 3, it becomes clearer why the conclusion of *Manfred* forces the reader to resolve Manfred's ultimate fate, for the Abbot merely implies—but does not assert—that Manfred's soul has gone to some dreadful and unthinkable doom. Byron leaves the question open, having the Abbot simply report the obvious, the substantiable: Manfred "is gone" (3.4.153). In determining the destination of Manfred's soul, the reader must evaluate the evidence in the words and actions of both these ultimately credible men.

Manfred's skeptical framework is reinforced in other ways. Both in the recurrent dualisms on which crucial passages in dialogue and monologue alike turn and in confrontations among characters, we encounter the mutually antagonistic and mutually destructive (or the mutually self-destructive) elements of the conventional skeptical debate. *Manfred* is filled with questions, most of which cannot be answered—or answered satisfactorily—by those to whom they are addressed. Most conspicuously, Astarte cannot answer the questions directed to her by Manfred, precisely because he is unable to answer them himself. A central lesson skepticism teaches is self-reliance. This is precisely the lesson Manfred learns in the course of Byron's drama and the lesson that enables him to recognize, as his final, punning line declares, that it is not so hard (difficult, but also unfortunate) to die. The reader or auditor intent on resolving a skeptical debate must perform a similar exercise in self-reliance, or self-sufficiency, untangling the mutually destructive dualisms on which such a debate turns by assuming responsibility for the "answer"—the new, third alternative—that emerges not through the calculated intervention of an authoritative narrator or arbiter but through his or her own independent judgment and consciousness as reader or listener.

Introducing the idea that *Manfred* constitutes an internal dialogue between its conscious, objectifying protagonist and various "selves," or aspects of his personality and experience that either arise from their suppressed or repressed positions in Manfred's psyche or are deliberately called up (the drama is full of conjurings, after all) also enables the instructor to consider the phenomenon of apparent irresolution that troubles some of Byron's critics. These addresses to and from the self, while they relate to Byron's manipulation of the Narcissus myth in creating in Manfred a figure whose process of self-completion is simultaneously one of self-consumption (Garber, *Self* 130–35), also dramatically reflect the intellectual impasse that occurs in the individual who is paralyzed by the powerful dualistic impulses these addresses embody. Especially with more advanced students, it is useful to discuss the unsympathetic view of *Manfred's* philosophical base represented by critics like Philip Martin, who has written that Byron's drama "does not propose a situation capable of supporting a psychological or emotional dimension worthy of serious interest" (110). Seen as anything but a virtuoso pastiche of "stagecraft," Martin writes, *Manfred* cannot be taken seriously. Even students for whom Byron is no great favorite are unwilling to accept such cavalier dismissals, perhaps because they see in Manfred a crisis of self-assurance not unlike those they face as students and, more important, as young adults confronting a world that is often both personally and professionally threatening.

Leslie Marchand offers a helpful insight when he observes of Manfred as a sort of stand-in for Byron that "the real drama was within his own mind" (*Byron: A Biography* 656). The apparent irresolution in *Manfred's* conclusion in fact reflects a spiritual (or even religious) irresolution that had long troubled Byron and that *Manfred* had rekindled in his thoughts. This problem can be effectively illustrated by quoting from a letter to his friend John Cam Hobhouse, written in April 1817 as he was revising act 3: "I do not know what to believe—or what to disbelieve—which is the devil—to have no religion at all—all sense & senses are against it—but all belief & much evidence is for it" (*Letters* 5: 212). Indeed, students can be encouraged to explore this very personal dimension of the drama if one asks them to consider these remarks to Hobhouse in light of Marchand's comment that Byron "had fought out, though he had arrived at no very satisfying philosophical conclusions, the metaphysical problems which had long been troubling him" (*Byron: A Biography* 698).

No very satisfying resolution? Perhaps not for Byron, but what about Manfred? Like the young visionary Poet in Shelley's *Alastor* (with which poem Byron had undoubtedly become acquainted, along with its author, in the summer of 1816), Manfred conjures up at the end of act 2 the image of a female prototype—an ideal counterpart—whom he cannot embrace and whose enigmatic separation from him renders him senseless. But unlike Shelley's Poet, who retires devastated to his mountain and a pitiful, solitary expiration, Manfred moves back into and through social contacts that, despite his retirement into his isolated tower to die, nevertheless humanize him for us (through his interaction with the Abbot) and for himself. He does learn something, students are increasingly quick to assert as they delve more deeply into the text, although they seem ultimately unsure just what that kernel of acquired wisdom might be.

Here skeptical philosophy's emphasis on experience can help elucidate what Manfred learns. "Old man! 'tis not so difficult to die" (3.4.151) points us in two different but related directions: dying is easier than living, and death is no misfortune. And yet Manfred's climactic encounter with Astarte, in which his perfected "better self" cannot answer for him the questions that he himself has been unable to answer, brings him not the despair we might expect in the circumstances but rather the serenity that characterizes his state in act 3: "There is a calm upon me— / Inexplicable stillness! which till now / Did not belong to what I knew of life" (3.1.6–8). This is a good speech to ask students to evaluate in detail, for it contains the clearest evidence that Manfred's struggle has been no mere exercise in Gothic self-indulgence but, instead, an intense trial of the soul and the mind in which something has indeed been gained—something of inestimable (albeit, iron-ically, inexpressible) value. Discounting philosophy (and by extension what might be termed, alternatively, spiritual gravity or intellectual seriousness), Manfred says that he almost believes himself to have found "the sought 'Kalon' " (which McGann glosses as "the Beautiful as morally conceived, the *summum bonum*" [4: 474n]).

What is this secret? I ask the students, and their replies are often sur-prisingly acute. If they have read this speech carefully, they recognize from its final lines that what Manfred has learned is that "calm" does exist in the universe and in the self and that it is experienced not through the meta-physics of philosophy but through the agency of human passion. It is a discovery, in other words, that both frustrates and transcends intellectual-ization and that operates in and through emotion. And yet to speak of this sensation—to the Abbot and, through him, to the reader—requires the dispassionate act of intellectualization inherent in the use of determinate language. *Knowing* and *experiencing* may be seen, in other words, to be both polar opposites and coincidental points on the continuum of human life. The instability and irresolution that are at the heart of *Manfred* as text, as drama, and as philosophical "case study" are those that inhabit skepticism generally.

All this is a lot to put into *Manfred*, as indeed it is to get out of Byron's drama. But the exercise is a useful one for several reasons. It demonstrates how the skeptical tradition both informs and helps elucidate the work, even as it exerted a powerful influence on the author's thinking, leading him to

create—particularly in the light of his revision of act 3—a serious representation of the crisis of self-knowledge and self-assurance. In short, it gets
students thinking, with increasing insight, about issues of credibility and
belief. In considering *Manfred*'s relationship to the skeptical tradition, students come more fully to appreciate both; and, in an interesting irony, they
arrive also at a fuller sense of self-reliance as readers, interpreters, and critics.

Teaching *Manfred* as Mental Theater

Alan Richardson

I first tried teaching *Manfred* as a graduate student running a discussion section in a large Romantic survey course. The lecturer, an eminent Victorianist, took the fairly common approach of presenting *Manfred* as a youthful aberration, more notable for its faults—metaphysical rant, clumsy stagecraft, and general attitudinizing—than for its virtues. His quavering renditions of scenes selected for their bombastic tone made for a particularly entertaining lecture. But the characterization of *Manfred* as a wrong turn on the road to *Don Juan* also made it nearly impossible for me to get my students to engage the work seriously in discussion.

Even without the recent work by Jerome McGann and Clifford Siskin suggesting that the developmental model, itself steeped in Romantic ideology, may be singularly inappropriate for understanding a literary career, we risk a great deal by teaching earlier works like *Manfred* or *Childe Harold* simply as foils for later, more "mature" efforts—beginning with the resulting distortion of the significance such apparently expendable works had for their original audiences. (College students are especially susceptible to the developmental myth, eager as they are to transcend their adolescent selves.) What we stand to lose more particularly in *Manfred* is a complex and rewarding text, valuable precisely because it does not readily fit with the Romantic canon, while at the same time seeming to confirm students' worst fears about the Romantic poet's antisocial, self-indulgent tendencies. Many students at first dismiss *Manfred* as the transparently confessional work of an egotistical, guilt-ridden *poète maudit*. But if the text of *Manfred*, and not only its protagonist, is seen as self-divided and self-critical, their initially negative reaction can generate a rethinking of received notions (however students have received them) about the Romantic self. A careful reading of *Manfred* can lead students to consider new perspectives on the poetic career and on the Romantic canon; it can throw into question, as well, standard conceptions of genre, of the discrete text, and of the poet's relation to tradition.

I usually begin with Byron's subtitle, *A Dramatic Poem*, and his related term for his verse dramas as "mental theatre" (Marchand, *Letters* 8: 186–87). Byron's indifference (if not hostility) to theatrical productions of his dramatic works is usually dismissed (following David V. Erdman) as "stage fright," but while Erdman's analysis may be appropriate for a more conventional tragedy like *Marino Faliero*, it can be reductive when applied to what Byron called his "metaphysical" dramas, *Manfred* and *Cain*. In teaching these works, I find Tilottama Rajan's speculations on the "dialogizing" of lyric poetry in the Romantic period (and her use of *Prometheus Unbound*, Shelley's "Lyrical Drama," as a key example) a better springboard for class discussions ("Romanticism"). Such an approach not only helps relate Byron's "dramatic poem" to other Romantic hybrids like the "lyrical ballad" or "conversation poem" but allows one to situate the form in a positive and iconoclastic program for dialogizing the subjective, univocal stance of lyric, rather than put off students in advance with the pejorative term "closet drama."

Byron's complication of conventional generic boundaries illustrates simultaneously the Romantic impatience with traditional forms and notions of decorum and the manner in which this seeming breakdown of genre in fact foregrounds our expectations and makes us more self-conscious regarding literary kinds. A discussion of readerly associations with lyric and drama, often viewed (in German Romantic criticism, for instance) as the most subjective and the most objective genres, can lead directly from a consideration of *Manfred*'s unconventional form to some of its thematic concerns. For tensions between dramatic (dialogical) and lyric (monological) modes, between objective and subjective, between social and private categories of experience arise not only in the text's ambivalent relation to the stage and its thwarting of generic expectations but in its protagonist's unusual career (as he describes it in retrospect) and his dealings with others in the drama as well.

Appropriately, *Manfred* begins with a soliloquy, one that can be read aloud in class to great effect. Manfred's opening speech describes an isolated, lyric consciousness alienated from "other beings," reacting to a prior fall both generic ("The Tree of Knowledge is not that of Life") and genetic ("Since that all nameless hour").[1] It sets up an intertextual engagement with *Paradise Lost* that recurs throughout the drama and reveals at the same time the protagonist's tendency to project his own sleepless agony and self-division (both inherited from Milton's Satan) onto the human condition as a whole. Soliloquy becomes incantation as Manfred attempts to shore up a fragmented psychic identity through exerting power over others. Here the others are the seven elemental spirits, but the scene can be analyzed as a model for all those in which Manfred confronts spirits in an agonistic relation (men he tends solipsistically to disregard; significantly, there are no earthly women in the drama). My students are sometimes bothered by the ontological status of the supernatural characters, unsure whether they are projections of Manfred's psyche or externalized antagonists, as they should be: Do these scenes represent dramatic interchange or a kind of ventriloquized monologue? Here too the work's fundamental generic tensions can be brought to bear on discussions of characterization and plot. How successful is this "dramatic poem" in breaking free of the closed, single-voiced character of lyric? At the same time, the Seventh Spirit's counterincantation (with Manfred "senseless"), condemning him to the isolation and sleeplessness he already suffers, makes simple answers ("It's all in his head") unlikely. And the momentary apparition of a "beautiful female figure" is worth noting as the first of several teasing references to Astarte and to incest ("And we again will be—").

From Manfred's first exchange with spirits, we usually move to his interaction—or rather, lack of it—with another human being, the Chamois Hunter of act 1, scene 2. This scene is easy to travesty in class; more difficult (and rewarding) is to generate a discussion of its thematic relation to the first scene. Manfred's attempt at suicide compares interestingly with the magical rites of the previous scene: though one seems an exertion of power and the other a gesture of powerlessness, both are motivated by a search for "self-oblivion." Increasingly another aspect of the term "mental theatre" (though one possibly not intended by Byron himself) emerges: that this "dramatic poem" not only is to be staged in the reader's mind but is a drama about consciousness. The history of Manfred's tormented, disintegral, and compulsively domineering psyche can then be traced through his autobiographical speeches in act 2 (scenes 1 and 2), which keep returning to the ambiguous figure of "Astarte." Although some Byron scholars have denied the presence of sibling incest in *Manfred*, students never do; I try to lead them toward connections between Manfred's narcissistic, specular relation to Astarte ("She was like me"), the unequal, cannibalizing relation underlying most instances of Romantic "androgyny," Manfred's apparent need to subordinate others to himself (related to his class status as feudal lord), and his obviously empty claims to autonomy ("The lion is alone, and so am I"). Once more, the "monological" character of Manfred's dealings with others can be related to the text's ambivalent generic status, as well as to issues of gender and class in Romantic poetry that may have come up previously.

If *Manfred* explores the problems inherent in posing an integral, autonomous mind, it also resists interpretation as a self-enclosed, free-standing text. Some students will pick up an echo of Goethe's *Faust* in Manfred's opening speech; others will notice how the entrances of the seven spirits (in 1.1) and of the Destinies (in 2.3) both resemble the entrance of the witches or "weird sisters" in *Macbeth*, a connection that can be reinforced by pointing out the etymological relation of *weird* and *destiny*. Another echo of *Macbeth* usually comes up in discussing Manfred's history, the (supernatural? hallucinatory?) transubstantiation of wine into blood in the Chamois Hunter's cottage (2.1). Moving toward the more extended echoes of Milton's Satan in Manfred's speeches in act 3, I invite students to connect Manfred's failure to maintain his pretence to psychic autonomy with the dependence of his very characterization on existing literary models: Faust, Macbeth, Satan. It is a difficult point to make in class, and a number of questions should come up: Is it a weakness in the poem that the central character is so indebted to earlier models, or is this part of Byron's design? Does the character's anxiety regarding his past and his dependence on others (or at least one other—Astarte) reflect the poet's anxiety about his dependence on literary precedents, the burden of the past? Does the drama end tragically, triumphantly, or ambivalently? Are our doubts as to whether Manfred succeeds or fails related to our uncertainty whether *Manfred* is a success or a failure? Working through these questions involves looking at Manfred's dismissal of the Abbot's offer of absolution (3.1.66–78) and his defiance of the "infernal god" who appears to summon him to hell (3.4.124–41), assertions of independence that are dependent on echoes of an earlier figure, Milton's Satan, and *his* assertion of psychic autonomy ("The mind is its own place . . .").

The discussion of intertextuality in *Manfred* depends, of course, on the context in which it is taught: I have been thinking here of the usual six-poet, chronological "Romantics" sequence. I can count on a few earlier discussions of the Romantics' ambivalent relation to Milton by this point, as found in works like Wordsworth's prospectus to *The Recluse* and Blake's *Marriage of Heaven and Hell*. Furthermore, questions regarding the "Romantic hero"—Do the Romantic poets celebrate or criticize the autonomous self? Do they identify with or critically parody Milton's Satan, or both?—have by then come up in examining, for example, Coleridge's supernatural poems. The class on *Manfred* similarly looks forward to discussions of *Alastor*, *Prometheus Unbound*, and Keats's "Hyperion" poems. I emphasize the context of anthology pieces because it is too easy to leave *Manfred* in the limbo region to which Abrams, in *Natural Supernaturalism*, consigns Byron's poetry as a whole; if one's implicit paradigm for Romantic poetry is the greater Romantic lyric, Byron will tend to seem extraneous. But in other contexts *Manfred* seems less eccentric: it teaches well, for example, with Mary Shelley's *Frankenstein* or, in a comparative Romanticism course, with works like Chateaubriand's *René* and Pushkin's *Eugene Onegin*. In the more usual British Romantics sequence, the class on *Manfred* can be included in a discussion, later in the term, on why Byron resists generalizations about British Romantic poetry despite his international status as the archetypal Romantic poet.

NOTE

[1]Quotations of Byron's poetry in this essay are from *The Poetical Works of Byron* (ed. More; rev. ed. Gleckner).

Contexts of Eden in *Don Juan* and the Mysteries
Wolf Z. Hirst

Students sometimes wonder why a poet who was denounced for sacrilege by his contemporaries (Steffan, *Lord Byron's* Cain 330–426) should continually allude to the Bible and base two plays on it. Does Byron simply "set out to subvert the religious tradition from within," and does his work then become "heretical and even blasphemous," as was assumed in the nineteenth century and was still claimed in 1984 (Cantor, "Byron's *Cain*" 50, *Creature* 135; Schaffner 7)? Although such questions have sometimes been dismissed as irrelevant today, they may yet serve as a starting point for examining not only Byron's religion or irreligion, his internal conflicts and unconscious urges, but also his works and poetry in general. In this essay I touch on points such as poetic license, verisimilitude, decorum, historic perspective, Romantic consciousness, generic distinctions, dramatic objectivity, tragic reversal, irony, parody, and allusion, but I concentrate on a poet's revision of a precursor text, in a manner that makes students more aware of how a new context extends and changes old meanings.

One approach is to compare Byron's manipulation of a specific scriptural motif in his two biblical dramas with his treatment of it in a nonbiblical work. I sometimes teach the early cantos of *Don Juan* (a work students invariably enjoy), go on to *Cain* (which usually stimulates a lively discussion) and *Heaven and Earth*, and then return to *Don Juan* in the later cantos while pointing out how centrally the fall from Eden figures in these three works (Ridenour, *Style*; Roston 198, 214; McGann, Don Juan *in Context* 143–47; Leigh 120), as it does in Byron's poetry in general (Gleckner, *Byron*; Storey, 164–81; Beatty, "Fiction's Limit"; and Looper 271–72, which provides a cross index to all references to the fall listed by Looper). I provoke my students to debate by suggesting that in his revisionary struggle with the Bible to impose his own novel meaning on the expulsion from paradise, Byron is more inhibited in the mysteries than in *Don Juan*, where he produces his most extravagant analogies and far-reaching reversals. Though a few students remain unconvinced, at the end of our discussion all come to see how Byron gives new significance to the traditional fall motif by the situations he invents for it and how this motif in turn enriches his works.

How meaning and effect depend on context can be brought home to students by drawing attention to the rapid shifts in *Don Juan*. In the first seven lines of canto 10, Byron describes Newton, who "saw an apple fall" and then supposedly discovered the law of gravity. The last line suddenly introduces Adam's fall: Newton was "the sole mortal who could grapple, / Since Adam, with a fall, or with an apple." Not only has the image of forbidden fruit been wrenched so far out of its original context that it creates an effect of burlesque (as it usually does in *Don Juan*), but new meanings

are generated: the juxtaposition of Adam's figurative fall with the literal fall
of Newton's apple and with "Gravitation" makes surrender to temptation
seem as inevitable as a law in physics, and the ludicrous rhyme word "grapple" evokes echoes of free will, *felix culpa*, and the shallowness of biblical
literalists. When Byron compares "first and passionate love" not with Eden
and the fall but with "Adam's *recollection* of his fall" (1.127; italics mine),
the motif encompasses the Romantic notion of consciousness foredooming
love to disillusion at its very inception. With the shift, at the end of the
stanza, from "The tree of knowledge" to "the unforgiven / Fire which Prometheus filch'd for us from heaven," Adam's act of disobedience is seen as
titanic aspiration for which he pays with pain and eternally frustrated desire.
Most subversive of the Bible is the implicit protest that, like the theft of
fire, the eating of forbidden fruit was "unforgiven." In the last line, however,
Byron trivializes his own rebellious stance by replacing the draft's "gave us
all" with the words "filch'd for us."

It can be shown from such passages how the poet's revisionism is held in
check by surviving scriptural impressions—for example, when he falls back
on diction reminiscent of Ecclesiastes: "all's known— / And life yields nothing further to recall" (1.127)—until he finally frees himself from the residual
pressure of the Bible and makes the Eden motif entirely his own (Hirst,
"Byron's Revisionary Struggle" 82–86). Old biblical associations offer less
resistance to an even more extreme subversion in the Haidée episode, in
which Byron builds on the literary tradition that has already extended the
meaning of Eden to comprise idyllic love. In one of the stanzas alluding to
"our first parents," who "[h]ad run the risk of being damn'd for ever," we
learn that Haidée, though "devout," conveniently "forgot" this risk when
consummating her love (2.193). Both Eve and Haidée surrender to temptation and disobey a divine edict, but their acts are viewed differently and,
it is implied, attain opposite results: the biblical sin punished by exile from
paradise becomes an innocent union of two lovers, "another Eden" (4.10).
This radical treatment of the fall is skillfully integrated and fits perfectly into
the pattern of reversals characterizing Byron's version of the Don Juan myth,
in which the traditionally callous seducer has been transformed into an
innocent youth pursued by women.

The proposition that usually arouses most controversy in class is that the
fall motif proves more resistant to subversion within the context of a work
derived from the same source as itself: the Bible. I argue that a story taken
from Holy Writ—unlike the Don Juan myth so brilliantly reversed by
Byron—tends to reassert itself more forcefully against attempts to change
it because of Scripture's distinct authority, and this authority, as Erich Auerbach has justly noted, is claimed not only for religious doctrine but also on
behalf of the episode in which such doctrine inheres (12). The authority of

religious doctrine had gradually waned, but poets (at least as late as 1820) tended to regard a biblical narrative as a series of agreed-on facts and felt it was their task to reinterpret these "facts." In his revisionary strife with the Bible in *Don Juan*, Byron exploits the motif of Adam and Eve's fall as his central metaphor (Ridenour, *Style*) and revises it by dozens of allusions, but he need not and does not retell the story of Adam and Eve. Thus while still subject to a residual pressure of the doctrine inherent in this episode, he is entirely freed from the inhibiting force of the biblical story *as story*. In his struggle for new meaning in *Cain* and *Heaven and Earth*, by contrast, he engages, in addition to the fall motif and its doctrinal implications, a given biblical episode—Abel's murder by Cain or the deluge—with *its* doctrinal implications, as a story to be rewritten in dramatic form with a certain fidelity to the "facts" of the biblical source. The fall motif too becomes more difficult to undermine in this change-resistant milieu.

Cain seems to open with as radical a subversion of its model as does *Don Juan*. Until the middle of the last act, Byron's Romanticized hero, frustrated by the "inadequacy of his state to his Conceptions" (Marchand, *Letters* 9: 54) but "thirst[ing] for good" (2.2.238), a tender husband, solicitous father, and even a loving brother to Abel, has so little in common with his model that we see in him no more of the murderer than we see in the new Juan the heartless destroyer of women's honor and happiness.[1] In other words, up to this point the poet appears to have revised the biblical Cain in a manner resembling his inversion of the Don Juan figure. What is most contradictory to the biblical worldview is the reversal of the relationship between God and humankind, for whereas in Genesis God judges man, in Byron's play Cain judges God. This judgment, it must be remembered, is chiefly based on the fall, as shown in Cain's most clearly formulated indictment, which occurs in his first soliloquy (1.1.72–79): his parents were entrapped and he was unjustly punished for their disobedience. Neither Adam's and Abel's expostulations nor Adah's pleas provide a logical counterargument to Cain's blasphemous allegations.

From the time of its publication in 1821, most critics have therefore regarded *Cain* as subversive of the Bible. (For recent exceptions, see Beatty, *Byron's* Don Juan 20–21; Corbett 155.) I try to convince my students that these critics are mistaken, because they fail to consider Cain's comments on Adam's fall and, for that matter, his other blasphemous utterances (as well as Lucifer's) in a wider context. What is most obvious is that they often overlook the fact that dramatic personages speak in character, as Byron repeatedly pointed out (Steffan, *Lord Byron's* Cain 11). Against this objection some critics have rightly maintained that the poet projects himself into his hero, who speaks for the author as much as for himself. Cain's first soliloquy, for example, reflects Byron's own torturing doubts about the intractable moral aspects of the fall. But a context that cannot be ignored is the long-established tradition in which *Cain* was written, far removed from the highly original parodic mode of *Don Juan*, in which "Byron's ploy . . . is to deconstruct satire" (Curran 196). Though the author gives *Cain* the subtitle *A Mystery*, the play assumes the absolute stance of a tragedy like *Oedipus Rex*, with its pattern of irony, conflict, peripeteia, and *anagnorisis* (Hirst, "Byron's Lapse" 152–56). The ironic overthrow of the idealistic hero who becomes a murderer constitutes a dramatic or poetic (though not a logical) refutation of his self-righteous accusations against a deity who ensnared humanity in Eden, by exposing him, the fratricide, as traitor to his own humanitarian aspirations. While no argument is vitiated by its advocate, we must point out that in a drama the ironic situation of a blinded protagonist tends to undercut his case. With the new (though still limited) insight that Cain gains at the end, readers and spectators too may ponder divine inscrutability, but they are no longer arrested by the initial impression of sacrilege.

In order to make the seeming subversion of Scripture a real one, Byron would have had to sustain to the end the impression of impious indignation, and he could have done so only by making a fundamental change in the plot of his source. He might have spared Abel's life or at least depicted his death as a moral victory. He might even, in a pure inversion of the Genesis story, have let Abel murder Cain—anything that would not have undermined Cain's moral posture so drastically. It was probably a sense of decorum and verisimilitude that prevented Byron from going so far in his revisionism. But if we maintain that the poet would have resisted the claim of Bible stories for fidelity no less than (say) Blake, we can only guess at the psychological reasons for his decision to follow Scripture in making Cain commit fratricide. Perhaps Byron found relief in the dramatic rebuttal of his own iconoclastic thoughts; indeed, he may have felt drawn unconsciously to Cain, because, unlike Adam and Eve's, Cain's guilt was clear to him and thus permitted him to undermine his hero's recalcitrance against the deity. Once, when I suggested that Byron's self-projection into a murderer might have freed him from the still greater torment of having to convict a God whose ways his reason failed to justify, a student responded with the analogy of a child of divorced parents who takes the blame for the failed marriage on herself. In order to attack God rather than a self-projection, Byron would have done better to dramatize the expulsion from Eden.

But Byron did actually rewrite the story of the fall. Part of the play's irony lies in Cain's repetition of the fall of his parents with which he is preoccupied throughout. Like the serpent of Genesis, Lucifer is a tempter, an analogy made instinctively by Adah (1.1.392, 401–05). Both serpent and Lucifer offer knowledge and cause death, which yet remains a mystery. Like his parents, Cain is undeterred by the threat of death: he would gaze on "the great double mysteries" even if he were to perish in the event, thus evoking Lucifer's apt retort, "There / The son of her who snatched the apple spake" (2.2.404–09). Cain implicitly identifies with Eve's act of disobedience (3.1.92). Those who see Byron succeed in his subversion of biblical theodicy from within confuse Cain's fall with Adam and Eve's and fail to take into account the new ground the poet has chosen for his revisionary struggle, one on which he is bound to lose. The theological dilemma of the Eden story is ultimately insoluble—the Bible's answer must have long ceased to be taken for granted, since Milton already found it necessary to make a heroic attempt to reassert its authority—but displaced into the context of Cain's temptation and fall, this problem finds at least a dramatic solution in the ironic reversal of the self-righteous hero that I have described. The transfer of the fall theme from Adam to Cain tends to restore the Bible's authority by moving the focus to some extent from the question "Are God's ways justified?" to "Is rebellion against God's ways justified?" Unlike Cain's protests, Adam's arguments against God's arbitrary temptation and excessive punishment would not have been dramatically undercut by the advocacy of a spokesman who, inflicting unmerited pain, commits the very injustice against which he inveighs. To regard *Cain* as iconoclastic is to accept the hero's judgment of God within the context he himself establishes: Why were his parents placed near the fatal tree "Where it grew / The fairest in the centre" (1.1.73–74)? The pivotal tragic question, however, concerns Cain's own conduct: Is he or is he not his "brother's keeper" (3.1.469)? The inevitable answer will either follow the doctrinal implications of the Cain episode or may be given in a secular context—but it will not run counter to biblical ethics.

Although in *Heaven and Earth* there is no such close analogy between the original temptation of Adam and Eve and its displacement into another's fate, this work too is "unmistakably concerned with the Fall of Man" (Roston 214), the third after Adam's and Cain's (Manning, *Byron* 157; Corbett 175). For Japhet, to bring on the Flood means to "[r]enew . . . Adam's Fall" (1.3.706). As in *Cain*, "man's fallen state coupled with an innate yearning for a mythic Eden" produces a state of "willful damnation" (Fitzpatrick 615). The side of Byron that (like Cain's and Lucifer's blasphemies) calls God's ways into question is expressed by Aholibamah's consistent rebellion and Japhet's occasional pleas for universal pardon, including the abolishment of hell and redemption of earth "in an endless paradise, / Where man no more can fall as once he fell" (1.3.201–02). Carrying the tradition that has extended the meaning of the fall to encompass the *felix culpa* a step further, Byron suggests that the "Eden . . . / . . . sometimes with our visions blent" (1.1.73–74) lies in the future.

Since *Heaven and Earth* is a fragment (and thus lacks the tragic closure of *Cain*), it is hard to decide whether the oldest connotation of Eden would eventually have reestablished itself. The context of *Heaven and Earth*—the drama breaks off with the rising waters of the deluge—seems to reassert the scriptural view of the fall by showing the "death and decay / Our mother Eve bequeathed us" (1.1.106–07), how "We are sent / Upon the earth to toil and die" (1.3.371–72) only because our first parents "listened to the voice / Of knowledge without power" (1.3.78–79). Perhaps that is why Byron pronounced the work "very pious" (*Letters* 9: 118), though he may also have been thinking of Raphael's denunciation of the rebellious angels and more mild dismissal of Japhet's heretical stance or the play's Calvinist division of characters into elect and damned. Or are the words "very pious" bitterly ironic? *Heaven and Earth* faithfully follows the Bible by telling how Noah's generation was destroyed while his own family was saved, but among the victims it singles out are a mother who vainly tries to save her infant and a pious mortal who blesses the Lord with his dying breath, which may suggest that Adam's fall was indeed "unforgiven" (*Don Juan* 1.127). That Byron refuses to resign himself to such an idea he tells us plainly through his spokesman Japhet, who is not disqualified by a crime like Cain's from serving as a dramatic vehicle for the expression of human grievances. Was Byron content to leave us with such a deconstructive reading of the third fall in the Bible? Or might he have preferred to repeat the pattern of *Cain*? But in order to do so he would have had to go radically against the source story by inventing some equivalent crime for the son of Noah, or he might have moved Aholibamah into the center and developed her criminal potential. Did Byron not simply abandon the project because it proved too recalcitrant? Be that as it may, what we have of *Heaven and Earth* "appears to be designed to create a mood rather than to develop a coherent plot or portray characters" (Kushwaha 165) and certainly lacks that clear dramatic vindication of the biblical world picture that the ironic overthrow of a rebellious hero confers on a tragedy like *Cain*. Whereas in the preface to *Cain* Byron insists that his depiction of the fall "has nothing to do with the *New Testament*," that it remains associated with the serpent (and not with Satan), "[w]hatever interpretation the Rabbins and the Fathers may have put upon this" (Steffan, *Lord Byron's* Cain 155), in *Heaven and Earth* Byron makes no such attempt to suppress his revisionary tendencies. Breaking free of the earliest narrow context of Genesis by (among other things) more explicitly voicing "Christian, as distinct from Hebraic, doctrine" (Corbett 179), Byron leaves the struggle between the original meaning of Eden and his reinterpretation of it unre-solved.

Nevertheless both mysteries show the limits—historical, aesthetic, psy-chological—that the resistance of a biblical motif in a biblical work imposes on the exercise of poetic license for revisionary purposes. Whether or not students accept my contention that Byron's struggle for new meanings of

Eden is more successful in his (nonbiblical) *Don Juan*, his revisionism shows them that just as a word is given its sense within the sentence, paragraph, or book in which it appears, so a recurrent motif like the fall must be read in its widest context. The same goes for any metaphor, for a speaker in internal monologue or dramatic dialogue, for a couplet in an ottava rima stanza, or for a rhyme. When Byron's words sound like a sermon, like a polemical attack on accepted beliefs, a political manifesto, or a philosophical worldview, and when characters in various works all speak as if they were the author in disguise, we must remind our students that a statement means different things in different contexts.

NOTE

[1]Quotations of Byron's *Cain* in this essay are from *Lord Byron's* Cain (ed. Steffan). Quotations of his *Heaven and Earth* are from *The Works of Lord Byron: Poetry* (ed. E. H. Coleridge).

DON JUAN

The Paradoxical Unity of *Don Juan*:
Hero, Narrator, World

Katherine Kernberger

Convinced that *Don Juan*'s skepticism and cynicism about human knowledge and society should speak particularly clearly to our modern relativistic world, I explore the poem with my undergraduate Romanticism survey course, looking at three potential grounds of unity: the hero, the narrator, and the real world that Byron incorporates into his literary work. Many students need help first to read and sort out such a long poem and then to begin to interpret it independently. I ask the students to live with a high level of anxiety, to exercise their Keatsean "negative capability," without any "irritable reaching" for certainty, while we assemble our impressions.

Initially, we establish the two conflicting forces most readers perceive in the poem: the hero and the narrator. Because most students cling to plot as their primary guide in reading a narrative poem, we explore the hero and his adventures first, looking for potential unity.

The opening stanza of canto 1 announces Byron's dilemma in choosing a hero appropriate for his time. What avenues are available for heroic endeavor in a world in decline, as Byron believed his was? The glory of battle of an Achilles, the quest for experience and knowledge of an Odysseus or a Faust, the patriotic piety of an Aeneas or a Dante, all are equally impossible in post-Napoleonic Europe. Public endeavor and spiritual strivings have shrunk to the only sphere left, the personal realm of sexual love. But in appropriating the legend of Don Juan, Byron deliberately cuts the story loose from its moorings. His Juan most emphatically is not the figure seen in the pantomime or Mozart's opera or enshrined in the popular imagination. Instead of presenting a hardened profligate who exults in seducing and abandoning his victims, Byron creates a passive and innocent hero who is himself seduced by the women he encounters. He is not a beneficiary of the reigning power paradigm that gives men hegemony over women. Because Juan approaches women without the trappings of power that men in their societies usually command, he offers them a chance for a relationship of equality rather than submission (as with Julia, Haidée, and Dudù).

Next, we chart Juan's picaresque wanderings, seeking within them a developmental thread. The Gulbeyaz, Ismail, and Catherine cantos show how Juan succumbs to corruption. His mind still occupied with visions of Haidée, Juan withstands the advances of the beautiful Gulbeyaz, enunciating a spirited defense of freedom in love. Within a few days, however, tainted by his unthinking participation in the unjust battle of Ismail, he accepts "that high official situation," serving Catherine the Great of Russia as a male mistress. (Significantly, Byron here clearly condemns war, the usual sphere of traditional, especially epic, heroism, as "a brain-spattering, windpipe-slitting art, / Unless her cause by right be sanctified" [9.4].) I find that comparing the Gulbeyaz and Catherine episodes helps students examine how Juan's capitulation to Catherine represents the climax of the plot.

What Byron does to the traditional homme fatal alerts the students that he had in mind something more than "to giggle and make giggle," as he asserted in correspondence with his publisher, John Murray. Many stanzas of the poem declare the poet's "plain, sworn, downright detestation / Of every despotism in every nation" (9.24). Embedded in sexual innuendo about the "lust" for power, these lines ostensibly on political tyranny appear in the Russian cantos and evoke the dual tyranny of Catherine herself. In each country Juan offers us an insight into and sometimes a liberating alternative to the sexual status quo, which itself reflects the political relations between the rulers and the ruled in that land. So, while Juan's adventures may seem random at first, I work with the class to establish how the plot development critiques society's hypocritical attitudes toward love and marriage and their implied connection with freedom and tyranny.

This analysis of the plot's content (and intent) leads us to examine the split between the hero and the narrator, whose interruptions irritate most students at the outset. They want Byron to get on with the story, to throw out all that digression and seemingly self-indulgent philosophizing. Yet after analyzing the hero's story, they can see the connection between Juan and the poet-narrator, one that creates the second potential unifying force, a shaping consciousness managing the fictive microcosm and offering the audience significant insight into life.

While some poems profit from the exclusion of authorial biography, *Don Juan* is not among them. Contemporaries would have recognized Byron's allusions to his domestic life (early exemplified by Donna Inez, whose favorite science was the "mathematical") even in the first anonymous publication. For the poet, notorious as his amatory exploits were, to choose Don Juan as the hero of his "modern epic," while clearly appropriate in our eyes, looked openly defiant, even Satanic, to the British of his day. The first reviewers perceived a political danger in the sexual freedom championed by Byron and his poem, condemning both as immoral and subversive.

But students note that, as the poem unfolds, Byron does not merely impose his point of view on the characters; his digressions seem ultimately to replace the narrative as the locus of the poem's interest:

> This narrative is not meant for narration,
> But a mere airy and fantastic basis
> To build up common things with common places.
> (14.7)

As they discover the options Byron's role as narrator opens up for him (and for the poem), most students withdraw their objections to the digressions and seek the thematic concerns that tie Juan's story to the narratorial commentary. They also note that the hero begins to resemble his narrator, becoming "gaté and blasé as he [grows] older" (Marchand, *Letters* 8: 78). By the English cantos, Byron has come "home," only thinly disguised in the cautious persona of Juan.

Byron refuses to confine himself to the story of his hero, but ponders boldly on all manner of topics; he insists on opening the poem up to admit the whole world. This brings us to the third unifying factor I emphasize: Byron deliberately tears down the boundaries traditionally imposed on literature, blurring the line between the literary and the real. He has followed Montaigne, Cervantes, Sterne, in discovering, as Virginia Woolf astutely observed, "an elastic shape which will hold whatever you choose to put into it" (Bostetter, *Twentieth Century Interpretations* 94). Are we wrongheaded from the start in applying the critical criterion of unity to a work that sets out to violate traditional principles of unity? Byron's fragment is unfinished *by design*, not merely by biographical accident.

Although we all know that the poem stops because its author died, abundant evidence in Byron's letters indicates that the poem would never have been "finished" regardless of how long Byron the poet had lived. Only a form whose openness refused to shut out any aspect of "history, tradition, [or the] facts" (1.203) could offer him limitless opportunity to explore the world and his thoughts on it. He had no reason to bring the poem to a close.

Literature can be managed and crafted to present consistency, but only by falsifying life:

> But if a writer should be quite consistent
> How could he possibly show things existent?
> (15.87)

And Byron wishes to present not potentiality but actuality:

> But now I'm going to be immoral, now
> I mean to show things really as they are,
> Not as they ought to be. . . .   (12.40)

His announced purpose in *Don Juan* goes beyond the creation of an artifact, divorced from "things really as they are." As McGann notes in Don Juan *in Context*, "Aesthetic form restricts the possible arrangements of the materials to the laws of internal coherence. The idea of poetic self-consistency closes the world either to the scope of the poem, or to the range of the poet's instilled imaginative conception" (110). To preserve unity, as traditionally understood by Aristotle or as propounded by Coleridge, writers must omit the inconvenient and recalcitrant facts that do not fit into a narrow scheme. But a "unified, integrative, or closed system" is precisely what Byron wishes to avoid (McGann, Don Juan *in Context* 103). As William A. Covino stresses in *The Art of Wondering*:

> With persistent references to events outside poetry, *Don Juan* reveals that the truth about the world is 1) not plain and 2) a function of the imaginative freedom which each of us allows himself.   (106)

The prevalence of the Romantic fragment poem represents something more significant than the chance deaths of various poets. The fragment is the perfect Romantic form, allowing the poet to avoid closing off possibilities. Byron's poem in particular asks us to suspend our desire for neatly arranged patterns of development and resolution—life does not operate that way; true art should not either. Surely we cannot ask the poem to do what Byron did not intend it to. It does not present a coherent moral universe because to do so would contradict the reality the poet knew. The poem does, however, assemble an attack on the world as it is:

> Without, or with, offence to friends or foes,
> I sketch your world exactly as it goes.
> (8.89)

Because "till we see what's in fact, we're far / From much improvement" (12.40). Perhaps because we no longer agree on the divinely ordained natural or human order most of Byron's contemporaries believed in, we find the thoroughgoing skepticism of the poem congenial; it suits our own uncertainty and tolerance.

The indeterminacy of the poem's larger components—plot, digressions, themes, aims—appears in the molecular unit, the stanza form itself. Students respond positively to the power of the ottava rima to build up an illusion in the first six lines and deflate it by striking back with the stinging rhyme of the couplet, a microcosmic model of what the episodes of the plot do. Students are not troubled, as Byron's contemporaries were, that Byron undercuts his readers' response. They do not resent having their expectations punctured; they are Romantic ironists already.

I think this sophistication is the result in part of a new medium, film, that can present in absolutely convincing reality a totally contrived and artificial world, punned on frequently as the "reel" world. As members of the audience at *The Rocky Horror Picture Show*, students come dressed in costume, bringing water pistols, rice, and playing cards, all to "participate" in the movie. While they may not have seen much live theater, they have grown up with movies and music videos that play with the conventions, breaking the illusion to reveal that the figures on the screen are only actors (the conclusions of *Blazing Saddles* and *Monty Python and the Holy Grail* both come to mind) or to call into doubt the reality of the world the viewers inhabit (*The Purple Rose of Cairo*). Perceiving these parallels, they appreciate Byron's interjection of his real world into the poem. In canto 5 Byron interrupts a digression on the conscience, appetite, and digestion of slave traders for a further digression on an occurrence from his own life. Finding the "military commandant / Stretched in the street," mortally wounded, Byron had him brought into the house, where he died before medical help could arrive. The incident evokes metaphysical musings, in the poem and in Byron's letters, but provides no answers. "But it was all a mystery. Here we are, / And there we go, but *where*? . . . / *We*, whose minds comprehend all things?" (5.39).

Surely this skepticism speaks directly to us, to our students, as a salutary reminder that our century has no more convincing answers to such questions than Byron did.

Teaching *Don Juan* from the Perspective of Cross-Dressing and the Politics of Gender

Susan Wolfson

Many of us find the complete *Don Juan* impossible to take on in a Romantic survey course. Its topicality, its allusiveness, and its wit often frustrate students unused to literature of this kind; its length allows us to teach only a few books or episodes. These difficulties may be partly met by focusing on the poem's politics of gender: this topic can draw on several important episodes and is one that undergraduates most likely have studied or have opinions about. For graduate seminars, an interesting set of theoretical, historical, and biographical material may be added to the study of the poem itself; an essay I published in 1987 develops one approach. Since that essay had its origin in my undergraduate teaching, however, I speak to that format.

Cross-dressing is a valuable point of entry into the subject of politics and gender precisely because dress is a customary signifier of gender difference; inverting that code thus calls into question the categories designed to discriminate "masculine" from "feminine"—even as such inversions provoke Byron to a series of conservative reactions and defensive reinscriptions of sexual orthodoxy. I open a discussion of the politics of dress with a look at how *Don Juan* links women and hypocrisy in the vocabulary of disguise. The narrator remarks of Lady Adeline: "[W]hatso'er she wished, she acted right" (14.57), using a "little genial sprinkling of hypocrisy" to succeed as one of the "loveliest Oligarchs of our Gynocrasy" (12.66). Students may remember that Byron calls on this rhyme again to advise all who would "take the tone of their society" to "wear the newest mantle of hypocrisy, / On pain of much displeasing the Gynocrasy" (16.52). With this material in hand, I ask whether the arts of hypocrisy are the property of the gynocracy alone. Might the male narrator's saying "*our* Gynocrasy" imply a certain pride of identification? And what about the third rhyme in the stanza from canto 12 quoted above, "aristocracy"? Might women be culpable of nothing more than disclosing the master trope of all social—and artistic—success? Students may think of hypocrisy only as a moral fault, but we can refer to etymology to show its involvement with artful acting. The narrator's confessed pleasure in performances both literary and social is relevant and revealing: by canto 16 he is praising his female muse as the "most sincere that ever dealt in fiction" (2).

Byron's ambivalence about the gender of hypocrisy provides a good point of departure for considering the poem's more visible transfers of the customary properties of gender—namely, its social and linguistic cross-dressings. These figures not only concentrate the energies of Byron's satire but compel attention to those crucial discriminations through which "masculine" and "feminine" have been culturally defined, and through which men and women have been psychologically compelled and historically confined. Students are usually able to identify the chief figures: the "odd travesty" of Juan in the slave market "femininely all array'd" (5.74, 80) and "her frolic Grace—Fitz-Fulke" disguised as the ghost of the Black Friar (16.123). I also point to the less obvious episodes in which Juan is covered by female clothes (first Julia's, then Haidée's and Zoe's) and to such linguistic transfers of verbal property as the narrator's calling himself "a male Mrs. Fry" (10.84); Antonia's references to Juan as a "pretty gentleman" with a "half-girlish face" (1.170–71), corroborated by the narrator's description of him as "a most beauteous Boy" (9.53), "feminine in feature" (8.52), dancing "like a flying Hour before Aurora, / In Guido's famous fresco" (14.40); and the application of masculine-toned terms to women: Empress Catherine as "handsome" and "fierce" (9.63). Some of these transfers and transgressions play as farce, but not exclusively, for the terms "male" and "female" are perplexed—both politically and psychologically—in ways that unsettle, even dismantle, the social structures to which gender has been assimilated. The result, I urge students to see, is a qualified but potent redefinition of conventional sexual politics. Citing Natalie Davis's remark that gender symbolism "is always available to make statements about social experience and to reflect (or conceal) contradictions within it" (127), I try to get students to see how the cross-dressings of *Don Juan* inhabit episodes and figures in which what has been customarily denied to one sex gets projected in terms of the other. While the figures on both sides of these transfers are often made to seem absurd or anomalous, it is their very anomaly that makes legible the ideology by which conventional codes are maintained and perpetuated.

With this territory sketched out, I take up the poem's two extended episodes of transvestism, Juan's conscription as an odalisque and Fitz-Fulke's masquerade in a friar's habit. Students usually have no difficulty in seeing how both derive their comic energy from the inversion of male privilege; less obvious is the way in which both provoke Byron's ambivalence about the cost. One aspect of that ambivalence that is helpful to understand is Byron's experience in Italy as "Cavalier Servente," the accepted escort and socially tolerated lover of a married woman. Byron was capable of a quasi-feminist analysis of this institution, assessing it as a by-product of fathers treating daughters as commodities on the marriage market. The successful bidder was often a man older than the father himself (the husband of Byron's mistress was about twice Byron's and three times her own age), and the resulting "preposterous connexion" made extramarital romance inevitable (Lovell, *Medwin's Conversations* 22). Yet as Cavalier Servente himself, Byron felt acutely his status as "a piece of female property" (Marchand, *Letters* 7: 28), complaining that "the system of *serventism* imposes a thousand times more restraint and slavery than marriage ever imposed" (Lovell, *Lady Bles-sington's Conversations* 180). The mistress's word is "the only law which he obeys," the narrator of *Beppo* reports, describing the role of this "super-numerary slave" in terms that figure such bondage, tellingly, as a kind of transvestism: he "stays / Close to the lady as a part of dress" (40).

Byron never developed his plan to submit Juan to the "ridicules" of being "a Cavalier Servente in Italy" (*Letters* 8: 78); even so, his mixed feelings about the office may be read in the poem's transvestite episodes. On the one hand, the spectacle of Juan in women's clothes and in the role of sex slave defamiliarizes, and so opens to scrutiny, the customary status of women as objects of trade in a male-centered economy. This is a world in which a Sultan may, by right, own four wives and fifteen hundred concubines. On the other hand, by marking this extreme system as Oriental, Byron deflects attention from less extreme but clearly analogous practices in the Western world; moreover, the emphasis is not on the oppression of women but on the violation of Western manhood. Juan's shock at learning he is owned by a Sultana who asks only, "Christian, canst thou love?" and who "[c]onceived that phrase was quite enough to move" (5. 116) is an implicit critique of the institution of sexual ownership; but much more explicit is the way Juan "in his feminine disguise" (6.26) registers Byron's male-centered discomfort at the sensation of being female property.

Students may sense that Juan has already been represented as something of an illicit or smuggled piece of property in his affairs with Julia and Haidée; if so, they will see that the harem episode explicitly equates his status as property with a loss of male social identity. The slave market is an omen, for not only do his captors make Juan a commodity, but they think of pack-aging him with one of the "*third* sex" (4.86), a castrato who inspires "some discussion and some doubt" if such a "soprano might be deem'd to be male" (4.92). It is scarcely an improvement that Juan is finally paired with an "odd female" in an allotment in which everyone else is paired "[l]ady to lady . . . man to man" (4.91–92). The status of Juan's gender in the marketplace becomes even more precarious when he is purchased by a eunuch and ordered to dress himself in "a suit / In which a Princess with great pleasure would / Array her limbs" (5.73). The narrator conspires in these travesties, not only by referring to him as "her" (6.35) but also by teasing at Juan's easy assimilation to the odalisques "all clad alike . . . a very nymph-like looking crew" (5.99). Juan's difference is scarcely apparent: "His youth and features favour'd the disguise" (5.115), and "no one doubted on the whole, that she / Was what her dress bespoke" (6.36).

Students invariably find these inversions comic. This response is valuable because it reveals the degree to which Byron's management of this episode at once approaches and retreats from progressive critical analysis. It is worth turning attention at this point to how Byron's total treatment of Juan cross-dressed contains its potential critique with renewed expressions of male power. That agenda is anticipated by Juan's steadfast adherence to the grounds of his identity: Byron allows him the dignity of protesting to his purchaser, "I'm not a lady," of worrying about his social reputation if "it e'er be told / That I unsexed my dress," and of declaring that his "soul loathes / The effeminate garb" (5.73–76). These statements of resistance to the effeminate find an ally in Byron's narrative mode, which (as is often the case with male transvestism in literary and theatrical tradition) gives the occasion over to farce—yet another means of containing the ideological disturbance. The political implications of Juan's feminization dissipate into a high-camp parody of the trappings of female subjection. Juan even has to be coached "to stint / That somewhat manly majesty of stride" (5.91). The Englishman who befriends him in the slave market sounds the cue with a jesting version of Laertes's caution to Ophelia—"Keep your good name"—and Juan and the narrator merrily play along: "Nay," quoth the maid, "the Sultan's self shan't carry me, / Unless his highness promises to marry me" (5.84). When the Sultan takes a shine to Juan's beauty, Juan shows how well he has learned to mimic feminine manners: "This compliment . . . made her blush and shake" (5.156). And quite beyond such campiness, Byron actually reverses the seeming impotence of Juan's travesty by introducing another kind of potency: Juan discovers he is not so much an unsexed man as a newly powerful woman. "Juanna" immediately becomes the center of attention and rivalry in the harem; all the girls want "her" to share their beds. This interest affords Juan a novel indirection by which to find directions out, for as the only phallic woman in the harem, he discovers a world of sexual opportunity. I point out that at the same time Juan is newly empowered by his female attire, Byron's narrative abases the "imperious" woman by whom Juan had been abased: the episode ends with the Sultana's will subverted and her character refeminized. When we first meet her, she is an interesting "mixture . . . half voluptuousness and half command" (5.108), but the destiny of biology—"Her form had all the softness of her sex" (109)—prevails. Not only is she unable to command Juan, but having been outwitted by him and his harem bed partner, she is reduced to a caricature of a woman scorned.

Students may note that while feminized men in *Don Juan* are treated as objects of contempt or subjects for farce, women such as Gulbeyaz and Catherine, with access to "male" purchasing power by virtue of political station, are almost always cast as dangerous figures of erotic desire. The episode of Duchess Fitz-Fulke's impersonation of the Black Friar offers an effective way to conclude this survey, not only because it is the provisional close of Byron's poem but also because it nicely complements the transvestite farce of Juan in the harem, restaging and making more flexible the issues of transvestism and female appropriation of male property. In contrast to Gul-beyaz's thwarted attempt to exercise male sexual prerogative, Fitz-Fulke's transvestism—even as a ghost hostile to the sexual productivity of the House of Amundeville—is a relatively successful scheme. It is not just a theatrical strategy tuned to the psychological advantage of shocking revelation; it also operates as an outlet for desire, granting her a kind of "male" power of action within the existing social structure and aligning her with its savvy craftsmen: those "[h]istorians, heroes, lawyers, priests" who put "truth in masquerade" and whose example inspires the narrator to urge Juan to "Be hypocritical . . . be / Not what you *seem*" (11.37, 86). Fitz-Fulke's disguise draws even fuller energy and ideological significance in this respect from the highly popular institution of the masquerade, at which, Terry Castle reports, transvestism was not only common but commonly suspected of encouraging "female sexual freedom, and beyond that, female emancipation generally" (164). Because Fitz-Fulke's cross-dressing has less to do with the specific hypocrisies of gynocracy than with the general ways of the world, the effect of her manipulations is ambiguous. If, as the narrator remarks, that "tender moonlight situation" in which she and Juan discover each other "enables Man to show his strength / Moral or physical," he remains coy about who the "Man" is—the girlish Juan or the transvestite Fitz-Fulke? Byron "leave[s] the thing a problem, like all things" (17.13).

The uncertain issue of this last episode helps students see what sort of problems accrue in trying to welcome Byron into the ranks of feminism on the basis of his comic assault on the constricting codes of gender. It is important to contemplate the nervous edge of these episodes. Not only do their inversions and reversals erode male power, but their plots involve images and threats of death. The dissolution of male power is apparent enough in the loss of male attire and the quasi transvestism involved in Juan's romances with Julia and Haidée. Julia "half-smother'd" a naked Juan in her bedding to hide from her husband's posse; it is a naked and half-dead Juan for whom "Haidée stripp'd her sables off" to make a couch—"and, that he might be more at ease, / And warm, in case by chance he should awake," she and Zoe "also gave a petticoat apiece" (2.133). Though not overtly trans-vestite, these coverings still compromise Juan's manhood, for each, while protective, also marks him as passive and dependent, the property of a woman's design. Significantly, after being discovered by Julia's husband, Don Alfonso, Juan can't recover his clothes but must escape "naked" (2.188) into the night. That reduction is also suggested by the garments Juan, "na-ked" once again, receives from Haidée. Though these are men's, the apparel does not proclaim the man: the "breeches" in which she "dress'd him" are rather too "spacious" (probably belonging to her father, Lambro) and, more tellingly, she withholds the real signifiers of male power: "turban, slippers, pistols, dirk" (2.160). With both Julia and Haidée, Juan remains a "boy" (Catherine, too, "sometimes liked a boy," "slight and slim," preferring such "a boy to men much bigger" [9.47,72]), and Byron underscores the corresponding impotence not only by confronting Juan with a genuine threat of death from the men betrayed by these affairs (Don Alfonso and Lambro) but by masculinizing the women. Julia is of "stature tall" (1.60). Haidée is "Even of the highest for a female mould . . . and in her air / There was a something which bespoke command" (2.116). The implied maleness of this manner is confirmed when she confronts her father: protecting Juan, "Haidée threw herself her boy before"; "Stern as her sire," "She stood . . . tall beyond her sex . . . and with a fix'd eye scann'd / Her father's face. . . . How like they look'd! the expression was the same. . . . their features and / Their stature differing but in sex and years" (4.42–45). Despite sexual difference, Haidée and Lambro differ less from each other than both differ from the "boy" Juan.

All these inversions fuel a lethal economy. A feminized Juan always invites death into the poem, in the form of threats either to his own life or to the lives of those implicated in his travesties. "Juan nearly died" (1.168) from affairs with Julia and Haidée, and the women exact full wages: the passionate Julia is sentenced to life-in-death in a convent; Haidée's nurturing of Juan is allied with figures of death, and she herself dies. The threat is all but perpetual: when Gulbeyaz discovers her designs for Juan usurped by Dudù, she issues a warrant for both their deaths, and Catherine's appetites all too soon reduce her "beauteous" favorite to "a condition / Which augured of the dead" (10.39). So, too, after his first sighting of the Black Friar's Ghost—itself a patent figure of death—Juan and Fitz-Fulke look "pale" (16.31); the morning after discovering her within that "sable frock and dreary cowl" (16.123), he appears "wan and worn, with eyes that hardly brooked / The light," and Her Grace seems scarcely better, "pale and shivered" (17.14).

Don Juan may not be able to conceive of any alternative to inversion and its costly consequences. Even so, students appreciate the ways in which Byron explores the problems of living with and within structures of social and psychological difference, and they are stimulated by the poem's capacity to draw our critical attention to the systems of power by which these differences are maintained.

"A plain man, and in a single station":
Byronic Self-Representation in *Don Juan*

Peter J. Manning

I most frequently teach *Don Juan* in courses in which it follows Wordsworth's *Prelude*. Students who have only just come to value Wordsworth's patient attempt to construct a self are often disconcerted by Byron's very different mode, and an introductory contrast with *The Prelude* is useful to suggest the improvisatory nature of *Don Juan* and to orient their reading.

In *The Prelude* Wordsworth seeks to accommodate his experience to an overall design in which "in the end / All [is] gratulant if rightly understood" (13.384–85). Though the text subverts this program and betrays the shifting intentions of its prolonged composition, Wordsworth characterizes *The Prelude* as an effort to "fix the wavering balance of [his] mind" (1.650) and to make the "rigorous inquisition" (1.159) necessary before advancing to the "honorable toil" (1.653) of his philosophic poem *The Recluse*. To compose *The Prelude* was also to compose his life and establish himself as the Poet. Such an urgent drama can be played only before an encouraging audience: the ideal reader projected by what Wordsworth referred to as "the poem to Coleridge" assumes Coleridge's attitude, "prompt / In sympathy" (1.645–46). *The Prelude* engages the French Revolution and other public events but remained private, unseen except by a circle of intimates and unpublished during Wordsworth's lifetime.

The dismay aroused when expectations formed by *The Prelude* confront *Don Juan* repeats the shock felt by the poem's early readers and the accusations of cynicism and insincerity levied at Byron down through the early part of this century; showing students that their questions about *Don Juan* run throughout the history of its reception authorizes, amplifies, and articulates their uncertainties. Biography too provides an entry into discussion of the kind of poem *Don Juan* is: "I'm a plain man, and in a single station" (1.22), says the narrator, but the poem was known to be Byron's despite appearing anonymously. The declaration, and the subsequent clinching couplet—"But—Oh! ye lords of ladies intellectual, / Inform us truly, have they not hen-peck'd you all?" (1.22)—depend for their wit on the reader's awareness of Lady Byron's mathematical interests and the scandal of the separation. If not every reader was privy to such jokes, which mark the coterie qualities of the poem, a general point also obtains: Byron's status as a notorious public figure, whose doings were reported in the newspapers and quarterlies, enables him to play with his image in *Don Juan* (the author of *Childe Harold's Pilgrimage* "a plain man"?) and flirt with the borders between life and art. The first line of the poem, "I want a hero: an uncommon want," replaces the grave invocations of epic tradition with the impulses of personal desire and acquires special force because spoken by the author who had stamped his name on the Byronic hero.

The exchange between Byron and his friend John Cam Hobhouse in the margins of stanzas 27–29 of canto 1, printed by Jerome McGann, usefully exemplifies the procedures of *Don Juan*. To Hobhouse's objection that the satire on Lady Byron was too "pointed" and that there was "some doubt" whether she had opened his letters, as Donna Inez is said to have done her husband's, Byron replied: "If people make applications it is their own fault. . . . What has the 'doubt' to do with the poem? It is at least poetically true— why apply everything to that absurd woman. I have no reference to living characters." The vehemence signals the disingenuousness of Byron's defense, and encountering an instance of malice at the root of creation often liberates students taught that literature embodies humanistic ideals. Yet Byron does not speak wholly falsely; rather, the exchange defines the equivocation between autobiography and fiction that typifies *Don Juan*.

Unlike Wordsworth, concerned to fashion an integrated self and a coherent narrative, Byron splits and multiplies into his characters. It is tempting to identify him with the narrator, but his upbringing with the widowed Mrs. Byron underlies Juan's with Donna Inez, and the strife of Inez and Don Jose echoes his marriage to Annabella Milbanke (as Hobhouse's rebuke witnesses). No single voice is authoritatively "Byron," and indeed the self represented in cantos 1 and 2 is not acknowledged as Byron's at all: the narrator is nameless, and no link is admitted between him and Juan. Wordsworth confesses that it is a "Hard task to analyse a soul, in which / . . . each most obvious and particular thought— / . . . / Hath no beginning" (2.232–37), but the project of *The Prelude* required grounding the self in formative childhood experience. In contrast to this search for unique origins, Byron proliferates fictions of the self. The Spanish cantos of *Don Juan* offer one oblique account of Byron's life in England; the English cantos, four years later, a revision, with the orphan Leila occupying the role of the innocent formerly taken by Juan. Truth in *Don Juan* is versional: "The very shadow of true Truth would shut / Up annals, revelations, poesy, / And prophecy" (11.37), proclaims the narrator, and shutting up is what he refuses to do. As he punningly remarks, "[T]he great *end* of travel . . . is driving" (10.72): unceasing invention, not stable and conclusive truth, is the goal of the poem. Despite the increasing presence of the narrator as *Don Juan* proceeds, Byron aims at rhetorical fertility rather than the evolution and maintenance of a privileged perspective from which to order experience. The story overrides generic conventions: *Don Juan* is slant autobiography, epic, picaresque adventure, satire, naturalistic narrative (in the shipwreck scenes), romance and idyll (on Haidée's island), quasi-novel (at Norman Abbey). Its variety serves the principle that life is too multiform for any one point of view to contain:

"if a writer should be quite consistent," queries the narrator, "[h]ow could he possibly show things existent" (15.87)?

Pondering the fluidity of the self, the narrator reflects: "I almost think that the same skin / For one without—has two or three within" (17.11). The corollary of this psychology is a narrative mode opportunistically ready to capitalize on any experience, to seize whatever occasions the moment of composition presents. "I *have* no plan—I *had* no plan—but I had or have materials," Byron told his publisher (Marchand, *Letters* 6: 207), or, as the narrator puts it: "I rattle on exactly as I'd talk / With any body in a ride or walk" (15.19). This digressiveness initially puzzles students accustomed to the roughly chronological sequence of *The Prelude* (let alone the architectonic integrity of *Paradise Lost*), but the ensuing plenitude usually wins them over. "I write what's uppermost, without delay," concedes (or boasts?) the narrator, forsaking Wordsworthian meditative depth for immediacy, and the sequel of his miniature manifesto deserves equal attention: "This narrative is not meant for narration, / But a mere airy and fantastic basis, / To build up common things with common places" (14.7). The world built up by *Don Juan* is extraordinarily rich: the double time scheme carries Juan from the late eighteenth century in Spain through the Siege of Ismail in 1790 to Catherine's court in Saint Petersburg and arrival in Regency England, while the narrator's commentary on politics and society tracks the production of the poem from 1818 forward, with backward glances at Byron's youth and fame. Together the two strands portray the Europe of Byron's era, torn by revolution, imperialism, and nationalism, subsiding into the post-Napoleonic reaction the poet excoriates. The societies depicted range from Greek pirates and Turkish slave markets to highwaymen and the house parties of the British aristocracy, and the level of style moves effortlessly from slang and jargon through factual reportage and colloquial speech to the sublime.

This panoramic context makes clear that in *Don Juan* the self is not an entity constructed in solitary introspection but a process or relation, in ongoing dialogue with the surrounding world. When in the later cantos Byron becomes the avowed narrator, he incorporates the hostile responses the poem had already provoked: "Some have accused me of a strange design / Against the creed and morals of the land, / And trace it in this poem every line" (4.5). Presenting himself as the reviewers painted him, Byron makes of their condemnation the springboard for new play and more stanzas, but even as he rebuts their changes, he preserves them. The continuous testing of, and influence by, the audience through which *Don Juan* develops is neatly illustrated by Byron's explanation in canto 4 that, having "hear[d] that several people take exception / At the first two books having too much truth," he will "make Don Juan leave the ship" before Juan and the brunette with whom he is chained become erotically involved, adding that "the publisher declares, in sooth, / Through needles' eyes it easier for the camel is / To pass, than those two cantos into families" (4.97). Byron never forgets, or lets us forget, that *Don Juan* is a text shaped within the literary market, subject to the pressures of opinion and the means of distribution. As the text, so the self represented in it: the sovereignty of the narrator is repeatedly checked by reminders of all that lies beyond his control, not merely physical frailties, on which the poem insists, but also the vividly conveyed reality of other works, other voices, other men, other sources of power with which *Don Juan* must compete for attention.

For a poet operating in such a world, the reader is the all-important point of contact, but the reader must be imagined, forever intrigued and seduced into further reading. Byron, writing from Italy for an expanding nineteenth-century audience that he could not directly know, had to create and sustain the partnership on which the "conversational facility" (15.20) of *Don Juan* relies for its success. The concordance reveals that forms of the first-person pronoun occur almost two thousand times in the poem; more surprising and as indicative of the nature of *Don Juan* is that forms of *you* and addresses to the reader occur more than five hundred times. In the theater of the poem in which Byron performs himself into being, readers find themselves represented too, encouraged to join and extend the dialogue Byron mimes; students who take up Byron's invitation pass from submissive readers of a masterpiece to engaged and critical countervoices.

Byron's London

John Clubbe

During the autumn 1988 semester I taught a graduate seminar, Literature and the Urban Experience. Focusing on literary responses to London, 1700–1850, I began with Dryden and Pope and ended with *Bleak House*, taking in, along the way, Swift, Johnson, Boswell, Blake, and Wordsworth. Almost as an afterthought, I had included Byron. Though I vaguely regarded Byron as the most urban (and urbane) of the Romantic poets, I had never —except for admiring his descriptions of Venice in letters and the stanzas on London in *Don Juan*—thought much about his responses to the city and urban life. I knew of course that Byron lived most of his life, in England and in Italy, in or near cities. But just what was his attitude toward urban civilization in general and London in particular? The question now had a more urgent interest for me since I had recently completed a lengthy study of Cincinnati. Writing a book about a city's architecture and history, a book that required emphases very different from those of the literary training I had received, forced me to rethink my responses to urban life as depicted in literature. For "Byron's London" the challenge was both to explore unfamiliar terrain and to explore it in an unfamiliar way. If Byron's comments about London were to be considered from multiple perspectives, what would we—the students and I—come up with?

Before approaching Byron, the class had in preceding weeks wrestled with the urban responses of Blake and Wordsworth. The course could well have considered, but did not, Lamb, De Quincey, Hunt, and Hazlitt, as well as other contemporaries like Benjamin Robert Haydon. Of the essayists, Lamb may have been the purest London lover. Hazlitt and Hunt often dealt with London life, and London, as every reader of the *Confessions* knows, haunted the young De Quincey. The traditional scholarly view has the Romantics, these exceptions aside, hostile to the city, London chiefly, hostile even more to urban values.

And Byron? Does he constitute another exception? After all, Byron chose to live in cities. Would his writings reveal, if not a wholehearted belief in urban civilization, at least a charitable regard for London and London life? That was the question the class and I faced.

In preparing for this seminar, I had come on numerous studies that discussed eighteenth-century and Victorian attitudes toward the city but almost none, aside from a few stray articles on Blake and Wordsworth, on the other Romantics. Even after writing a lengthy bibliographical essay on Byron for another MLA book, I could find no study that took up Byron's response to urban life or to London. Why this lacuna? My puzzlement was all the greater in that I felt the subject had interest not only for students of Byron and English Romanticism but also for students of London and urban life. Byron was born in the eighteenth-century Georgian city; as an adult he experienced a London poised at the beginning of its extraordinary nineteenth-century growth.

We began by examining the passages in *Don Juan* that consider, if only by implication, urban civilization. These include the stanzas in canto 1 (130–33) in which the Byronic narrator assesses the nature and benefits of "progress"; the Daniel Boone stanzas in canto 8 (60–68) that pit city against country; finally, Juan's and the narrator's divergent responses to London and London life in the English cantos.

Byron's attitude toward London in *Don Juan*, we discovered, is linked to his attitude toward progress. In canto 1 he speculates about the origin and role of disease in society. If technology now permits the making of (indifferent) bread from potatoes, if galvanism can cause a corpse to twitch, what, Byron asks, will people do next? "What wondrous new machines have late been spinning! / I said the small-pox has gone out of late; / Perhaps it may be follow'd by the great" (1.130). Such not wholly ironic speculation inevitably leads Byron to take up Malthus. If America's population has increased too rapidly, maybe, like Europe's, it needs thinning: "With war, or plague, or famine, any way, / And which in ravage the more loathesome evil is— / Their real lues, or our pseudo-syphilis?" (1.131). "Pseudo-syphilis" refers, as McGann observes in his note, to the "civilized European diseases of war, plague, and famine." On the whole, then, Byron remains skeptical toward progress.

In the Boone passage Byron ponders the possibilities of a life far distant from Europe's urban centers. He contrasts civilization with Eden, town with country. Cities rise and fall but nature, Byron implies, goes on forever. Boone's sylvan arcadia exists in a timeless continuum, against which Byron sets the fragility of "Rome—Babylon—Tyre—Carthage—Nineveh" (8.60). Though Byron had not seen the ruined cities of antiquity, Rome he had visited, and other cities central to Western civilization—Athens, Constantinople, and Venice—he knew very well. Byron could identify with Boone's recurring need to escape from the nagging problems of society or, more simply, to get away from the pressure of other human beings. But that Europeans could still *live* Boone's life he doubted. "The inconvenience of civilization," he concludes, "[i]s, that you neither can be pleased nor please" (8.64).

Later in the poem Byron observes that, "of all nature's discrepancies, none . . . is greater than the difference . . . between the country and the town." Urban life, he asserts, "merits every preference / From those who have few resources of their own" (16.85). Although the city provides constant distraction to the mindless, for those with resources of their own there remains the challenge of a life in nature. In the end, however, Byron shied away from committing himself either to city or to country. Keeping alternatives open had more appeal to him than opting for any one of them. New World simplicity cut off from, yet the inheritor of, Old World civilization —Byron teases us with the paradox. Only to conclude: "So much for Nature" (8.68). So much indeed!

Before considering Juan's response to London, it made sense for the class and me to investigate Byron's own response. During 1812–16 he had lived in London at several West End addresses, most of them within a few blocks of his publisher, John Murray, at 50, Albemarle Street. In Murray's "Senate" he found a group—William Gifford, Samuel Rogers, Thomas Moore, Richard Brinsley Sheridan—sympathetic to his poetry and literary ideals. Melbourne House and Holland House, the mansions of the great Whig families, were open to him. At intervals Byron left London for visits to country houses and spas, but always he came back. London was where he spent much of his time and where he felt most at home. And Byron relished the city to the full: the diversity of its people, the opportunities for social and intellectual discourse, the parties and the balls, the nearness of Covent Garden and Drury Lane—in short, all the advantages offered by London's concentration of resources. If the choice had been his to make, Byron would never have lived elsewhere. But the exile of 1816 precluded such a choice.

Byron waxes most eloquent about London's advantages in several letters to, or about, James Hogg, the Ettrick Shepherd, the least urban in his interests, probably, of all Byron's literary contemporaries. "The first time all the poets of the age meet—it must be London," Byron wrote Hogg in March 1814; "glorious London is the place after all" (Marchand, *Letters* 4: 86). In March 1816 Byron described London to Hogg, as "a dammed place—to be sure—but the only one in the world—(at least in the English world) for fun—though I have seen parts of the Globe that I like better— still upon the whole it is the completest either to help one in feeling oneself alive—or forgetting that one is so" (*Letters* 5: 38). Two months later Byron exiled himself to the Continent. After a turbulent summer in Switzerland, he had settled, by November, in Venice. From there he wrote Moore in March 1817 that, in regard to London, he "liked it as well as any body, myself, now and then" (*Letters* 5: 201). What Byron remembered most about London in after years were the "fogs" (that is, smog), the quiet Sundays, the ghastly climate ("the London winter ends in July" [*Don Juan* 13.43]), and, particularly, the gas lamps that turned midnight into "London's noon" (13.111). Recalling London in *Don Juan* as "that pleasant place" (12.23), he exempted it from the general disesteem for things English that characterized his years abroad.

Throughout his life Byron opposed London and its cosmopolitanism to the Lake Poets and self-contained literary groups. City life was diverse, varied, mind-expanding; country life, provincial. Writers needed the city to widen their experience of life, to grow and develop as interpreters of humankind. "London and the world," Byron wrote Moore in 1814, "is the only place to take the conceit out of a man" *(Letters* 4: 152). There cosmopolitan men and women could test themselves in the arena of life; there literary energies could flourish. Byron himself responded most to writers whom he considered men of the world. To become a good writer, he believed, a man must become more than a writer, for without knowledge of or entrance to the great world of the city, a writer cannot communicate adequately on social subjects. The city makes possible a wider social experience. Purely literary men Byron professed to abhor. In London he could associate with other kinds of men. London may have had less pleasant associations for him than Rome, Athens, or Venice, but it was still a city where he had found life worth living. There he had become a poet.

In London Byron could be solitary whenever he wished, for days at a time, accountable to no one. No less than solitude, the city permitted anonymity. Anonymity was also part of the appeal of Venice, the Italian city he resided in the longest. In Byron's day Venice was far from being the tourist mecca it has since become. Few English disturbed him there. He took "delight in the dialect & naivete of the people—and the romance of it's old history & institutions & appearance all it's disadvantages are more than compensated by the sight of a single Gondola—The view of the Rialto—of the piazza—& the Chaunt of Tasso (though less frequent than of old) are to me worth all the cities on earth—save Rome & Athens" *(Letters* 6: 66). Nor did opportunities lack for amorous dalliance. Venice's appeal to Byron, different from London's, was no less multifaceted.

By the time Byron came to describe London in *Don Juan*, he had lived in cities most of his life and knew London both in itself and in relation to the cities of Europe. In 1816 Byron had gone from London, via Canterbury, to Dover, then across the Channel. Juan reverses his creator's last English journey. In 1816 Byron had been disillusioned, hostile to England and English values. Six years later much of this hostility remained. His protagonist, a young Spaniard, a Catholic who neither reads nor writes English, enters England buoyant, optimistic, naive. Juan sees, not for himself, but through stereotypes provided by visitors such as Voltaire, who hymned England as a land of superior laws, personal liberty, and parliamentary democracy—in short, a modern utopia. At sunset Juan reaches Shooter's Hill, overlooking London from the southeast:

> A mighty mass of brick, and smoke, and shipping,
> Dirty and dusky, but as wide as eye
> Could reach, with here and there a sail just skipping

In sight, then lost amidst the forestry
Of masts: a wilderness of steeples peeping
On tiptoe through their sea-coal canopy;
A huge, dun cupola, like a foolscap crown
On a fool's head—and there is London Town.
(10.82)

Byron's description ironically recalls Wordsworth's vision of a sleeping city clad in the silent dawn in "Composed upon Westminster Bridge." Significantly, it is not Juan but the worldly-wise narrator who thus realistically envisions London. Juan sees, not with his eyes, but with his imagination (10.83). What enchants him is London's magic, not its grimy reality. Even the clouds of coal dust he finds "extremely wholesome."

But we anticipate. Juan has not yet arrived *in* London. Suddenly, four footpads assault him, and Juan, in defending himself, runs one through. Only a few hours in the land of law and order and his English education has begun. But however problematic an event for him, Juan's arrival before London releases Byron's linguistic energies. Stanza 19 of canto 11, dazzling in its verbal exuberance, shows the poet reveling in contemporary slang, flash language, and cant words. Byron can now speak as he wishes. He has come home. His realistic epic vision demands a language commensurate with the city's chaotic vitality.

The eleven memorable stanzas that follow evoke sound as well as sight to render the city's pulse: the roar of its many voices, the clatter of the mails, even the gentle lapping of the Thames itself (11.21–31). Having his hero enter London at night allows Byron to praise its new gas lamps. As at Dover, Juan in London lands at an unnamed but too-expensive hotel for foreigners—possibly, conjecture the editors of the *Don Juan Variorum Edition*, Grillon's in Albemarle Street (Steffan and Pratt). But Byron does not say, and in subsequent depictions of the social scene he coyly avoids specificity. Lord Henry's mansion, for example, stands in "Blank-Blank Square" (13.25). Enough that the general setting has been established and Juan grounded in a realistically introduced London. Readers may imagine locales for themselves. Juan has now moved out of the world of romance into a world that his creator knew more intimately than any other. His situation somewhat parallels Byron's in 1812–13 as the poet renders the tone and atmosphere of the Regency beau monde he remembered. Juan is not corrupted by his experiences, as Byron was not by his, and neither London nor English society corrupts him in the poem we have.

On the whole, then, despite the yearning to identify with nature that still occasionally overtook him, Byron remained essentially partisan to urban civilization and urban pleasures. In the country he suffered, as does Juan, from ennui. Urban existence, and the good talk and fun that came with it, was tonic for him and for Juan. Babylon and Nineveh may have fallen, but Venice—and London—remain. Only urban men and women, Byron concludes, can appreciate a life in nature—and they live in the city, preferably, perhaps, the city to which Juan ventures in canto 10. Byron, in sum, was an urban poet.

Re-Reading (in) Byron: Intertextuality in *Don Juan*

Paul Elledge

Don Juan fascinates by its dialogue with other texts. A noisy ensemble of quotations, allusions, traditions, conventions, archetypes, rhetorical formulas, clichés, puns, cultural signs, street talk, journalistic sound bites, reviews of itself, self-quotations—a medley of gossip, folklore, confession, travelog, hymns, ballads, diary entries, menus, historical narratives, political debate, scientific data, and metaphysical speculation, it conducts with a host of other discourses a running conversation on which students should be trained to eavesdrop for fullest experience of Byron's epic. I write here generally about the pedagogical opportunities afforded by intertextuality in *Don Juan*, cite potentially serviceable subjects for intertextual address, and, for purposes of illustrating interpretative possibilities, examine several allied instances of intertextuality in frequently anthologized portions of the poem.[1]

To propose re-reading *of* as well as in Byron is less radical these days than it was in the 1970s. But to counter those editorial voices that advise rapid, passive perusal of the Byronic canon, we must urge students to assume a craftsmanship, an aesthetic subtlety, and an ideological complexity that patient analytical reading will always disclose in the major verse. Intelligent re-reading *in* Byron approximates a program of cultural literacy, so extensive is his range of reference. Any informed reader glancing through several pages of *Don Juan* will recognize reflections of the Bible, Shakespeare, Dante, Homer, Vergil, Horace, Ovid, Petrarch, Cervantes, and scores of Byron's contemporaries and near-contemporaries in England and on the Continent. Beyond Shakespeare and the Bible (and possibly Homer, Dante, and Cervantes?), not many of our undergraduates will be suitably prepared to remark on Byron's use of his sources; hence our opportunity to expose them, by carefully defined assignments, to masterworks—a chance, by the way, that most students welcome. With Shakespeare, however, many can engage in confidence-building displays of their familiarity while we gently identify its limits and send them back to review the original in the light of Byron's appropriations. Pertinence and importance should govern students' investigations of sources. Attention to the full textual and dramatic context and implication of a Shakespearean allusion can result not merely in a more resonant Byronic text but in heightened student awareness of the mutual benefits of literary cross-pollination—the enrichment of a Homeric line, for example, by linkage with Byron's.

Further, the flagging of authored intertexts in *Don Juan*, and their chronological arrangement in relation to Byron's poem and to each other, will smuggle into classrooms necessary instruction in the historical development of literary tradition. As simple-minded as it sounds, students need to be reminded that not all imaginative literature originated at approximately the same moment in an unthinkably distant past before, say, 1970. It may be helpful to state that each writer exists in a historically unique, spatially particular, temporally specific moment, and that one follows another in time; that later ones read earlier ones and respond to them in manifold ways— and even that earlier ones "read" and answer their successors, inasmuch as older texts are reshaped by every use of them; that authors exploit, manipulate, rewrite, brutalize, furbish, and perpetuate the predecessors they simultaneously seek to surpass; that all writing depends on and develops from all previous writing. Alertness to the intertextual dimensions of *Don Juan* offers one means of making students aware of these processes.

Such instruction will of course include attention to conventions Byron inherits. Among the obvious items for study here are his use and abuse of epic tradition; his English and Italian models for ottava rima; his variation on the fabliau form; his employment of the fall archetype, as skillfully elucidated by George Ridenour; his subscription to and modifications of classical and Augustan satiric prescript; his perhaps surprising manipulation of Petrarchan convention; his alternating and complementary assumptions of Horatian and Juvenalian voices and tactics throughout the poem; and, perhaps most important and of signal curiosity to students, his transformation of a fabled hero. (Scholarly assistance with subjects mentioned here may be found in the following sources, among many others: Beaty; Boyd; de Almeida; Fuess; McGann, Don Juan *in Context*; Ridenour, *Style*; Shilstone, *Byron and the Myth*; Steffan and Pratt, *Variorum*; Weinstein; and Wilkie, "Byron and the Epic.") Well before meeting any generic or rhetorical customs when encountering this poem, our students read a title, a name, around which clusters a host of associations mustered by their experiences with textual, musical, cinematic, and theatrical expressions of a legend presumably featuring the same hero—powerful associations that persist through many reencounters. All of us always come to Byron's Juan, as he does, through the character's prior incarnation(s)—hence in part the continuing freshness of the poet's revision. Byron promptly sets about disappointing our every expectation, challenging every complacent assumption, beginning with our mispronunciation of Juan's name. His "correction" is a metonymic prolepsis of the reconstituting procedure—the assault on received myth—he thus launches. Byron's renaming usually elicits skeptical interest from students, who will demand proof, and thus open the door for discussion of prosody in *Don Juan*. Too much of the scholarship on Byron's reformulation of the Juan myth uncritically rewrites the foundation texts and accordingly leaves abundant room for students to trace, through interdisciplinary and international channels, the evolution of the figure Byron received. I should add that Juan's intertextuality deserves to be plotted through sixteen cantos, not merely the inaugural one.

But these matters are relatively familiar to the experienced teacher of Byron, and most of them may be introduced without reference to intertextuality as such. I want now to suggest the pedagogical value of intertextual reading by a selective look in cantos 1 and 2 at Byron's quotations of other texts, his allusions to other texts, and his quotations of himself, this last a habitual and fascinating occurrence throughout the epic. Byron's direct quotations usually identify themselves by proper punctuation, but purpose and relevance sometimes seem problematic. Two may be treated as exemplary of his more subtle appropriation of another's text.

Stanza 212 of canto 1 opens with a Horatian line and closes with Byron's rough translation of it, together with his substitution of George III for Plancus: "*Non ego hoc ferrem calida juventa / Consule Planco*": "I had not borne such an insult in the heat of my youth." Why, we might inquire of students, does Byron quote when he goes on to state in plain English that he was, once, more vengeful than now? Well, the quotation authorizes abatement of his avenging impulse; it provides classical precedent and permission for passive acceptance of literary abuse (we must of course be attuned to the ironic potential of such announced acceptance). Linking the speaker with the temperance illustrated in the quotation will remind students of the constituents of Horatian satire. Advanced students may recognize reinforcement of a pattern: the stanza twice presses a borrowed text into the service of surrogate articulation, of substitute expression of the poet's despondency. Within the framework of surrender and privation that defines much of Byron's closural procedure for canto 1, this stanza specifies a particular loss—the retributive urge—and its compensatory gain—moderation—at the same time that by a clever rhetorical maneuver it initially evades admission of loss and even terminally acknowledges it in an oblique way. Students may need to be shown that the stanza and its context centrally concern the poet's relations with a (supposed) hostile audience poised to respond with heavy artillery to his confession of a diminished retaliatory impulse: the passage signals Byron's withdrawal from the field. They will then understand that the Horatian line, as another's admission of a reluctance to engage, insulates the narrator by absorbing some of the shock of a disturbing recognition; it consoles and reassures him in bereavement merely by being the pronouncement of an authoritative model in similar circumstances. Horatian and Hanoverian allusions, markers for the poet of a great historical diminishment, bracket his notation of the decline of certain Byronic energies, but within their boundaries we glance with him nostalgically back to the avenging, albeit repressed, "Brougham" stanzas (McGann, *Poetical Works* 5: 85–88, 685–87) for which these closural stanzas partially substitute, and more inclusively to a pre-exilic life when location on home turf gave embattled association an attraction and an immediacy unavailable from the Continent.

The deflection onto and transmission through Horace of the poet's mellowing temperance laments the loss without desiring the restoration of a combative will and of an era when Byron's response to rejection was engagement, and to hostility, decisive encounter.

Ten stanzas later (1.222), Byron similarly deflects onto another a long deferred and still unwelcome task—the termination of canto 1. Editorial commentary should alert students to the Italian and Chaucerian resonances in these lines and provide background information (if not noted in the "Dedication") on the Byron-Southey antipathy (a subject students find intriguing). But we may invite inquiry into possible reasons why Byron should quote a literary opponent just here. Discerning readers will detect the suggestive circularity in the terminal stanza's proximate reprise of the canto's first stanza, in which the poet rescues Juan from demonic to benign relationship partly because he is not among those heroes regularly "sen[t] forth" (and yet he is of course pirated from other texts). Desire and need join hero and narrator there. But the "heroic" Juan embraced at the outset has been transformed into a text requiring an authorial surrender and dispatch that will reinstate the actuating conditions of impoverishment and desire. As he gives up his book, Byron's self-association with that hyperactive tribe chastised in canto 1, stanza 1, cannot be agreeable, but it invites us to "re-read" by recalling the initial dispatching act and its multiple replications throughout the canto, and thus partially to neutralize the ending that this stanza designates. More important, however, Byron transfers to Southey the dispossessing act, displaces onto him even the appropriation of traditional valedictory formulas, and so spares himself that hardship and shame. In the light of the disparactive context of the entire canto, Southey's insistently dismissive language and the solitude into which ejecting action casts him fix the laureate as archetypal abandoner, orphaning the child of his imagination. Southey's unprincipled recantation of liberal "texts" in Byron's view deserved this attack on apostasy. But the quotation is also a skillful rhetorical expedient that indicts with his own words an enemy for the sin of abandonment his accuser thus escapes. And when the couplet rejects a linguistic structure and the action it signified and implemented—for renunciation of the other's language dismantles the results he used the stolen discourse to accomplish—Byron reinstates the relationship that Southey's lines terminated . . . as canto 2 then witnesses.

Students may be happier, however, with what they suppose to be the greater latitude for imaginative interpretation encouraged by allusion to, rather than reproduction of, other texts. Some, for example, will see that Byron's denunciation of Plato in canto 1, stanzas 115–16, ironically endorses the clucking interdict implicit in his suspension of the narrative just before coition, and that misemployed amorous Platonism engineers its own defeat.

Those trained in aesthetics should be invited to investigate the Aristotelian and Longinian allusions of stanzas 201 and 204 and the ironies developed both there and by the reminder of "epical pretensions" (the pun is probably deliberate) in stanza 209; for each either oversets itself (as in st. 200) or is subverted by the citation of Homeric and Vergilian paradigms to which the present "epic" already and manifestly fails to conform. More independent and ambitious students might work solely with stanza 209—a swarm of generic "texts"—not merely (or at all) by tracking likely historical referents for scripts there named but by wrestling with the problematics of verification by intertextual means—with the difficulties of identifying the "factual," reliable testimony among highly unstable texts, both imaginative and "true." Old Testament readers may wish to tease out the implications of Byron's comparison of Juan's night flight to Joseph's (1.186); but the more sophisticated among them will see that the episode reconstitutes from stanza 64 the figure of sin sent "shivering forth" "without a rag on" into the covering darkness, and should explore not only the verbal reminiscence but the curious moral statement implied by the analogy. Most classes will be familiar with the Decalogue and should easily grasp the main point of Byron's parody (1.205–06); the better trained can enlighten their inferiors on what in "Milton, Dryden and Pope" recommends itself to Byron's "belief" and what excludes Wordsworth and Coleridge from creedal incorporation. Our assistance with the identification of Byron's other contemporaries appearing here should include sensitivity to the intertextual and self-reflexive potential of his citations, for relationships among texts and their makers control this passage. We will also wish to point out that Byron strategically situates his exodus discourse as part of his own exiting procedure and that, like their model, his "poetical commandments" serve a covenantal purpose: observance of the code they articulate will secure honorable attachment between giver and receiver, author and reader. The poet's Mosaic posture (sliding into a punitive pedagogical one, as our students will knowingly point out) combines with the tyrannical content of his imperatives to invalidate the democratic title proposed for them (1.204); and Byron reveals himself by the parody as literary thief even as he forbids theft, thus grandly enacting the hypocrisy he so fervently decries.

Sometimes Byron self-consciously spotlights a borrowing by naming its source or otherwise remarking on it—as though anxious that we consider its effects. One such occasion occurs in canto 2, stanza 17, as Juan from shipboard laments his departure from Cadiz:

> And Juan wept, and much he sigh'd and thought,
>   While his salt tears dropp'd into the salt sea,

'Sweets to the sweet;' (I like so much to quote;
    You must excuse this extract, 'tis where she,
The Queen of Denmark, for Ophelia brought
    Flowers to the grave). . . .

Students will enjoy discovering how Byron's quotation deliberately misunderstands its source (that is, it rewrites Shakespeare by altering the referents for both nouns) and comments ironically on both saline solutions and on the trivialization of tears by the oceanic element. They will also see that he introduces a second valedictory text, on its face wholly inappropriate, to empower and enhance the dramatization of Juan's. Lifted from a tragic context, the quotation repeats the design of the Juan-Israelite analogy from canto 2, stanza 16, in which Byron ironically likens Juan's disjunctive sorrow to the Jews' "[b]y Babel's waters" and through the boy protests enforced separation while lamenting it: the Psalmic intertext sings the difficulty of exilic singing and enjoins upon the singer remembrance of what has been lost, lest such radical consequences follow forgetfulness as those Juan apocalyptically imagines in stanza 19. Gertrude's words bid farewell to an Ophelia herself the victim of an enforced separation from Hamlet eventuating in her own voluntary exit from the world. The tragic valedictory context, then, balances the comedic one about to be elaborated in Juan's hyperbolic cries.

Further, the parenthetical remark with which Byron interrupts his narrative is the comic analogue of the textual substitutions concluding canto 1, for here neither deference to such discourses nor evasion of the subject they are adduced to manage marks his allusiveness. On the contrary, Byron's pedantic glossing of his quotation belabors the termination of relationship. And the two clauses introducing the gloss are superfluous except as pointers to it. Well might Byron solicit our attention, for his Shakespearean appropriation constitutes a deft and witty response to a hypothesized use of poetry in canto 2, stanza 16:

Young men should travel, if but to amuse
    Themselves; and the next time their servants tie on
Behind their carriages their new portmanteau,
Perhaps it may be lined with this my canto.

Amusement replaces grief as the proper temper of departing youth; but the ensuing disparagement of his own verse subverts the authority of his advice and provides one source of the amusement it recommends, for as a text lining portmanteaus (with the pun on "lined"), it may attend travelers on the journeys it endorses. The carriage-loading scene repeats on land the nautical occasion it suspends, the one separative event underscoring the other as the vision of exiled Jews underscores the serious implications of the exile that parodies it. Byron's expectations for the disposition of his canto grant the verses a utilitarian purpose, however demeaning, and link them as departure discourse with the practical usefulness eventually accorded the otherwise impractical Julian letter, and with the combination of useful and useless in the epistolary package Inez presents to Juan. As, then, Byron in these lines anticipates being done unto, in stanza 17 he does unto, preemptively. With a mocking show of editorial scrupulousness, he sets the *Hamlet* passage in its immediate context while outrageously misappropriating and insulting its larger one to serve comic ends. That is, he puts another's text to the imminently practical if irreverent use of literally *lining* and *underlining* —of making and reinforcing—his own. Using Shakespeare's verse in one stanza, Byron neatly executes against another's poetry the fate his previous stanza had prophesied for itself.

Remembering Julia, the lamenting Juan in Byron's next stanza (18) occasions one of the poet's most complex intertextual events, an absorbing instance of Byronic self-quotation, with the examination of which this discussion must close. Declaiming farewells, Juan, parenthetically, "drew / Her [Julia's] letter out again, and read it through" (2.18). Whether he has read it previously, we cannot certainly know; but it seems plausible that the idea for an answering farewell originates in Julia's letter, and the internal evidence of his text, particularly the verbal echo of hers in stanza 18, line 6, suggests her influence. Float the notion to students—and watch them run with it— that Julia has partially scripted Juan's performance with her own, that his theatricality is the coarsened, male parodic version of her own more subtle thespian and epistolary art. Concluding his apostrophes, Juan draws out her letter for consultative purposes, to review valedictory procedures, to shape from a prototype his own role in this one. Students will be quick to observe that he continues as subject to seek direction from a still powerful influence. They may also discover that in Juan's consultative procedure, Byron satirizes his own recourse to other texts for assistance with and as alternatives to invention, with the triumphant irony on the present occasion that the imported text is also his, and so as instrument yet becomes the victim of its own satire. Finally, in Juan's consultation of Julia's letter, Byron represents another use of poetry: the boy's evidently flattering (mis)appropriation of a poetic text recalls the earlier one we have just examined—the "lining" of one's own farewell with another's itself reformulates the trunk-as-book configuration from stanza 16—but more egregiously insults the letter than the ultimate disposition of it, for the epistolary text becomes in his hands a guide to attitudinized affectation, a handbook of humbuggery. Julia's cant inspires more cant in an apparently endless, self-perpetuating proliferation checked only by the explosive rebellion of those physical exigencies it has repeatedly sought to deny. In evacuating his hero of a psychic and verbal corruption, Byron offers a moral and, incidentally, a pedagogical, point worth remembering as we strive to eliminate the critical rubbish in our students' writing and our own.

NOTE

[1]The definition of *intertextuality* assumed and illustrated in this essay is perhaps narrower, less sophisticated, more conservative than some instructors might wish, but I believe it a suitable and practical one for the undergraduate classroom. Advanced and graduate students interested in the subject should consult the excellent presentation by Jay Clayton and Eric Rothstein on the conceptual development and critical use of intertextuality, "Figures in the Corpus: Theories of Influence and Intertextuality."

Don Juan: From Classic to Modern

Hermione de Almeida

From the first moments of the declamation for a contemporary hero of appropriate epic stature in the opening stanzas of *Don Juan* to the suspended "in medias res" time of canto 17 where the poem abruptly rests, through Byron's repeated invocations of Homer and "ancient epic laws" in cantos 1–10 and even during his rehearsal of a pact with "us moderns" in the English cantos, we find ourselves confronted, recurringly, with the poet's audacious claim: "My poem's epic." Byron's challenge to his readers cannot be dodged: we are to place *Don Juan* within epic tradition despite its peremptory dismissals of the classics from the past, and we are to perceive in the poem's epic modernity a contemporary relevance wholly without precedent. Fortunately for those of us who teach *Don Juan*, students are quick to recognize Byron's challenge. They respond swiftly to the poem's epic claims and counters, usually with whatever knowledge they might have of literatures past and present. They do so, I have found, even when they are disturbed by the poem's many topics and multiple styles.

Because *Don Juan* is cast as an extended inquiry into what might constitute epic heroism, epic social manners, and epic style in a democratic, post-Waterloo age, Byron is able to write a long poem that is at once accumulative of and culminative to its heritage. The poem is packed with allusions to the literature that has preceded it: it appropriates patterns from epic so as to encompass literary history from Homer and Vergil to Milton and Fielding; it evokes the comic derivations of epic and uses the examples of writers like Rabelais, Pope, and Sterne to inform its own mocking style; and it recalls literary genres like the personal essay (in writers like Montaigne) and the confessional memoir (in writers like Rousseau) to justify its own whimsical choice of topics. These topics, moreover, pass effortlessly between the cultural legacies and current affairs of Western Europe. Thus, cheerful, irreverent, but always comprehensive, Byron's summary poem of literature and culture since Homer serves as a remarkably useful survey for students regardless of their preparation. It fills in for those students who have gleaned but a passing knowledge of classical literature or epic tradition from a sophomoric course such as World Literature, Part 1; it provides quick comparative medicine for those would-be English majors who might have taken the requisite sophomore survey from Beowulf to Pope but who have no knowledge of the European tradition; it intimates of startling literary precedents to students who might have taken a course or two in modern or contemporary authors but never thought to know where all these blockbusters came from. Indeed, much as the young protagonist of *Don Juan* once learned his Greeks through the appendixes of his expurgated textbooks, our students, too, can learn of epic and classical tradition and of the genesis of the novel through the interstices and grand-scale mockeries of Byron's modern epic.

Homer is always a good starting point, as Vergil, Dante, Milton, and countless writers since, including Byron, discovered. The Homeric parallels in *Don Juan* are also an easy beginning place for classroom discussion. These parallels are, of course, quite numerous, because *Don Juan* is consciously patterned after the *Odyssey* and its exemplary civility; the poem's action is deliberately set against the *Iliad* and its example of warmongering and masculine boredom. Byron's poem loosely follows the *Odyssey*'s tripartite structure: the setting forth of a young man, an odyssey abroad, and a return (to the poet's) home. Characters and episodes also follow the *Odyssey* and, occasionally, merge with those in the *Iliad*: Juan journeys forth like Odysseus but also like Telemachus; the idyll with Haidée on the Greek isle echoes Odysseus's tranquil experience at Phaeacia with Nausicaä and her family; Lambro functions well as a Byronic blind and mad Cyclops; Pedrillo is Byron's approximation of Homer's high-voiced elder statesman, Nestor; Juan's sojourn in the belly of the slave ship and Haidée's nervous breakdown combine as underworld experiences to rival Odysseus's visit to Hades; Gulbayez is a sufficiently exotic Circe plucked from Byron's juvenile experience of the East (she turns Juan into a woman, not a pig); Johnson the mercenary and the heroic but doomed old Turk together represent the two sides of Achilles; Lady Adeline plays well the role of a bored and conniving Circe with a seven-year itch; and so on.

Nor are the Homeric parallels of *Don Juan* necessarily parodic and reductive. Byron uses the noncombative manner and comic humanity of Odysseus as a model for his passive and vulnerable protagonist, and the example of elegant civility in the city courts of Ithaca and Phaeacia in Homer's ideal world serves as a serious backdrop against which we are to view the follies of Seville, Saint Petersburg, Ismail, and London. Indeed, much as the Homeric epics are vital to our reconstruction of early Aegean civilization, so also is *Don Juan* essential to our comprehension of the civilities and mores of Europe and England during the revolutionary and Waterloo periods. Individual classes and teachers may hear differing echoes of the Homeric example in Byron's poem, but, in all cases, a discussion of the parallels between *Don Juan* and the *Odyssey* can lead to a larger recognition of the literary distinctions between the two epics and, beyond these, to the profound associations in terms of human values that link them across some thirty centuries.

Evocations and responses to Homer necessarily take into account, as Byron knew, all previous responses to Homeric tradition. Certainly, the transition from Greek hero to late-eighteenth-century Spanish youth in the poem occurs by way of the overall descent of the European literary hero through the mock-heroic indistinctions of the likes of Tristram Shandy, Tom Jones, Joseph Andrews, Gulliver, Candide, Rameau's nephew, Don Quixote, Orlando, and Pantagruel. So, also, do the journeys of Don Juan through revolutionary Europe and Regency England follow the winding and ever-descending paths taken before him by the characters of eighteenth-century French and English novels, seventeenth-century picaresque tales, and the gargantuan stories of Rabelais. The discussion of epic pattern in the classroom can thus lead, quite effortlessly, into a wider consideration of the varied range in mock-heroic literature available from Pulci to Pope. Few teachers and fewer students will know all the players in the mock-heroic cosmos. Nevertheless, I have found that the classroom recollection of even a few of the reductive characters or episodes from some of the authors listed above, coupled with free association by the teacher, to be sufficient material for building a ladder from the lofty epic down to the mock epic, past the comic slopes of the eighteenth-century English novel, and up again to the nineteenth-century novel of social consequence of France and England.

Fielding was correct when he proposed in the preface to *Joseph Andrews* that the energy of the epic had to pass into the new and "modern" form of the novel. His novels were modified epics, seriocomic reflections of their environment that were at once funny and more real than their epic examples. Fielding's heirs, like Smollett and Sterne, wrote comic novels that evoked epic style and circumstance in parody; their multiplicity of styles did not respond to the comprehensive challenge of Homer, but they did provide examples for the fictive forms of the centuries that followed them. Byron certainly learned from his eighteenth-century forebears—*Don Juan* has often been called "a versified *Tristram Shandy*" and described as a novel in verse—but he did more than this: he wrote a modern epic that fulfilled Fielding's intentions in the preface to *Joseph Andrews* and was at once true to its democratic milieu and responsible to the challenge (in substance and in style) of Homer's example.[1] Byron wrote *Don Juan* as the last epic of an overburdened literary and cultural tradition; as the first to express this spirit of decadence and sense of ending in Western culture, Byron proved exemplary to later generations who also sought to write summary epics of their times. In my study of *Don Juan* and Joyce's *Ulysses* as Homeric but also contemporary forms of fiction (*Byron and Joyce through Homer*), I describe the style of the modern epic as parallactic, *parallax* being the term that the Greeks used to explain Odysseus's shifting perspective when he thought he saw the rocks of the sea move about his ship. The term suggests the kind of fluidity of situation, undependability of stance, disconcerting shifting of voice, and antipodal tones that are characteristic of the multiple style shared by *Don Juan, Ulysses, Faust, Le rouge et le noir,* and countless other fictional efforts in prose or verse of the nineteenth and twentieth centuries. Any discussion of *Don Juan*'s "transcendental buffoonery" of style (Friedrich Schlegel's descriptive phrase for the wholesale irony of most Romantic art), of the poem's unreliable narrator and shifting forms of expression, can stimulate discussion of the parallels and distinctions in other modern epics, a discussion that would be limited only by the teacher's and students' experience and literary recollections.

Contemporary odysseys (and epic mockeries) by writers like Joyce, Kafka, Faulkner, Durrell, Golding, Nabokov, Kazantzakis, Lessing, Barth, Pynchon, and Rushdie can profit from a juxtaposition with *Don Juan* in the classroom. True to Homeric precedent in his epic, Byron was also true to his democratic and revolutionary age; his poem serves, moreover, as a true anticipation of the literary styles and cultural preoccupations of our own age. Had I my druthers, I would make *Don Juan* required secondary reading for all university courses in modern and contemporary literature, and I mean *all* of Byron's epic poem, for, despite its piecemeal publication history, it does not lend itself to being taught in parts. Indeed, the poem's reputation as a teaching catalyst among teachers has suffered seriously from its being dismembered by anthologizers according to their national or sequential passions—early, middle, or late cantos, the Greek episodes, English cantos, and so on. The parts of *Don Juan* do not function well in isolation; but the whole in its diverse parts, by itself or among other great works, occasions a splendid pedagogic odyssey.

NOTE

[1]Among the studies that address Byron's epic responsibility in *Don Juan*, I would recommend in particular Elizabeth Boyd, *Byron's* Don Juan: *A Critical Study*; Brian Wilkie, *Romantic Poets and Epic Tradition*; Karl Kroeber, *Romantic Narrative Art*; Alvin Kernan, *Plot of Satire*; Edward Bostetter, *Romantic Ventriloquists*; and Donald Reiman, *"Don Juan* in Epic Context."

CONTRIBUTORS AND SURVEY PARTICIPANTS

Roy A. Ball, Clinch Valley Coll.; Frederick L. Beaty, Indiana Univ.; Stephen C. Behrendt, Univ. of Nebraska; G. K. Blank, Univ. of Victoria; Hallman B. Bryant, Clemson Univ.; James Chandler, Univ. of Chicago; John Clubbe, Univ. of Kentucky; Louis Crompton, Univ. of Nebraska; Frank Day, Clemson Univ.; Hermione de Almeida, Univ. of Miami; Paul Elledge, Vanderbilt Univ.; David V. Erdman, emeritus, State Univ. of New York, Stony Brook; Bernard J. Gallagher, Central Methodist Coll.; Robert F. Gleckner, Duke Univ.; John E. Hankins, emeritus, Univ. of Maine; Bernard A. Hirsch, Univ. of Kansas; Wolf Z. Hirst, Univ. of Haifa; Katherine Kernberger, Linfield Coll.; Mark Kipperman, Northern Illinois Univ.; Karl Kroeber, Columbia Univ.; Peter J. Manning, Univ. of Southern California; Jerome J. McGann, Univ. of Virginia; Anne K. Mellor, Univ. of California, Los Angeles; Judith Plotz, George Washington Univ.; Joanna E. Rapf, Univ. of Oklahoma; Mark Reynolds, Jefferson Davis Junior Coll.; Alan Richardson, Boston Coll.; Charles J. Rzepka, Boston Univ.; Ronald A. Schroeder, Univ. of Mississippi; Frederick W. Shilstone, Clemson Univ.; Scott Simpkins, Univ. of North Texas; James L. Skinner, Presbyterian Coll.; Robert Snyder, Seattle Pacific Univ.; Stuart M. Sperry, Indiana Univ.; Eugene Stelzig, State Univ. of New York, Geneseo; Gordon K. Thomas, Brigham Young Univ.; Nicholas O. Warner, Claremont McKenna Coll.; Nancy Watanabe, Boise State Univ.; Daniel P. Watkins, Duquesne Univ.; Brian Wilkie, Univ. of Arkansas; Susan Wolfson, Rutgers Univ.

WORKS CITED

Abrams, M. H., ed. *English Romantic Poets: Modern Essays in Criticism*. New York: Oxford UP, 1960.

———. *The Mirror and the Lamp: Romantic Theory and the Critical Tradition*. 1953. New York: Oxford UP, 1971.

———. *Natural Supernaturalism: Tradition and Revolution in Romantic Literature*. New York: Norton, 1971.

———, gen. ed. *The Norton Anthology of English Literature*. 5th ed. Vol. 2. New York: Norton, 1986.

———, gen. ed. *The Norton Anthology of English Literature*. Major Authors edition. 5th ed. New York: Norton, 1987.

Adams, Robert Martin. *NIL: Episodes in the Literary Conquest of Void during the Nineteenth Century*. New York: Oxford UP, 1966.

Altick, Richard D. *Paintings from Books: Art and Literature in Britain, 1760–1900*. Columbus: Ohio State UP, 1985.

Arnold, Matthew. "The Study of Poetry." *Poetry and Criticism of Matthew Arnold*. Ed. A. Dwight Culler. Riverside edition. Boston: Houghton, 1961. 306–27.

Ashton, Thomas L., ed. *Byron's* Hebrew Melodies. Austin: U of Texas P, 1972.

———. "*Marino Faliero*: Byron's 'Poetry of Politics.' " *Studies in Romanticism* 13 (1974): 1–13.

Auden, W. H., ed. *The Selected Poetry and Prose of Byron*. New York: NAL, 1983.

Auerbach, Erich. *Mimesis: The Representation of Reality in Western Literature*. Trans. Willard Trask. 1953. Garden City: Doubleday, n.d.

Baker, Carlos. *The Echoing Green: Romanticism, Modernism, and the Phenomena of Transference in Poetry*. Princeton: Princeton UP, 1984.

———. *Shelley's Major Poetry: The Fabric of a Vision*. Princeton: Princeton UP, 1948.

Barnes, Julian. "Shipwreck." *New Yorker* 12 June 1989: 40–50.

Barzun, Jacques. *Berlioz and the Romantic Century*. 3rd ed. 2 vols. New York: Columbia UP, 1969.

Bathurst, Cynthia L. "Illustrating Byron's Poetry: Cruikshank's Byron." *Byron Society Newsletter* 8 (1982–84): 4–11.

Beatty, Bernard. *Byron:* Don Juan *and Other Poems: A Critical Study*. Penguin Masterstudies. London: Penguin, 1987.

———. *Byron's* Don Juan. Totowa: Barnes, 1985.

———. "Fiction's Limit and Eden's Door." Beatty and Newey 1–38.

Beatty, Bernard, and Vincent Newey, eds. *Byron and the Limits of Fiction*. Totowa: Barnes, 1988.

Beaty, Frederick L. *Byron the Satirist*. DeKalb: Northern Illinois UP, 1985.

Beerbohm, Max. *The Poet's Corner*. London: Heinemann, 1904.

Bernbaum, Ernest. *Guide through the Romantic Movement*. 2nd ed. New York: Ronald, 1949.

Berry, Francis. "The Poet of *Childe Harold*." Jump, *Byron: A Symposium* 35–51.

Blackstone, Bernard. *Byron: A Survey*. London: Longman, 1975.

Blank, G. Kim, ed. *The New Shelley: Later Twentieth-Century Views*. London: Macmillan, 1990.

———. *Wordsworth's Influence on Shelley: A Study of Poetic Authority*. London: Macmillan, 1988.

Bloom, Harold, ed. *George Gordon, Lord Byron: Modern Critical Views*. New York: Chelsea House, 1986.

———, ed. *Lord Byron's* Don Juan: *Modern Critical Interpretations*. New York: Chelsea House, 1987.

———, ed. *Romanticism and Consciousness: Essays in Criticism*. New York: Norton, 1970.

———. *The Visionary Company: A Reading of English Romantic Poetry*. Rev. ed. Ithaca: Cornell UP, 1971.

Bloom, Harold, and Lionel Trilling, eds. *Romantic Poetry and Prose*. Vol. 4 of *The Oxford Anthology of English Literature*. 6 vols. New York: Oxford UP, 1973.

Bold, Alan, ed. *Byron: Wrath and Rhyme*. Totowa: Barnes, 1983.

Borst, William A. *Lord Byron's First Pilgrimage*. 1948. New York: Archon, 1969.

Bostetter, Edward E., ed. *George Gordon, Lord Byron: Selected Works*. Rev. and enl. ed. Rinehart edition. New York: Holt, 1972.

———. "Masses and Solids: Byron's View of the External World." *Modern Language Quarterly* 35 (1974): 257–71.

———. *The Romantic Ventriloquists: Wordsworth, Coleridge, Keats, Shelley, Byron*. Rev. ed. Seattle: U of Washington P, 1975.

———, ed. *Twentieth Century Interpretations of* Don Juan. Englewood Cliffs: Prentice, 1969.

Boyd, Elizabeth French. *Byron's* Don Juan: *A Critical Study*. 1945. New York: Humanities, 1958.

Bredvold, Louis I., Alan D. McKillop, and Lois Whitney, eds. *Eighteenth Century Poetry and Prose*. 2nd ed. New York: Ronald, 1956.

Brenton, Howard. *Bloody Poetry*. London: Methuen, 1985.

Brown, Nathaniel. *Sexuality and Feminism in Shelley*. Cambridge: Harvard UP, 1979.

Burnett, T. A. J., ed. Childe Harold's Pilgrimage, Canto III: *A Facsimile of the Autograph Fair Copy Found in the "Scrope Davies" Notebook*. Garland Manuscripts of the Younger Romantics. New York: Garland, 1988.

Burwick, Frederick, and Paul Douglass, eds. *A Selection of* Hebrew Melodies,

Ancient and Modern, *by Isaac Nathan and Lord Byron*. Tuscaloosa: U of Alabama P, 1988.

Bush, Douglas. *Mythology and the Romantic Tradition in English Poetry*. Cambridge: Harvard UP, 1937.

Butler, Marilyn. "The Orientalism of Byron's *Giaour*." Beatty and Newey 78–96.

———. *Romantics, Rebels and Reactionaries: English Literature and Its Background, 1760–1830*. Oxford: Oxford UP, 1981.

Calvert, William J. *Byron: Romantic Paradox*. 1935. New York: Russell, 1962.

Cantor, Paul A. "Byron's *Cain*: A Romantic Version of the Fall." *Kenyon Review* ns 2 (1980): 50–71.

———. *Creature and Creator: Myth-Making and English Romanticism*. Cambridge: Cambridge UP, 1984.

Castle, Terry. "Eros and Liberty at the English Masquerade, 1710–90." *Eighteenth-Century Studies* 17 (1983–84): 156–76.

Chew, Samuel C. *The Dramas of Lord Byron: A Critical Study*. Baltimore: Johns Hopkins UP, 1915.

———. *The Nineteenth Century and After, 1789–1939*. Pt. 4 of *A Literary History of England*. Ed. A. C. Baugh. New York: Appleton, 1948.

Christensen, Jerome. "Byron's Career: The Speculative Stage." *ELH* 52 (1985): 59–84.

———. "*Marino Faliero* and the Fault of Byron's Satire." *Studies in Romanticism* 24 (1985): 313–33.

Clark, Kenneth. *The Romantic Rebellion: Romantic versus Classic Art*. London: Murray, 1973.

Clayton, Jay, and Eric Rothstein. "Figures in the Corpus: Theories of Influence and Intertextuality." *Influence and Intertextuality in Literary History*. Ed. Clayton and Rothstein. Madison: U of Wisconsin P, 1990. 3–36.

Clinton, George [Sir James Bacon]. *Memoirs of the Life and Writings of Lord Byron*. Illus. George Cruikshank. London, 1827.

Clubbe, John. "George Gordon, Lord Byron." Jordan, *English Romantic Poets* 465–592.

———. "'The New Prometheus of New Men': Byron's 1816 Poems and *Manfred*." *Nineteenth Century Literary Perspectives: Essays in Honor of Lionel Stevenson*. Ed. Clyde de L. Ryals et al. Durham: Duke UP, 1974. 17–47.

Clubbe, John, and Ernest J. Lovell, Jr. *English Romanticism: The Grounds of Belief*. DeKalb: Northern Illinois UP, 1983.

Coleridge, E. H., ed. *The Works of Lord Byron: Poetry*. 7 vols. 1898–1904. New York: Octagon, 1966.

Coleridge, Samuel Taylor. *The Portable Coleridge*. Ed. I. A. Richards. New York: Viking, 1961.

Cooke, Michael G. *Acts of Inclusion: Studies Bearing on an Elementary Theory of Romanticism*. New Haven: Yale UP, 1979.

————. *The Blind Man Traces the Circle: On the Patterns and Philosophy of Byron's Poetry*. Princeton: Princeton UP, 1969.

Corbett, Martyn. *Byron and Tragedy*. London: Macmillan, 1988.

Covino, William A. *The Art of Wondering: A Revisionist Return to the History of Rhetoric*. Portsmouth: Heinemann, 1988.

Crompton, Louis. *Byron and Greek Love: Homophobia in Nineteenth-Century England*. Berkeley: U of California P, 1985.

Curran, Stuart. *Poetic Form and British Romanticism*. New York: Oxford UP, 1986.

Daiches, David. *A Critical History of English Literature*. 2nd ed. New York: Ronald, 1970.

David, Alfred. *Teaching with the* Norton Anthology of English Literature, *Fifth Edition*. New York: Norton, 1988.

Davis, Natalie Zemon. "Women on Top." *Society and Culture in Early Modern France*. Stanford: Stanford UP, 1975. 124–51.

de Almeida, Hermione. *Byron and Joyce through Homer:* Don Juan *and* Ulysses. New York: Columbia UP, 1981.

Deneau, Daniel P. *Byron's Narrative Poems of 1813: Two Essays*. Salzburg: Institut für Englische Sprache und Literatur, 1975.

Dingley, R. J. " 'I had a dream . . .': Byron's 'Darkness.' " *Byron Journal* 9 (1981): 20–33.

Doherty, Francis M. *Byron*. Arco Literary Critiques. New York: Arco, 1969.

Drinkwater, John. *The Pilgrim of Eternity: Byron—a Conflict*. New York: Doran, 1925.

du Bos, Charles. *Byron and the Need of Fatality*. Trans. Ethel C. Mayne. 1932. New York: Haskell, 1970.

Ehrstine, John W. "The Drama and Romantic Theory: The Cloudy Symbols of High Romance." *Research Studies* 34 (1966): 85–106.

————. *The Metaphysics of Byron: A Reading of the Plays*. The Hague: Mouton, 1976.

Elledge, W. Paul. *Byron and the Dynamics of Metaphor*. Nashville: Vanderbilt UP, 1968.

Elledge, W. Paul, and Richard L. Hoffman, eds. *Romantic and Victorian: Studies in Memory of William H. Marshall*. Rutherford: Fairleigh Dickinson UP, 1971.

Elwin, Malcolm. *Lord Byron's Wife*. New York: Harcourt, 1963.

Emerson, Sheila. "Byron's 'one word': The Language of Self-Expression in *Childe Harold* III." *Studies in Romanticism* 20 (1981): 363–82.

Engell, James. *The Creative Imagination: Enlightenment to Romanticism*. Cambridge: Harvard UP, 1981.

Erdman, David V. "Byron and Revolt in England." *Science and Society* 11 (1947): 234–48.

————. "Byron and 'the New Force of the People.' " *Keats-Shelley Journal* 11 (1962): 47–64.

―――. "Byron's Stage Fright: The History of His Ambition and Fear of Writing for the Stage." *ELH* 6 (1939): 219–43.

―――. "Lord Byron and the Genteel Reformers." *PMLA* 56 (1941): 1065–94.

―――. "Lord Byron as Rinaldo." *PMLA* 57 (1942): 189–231.

―――, ed. *The Romantic Movement: A Selective and Critical Bibliography*. New York: Garland, 1979–87; West Cornwall: Locust Hill, 1988–

Erdman, David V., and David Worrall, eds. Childe Harold's Pilgrimage: *A Critical, Composite Edition*. Garland Manuscripts of the Younger Romantics. New York: Garland, forthcoming.

Erickson, Carolly. *Our Tempestuous Day: A History of Regency England*. New York: Morrow, 1986.

Escarpit, Robert. *Lord Byron, un tempérament littéraire*. Paris: Cercle du livre, 1955.

Evans, Bertrand. "Manfred's Remorse and Dramatic Tradition." *PMLA* 62 (1947): 752–74.

Farrell, John P. "Byron: Rebellion and Revolution." *Revolution as Tragedy: The Dilemma of the Moderate from Scott to Arnold*. Ithaca: Cornell UP, 1980. 131–86.

Fetzer, John Francis. "The Evolution of a Revolution: Romantic Irony." *The Comparatist* 11 (1987): 45–53.

Fitzpatrick, William P. "Byron's Mysteries: The Paradoxical Drive toward Eden." *SEL* 15 (1975): 615–25.

Fogle, R. H., comp. *Romantic Poets and Prose Writers*. Goldentree Bibliographies. New York: Appleton, 1967.

Ford, Boris, ed. *The Pelican Guide to English Literature*. Vol. 5. Baltimore: Penguin, 1957.

Freud, Sigmund. *Civilization and Its Discontents*. Trans. James Strachy. New York: Norton, 1961.

Frye, Northrop. *Fables of Identity: Studies in Poetic Mythology*. New York: Harcourt, 1963.

―――, ed. *Romanticism Reconsidered: Selected Papers from the English Institute*. New York: Columbia UP, 1963.

Fuentes, Carlos. "The Discreet Charm of Luis Buñuel." *The World of Luis Buñuel*. Ed. Joan Mellen. New York: Oxford UP, 1978. 51–71.

Fuess, Claude Moore. *Lord Byron as a Satirist in Verse*. 1912. New York: Haskell, 1973.

Furst, Lilian. *Fictions of Romantic Irony*. Cambridge: Harvard UP, 1984.

Galt, John. *The Life of Lord Byron*. New York: Fowle, 1900.

Garber, Frederick. "Beckford, Delacroix, and Byronic Orientalism." *Comparative Literature Studies* 18 (1981): 321–32.

―――. *Self, Text, and Romantic Irony: The Example of Byron*. Princeton: Princeton UP, 1988.

Gatton, John Spalding. "Portraits of a Doge: Delacroix's Reading of Byron's *Marino Faliero*." *Byron Journal* 9 (1981): 74–84.

Gaull, Marilyn. *English Romanticism: The Human Context*. New York: Norton, 1988.

Gill, Stephen, ed. *William Wordsworth*. Oxford: Oxford UP, 1984.

Gleckner, Robert F. *Byron and the Ruins of Paradise*. Baltimore: Johns Hopkins UP, 1967.

———. "From Selfish Spleen to Equanimity: Byron's Satires." *Studies in Romanticism* 18 (1979): 173–205.

Gleckner, Robert F., and Gerald E. Enscoe, eds. *Romanticism: Points of View*. Englewood Cliffs: Prentice, 1962.

Glover, A. S. B., ed. *Byron: Poems*. New York: Penguin, 1985.

Goode, Clement Tyson. "A Critical Review of Research [on Byron]." Santucho 3–166.

Gunn, Peter, ed. *Byron: Selected Prose*. Hammondsworth, Eng.: Penguin, 1972.

Hagelman, Charles W., Jr., and Robert J. Barnes. *A Concordance to Byron's Don Juan*. Ithaca: Cornell UP, 1967.

Hamilton, G. H. "Delacroix, Byron, and the English Illustrators." *Gazette des Beaux Arts* 36 (1949): 261–78.

———. "Eugène Delacroix and Lord Byron." *Gazette des Beaux Arts* 23 (1943): 99–110.

Hartley, Robert A., ed. *Keats, Shelley, Byron, Hunt, and Their Circles: A Bibliography: July 1, 1962–December 31, 1974*. Lincoln: U of Nebraska P, 1978.

Harvey, A. D. *Britain in the Early Nineteenth Century*. New York: St. Martin's, 1978.

———. *English Poetry in a Changing Society, 1780–1825*. New York: St. Martin's, 1980.

Hayden, John O., ed. *Romantic Bards and British Reviewers: A Selected Edition of Contemporary Reviews of the Works of Wordsworth, Coleridge, Byron, Keats, and Shelley*. Lincoln: U of Nebraska P, 1971.

Hazlitt, William. "Lord Byron." *Lectures on the English Poets* [and] *The Spirit of the Age: Or, Contemporary Portraits*. Ed. Catherine MacDonald Maclean. New York: Dutton, 1910. 235–44.

Hearn, Ronald B. *Byron Criticism since 1952: A Bibliography*. Wolfeboro: Longwood, 1980.

Heath, William, ed. *Major British Poets of the Romantic Period*. New York: Macmillan, 1973.

Heinzelman, Kurt. "Byron's Poetry of Politics: The Economic Basis of the 'Poetical Character.'" *Texas Studies in Literature and Language* 23 (1981): 361–88.

———. "Politics, Memory, and the Lyric: Collaboration as Style in Byron's *Hebrew Melodies*." *Studies in Romanticism* 27 (1988): 515–27.

Hirsch, Bernard A. "The Erosion of the Narrator's World View in *Childe Harold's Pilgrimage*, I–II." *Modern Language Quarterly* 42 (1981): 347–68.

————. " 'A Want of That True Theory': *Julian and Maddalo* as Dramatic Monologue." *Studies in Romanticism* 17 (1978): 13–34.

Hirst, Wolf Z. "Byron's Lapse into Orthodoxy: An Unorthodox Reading of *Cain*." *Keats-Shelley Journal* 29 (1980): 151–72.

————. "Byron's Revisionary Struggle with the Bible." *Byron, the Bible, and Religion*. Ed. Hirst. Newark: U of Delaware P, 1991. 77–100.

Hobhouse, John Cam. *Recollections of a Long Life*. Ed. Lady Dorcester. 6 vols. 1911. New York: AMS, 1968.

Hobsbawm, Edward J. *The Age of Revolution: 1789–1848*. New York: NAL, 1962.

Hodgson, John A. "The Structures of *Childe Harold* III." *Studies in Romanticism* 18 (1979): 363–82.

Hofkosh, Sonia. "Women and the Romantic Author: The Example of Byron." Mellor, *Romanticism and Feminism* 93–114.

Honour, Hugh, and John Fleming. *The Visual Arts: A History*. Englewood Cliffs: Prentice, 1982.

Hume, Robert D. "*The Island* and the Evolution of Byron's 'Tales.' " Elledge and Hoffman 158–80.

Jack, Ian. *English Literature 1815–1832*. Vol. 10 of *The Oxford History of English Literature*. Oxford: Clarendon–Oxford UP, 1963.

Jones, Frederick L., ed. *The Letters of Percy Bysshe Shelley*. 2 vols. Oxford: Clarendon–Oxford UP, 1964.

Jordan, Frank, ed. *The English Romantic Poets: A Review of Research and Criticism*. 4th ed. New York: MLA, 1985.

————. "Natural Supernaturalism and Romantic Irony." Jordan, *English Romantic Poets* 11–19.

Joseph, M. K. *Byron the Poet*. London: Gollancz, 1966.

Jump, John D. *Byron*. Routledge Authors Guides. London: Routledge, 1972.

————, ed. *Byron: A Symposium*. London: Macmillan, 1975.

Kelsall, Malcolm. *Byron's Politics*. Totowa: Barnes, 1987.

Kermode, Frank, and John Hollander, gen. eds. *The Oxford Anthology of English Literature*. 2 vols. New York: Oxford UP, 1973.

Kernan, Alvin B. "The Perspective of Satire: *Don Juan*." Kernan, *Plot of Satire* 171–222.

————. *The Plot of Satire*. New Haven: Yale UP, 1965.

Knight, G. Wilson. *Byron and Shakespeare*. New York: Barnes, 1966.

————. *Lord Byron: Christian Virtues*. London: Routledge, 1952.

————. *Lord Byron's Marriage: The Evidence of Asterisks*. New York: Macmillan, 1957.

Kroeber, Karl, ed. *Backgrounds to British Romantic Literature*. San Francisco: Chandler, 1968.

————, ed. *Beginning Byron's Third Century*. Spec. issue of *Studies in Romanticism* 27 (1988): 473–645.

————. *Romantic Narrative Art.* Madison: U of Wisconsin P, 1960.

Kronenberger, Louis, ed. *Byron, Don Juan.* New York: Modern Library, 1984.

Kumar, Shiv K., ed. *British Romantic Poets: Recent Revaluations.* New York: New York UP, 1966.

Kushwaha, M. S. *Byron and the Dramatic Form.* Salzburg: U of Salzburg, 1980.

Lacoue-Labarthe, Philippe, and Jean-Luc Nancy. *The Literary Absolute: The Theory of Literature in German Romanticism.* Trans. Philip Barnard and Cheryl Lester. Albany: State U of New York P, 1988.

Lamm, Robert C., and Neal M. Cross, eds. *The Humanities in Western Culture: A Search for Human Values.* 8th ed. 2 vols. Dubuque: Brown, 1988.

Lang, Cecil Y. "Narcissus Jilted: Byron, *Don Juan*, and the Biographical Imperative." *Historical Studies and Literary Criticism.* Ed. Jerome J. McGann. Madison: U of Wisconsin P, 1985. 143–79.

Larrabee, Stephen. *English Bards and Grecian Marbles.* New York: Columbia UP, 1943.

Leigh, David J. "*Infelix Culpa*: Poetry and the Skeptic's Faith in *Don Juan.*" *Keats-Shelley Journal* 28 (1979): 120–38.

Lessenich, Rolf P. *Lord Byron and the Nature of Man.* Wien: B'ohlau, 1978.

Levine, Alice, and Jerome J. McGann, eds. *Byron, Miscellaneous Poems: A Facsimile of the Manuscripts in the Pierpont Morgan Library.* Garland Manuscripts of the Younger Romantics. New York: Garland, 1988.

Levinson, Marjorie. *The Romantic Fragment Poem: A Critique of a Form.* Chapel Hill: U of North Carolina P, 1986.

Looper, Travis. *Byron and the Bible: A Compendium of Biblical Usage in the Poetry of Lord Byron.* Metuchen: Scarecrow, 1978.

Lovejoy, A. O. "On the Discrimination of Romanticisms." *PMLA* 39 (1924): 229–53.

Lovell, Ernest J., Jr. *Byron: The Record of a Quest. Studies in a Poet's Concept and Treatment of Nature.* Austin: U of Texas P, 1949.

————, ed. *His Very Self and Voice: Collected Conversations of Lord Byron.* New York: Macmillan, 1954.

————, ed. *Lady Blessington's Conversations of Lord Byron.* Princeton: Princeton UP, 1969.

————, ed. *Medwin's Conversations of Lord Byron.* Princeton: Princeton UP, 1966.

Low, Donald A. *That Sunny Dome: A Portrait of Regency England.* London: Dent, 1977.

Mack, Maynard, gen. ed. *The Norton Anthology of World Masterpieces.* 5th ed. 2 vols. New York: Norton, 1985.

Magill, Frank N., ed. *Critical Survey of Poetry.* English Language Series. Englewood Cliffs: Salem, 1982, 1987.

Mahoney, John L., ed. *The English Romantics: Major Poetry and Critical Theory.* Lexington: Heath, 1978.

Manning, Peter J. *Byron and His Fictions.* Detroit: Wayne State UP, 1978.

———. "*Don Juan* and Byron's Imperceptiveness to the English Word." *Studies in Romanticism* 18 (1979): 207–33.

———. "Tales and Politics: *The Corsair, Lara,* and *The White Doe of Rylstone.*" Stürzl and Hogg 204–30.

Marchand, Leslie A. *Byron: A Biography.* 3 vols. New York: Knopf, 1957.

———. *Byron: A Portrait.* 1970. Chicago: U of Chicago P, 1979.

———, ed. *Byron, Don Juan.* Riverside edition. Boston: Houghton, 1972.

———, ed. *Byron's Letters and Journals.* 12 vols. Cambridge: Belknap–Harvard UP, 1973–82.

———. *Byron's Poetry: A Critical Introduction.* Boston: Houghton, 1965.

———, ed. *Lord Byron: Selected Letters and Journals.* Cambridge: Belknap–Harvard UP, 1982.

Marjarum, E. W. *Byron as Skeptic and Believer.* 1938. New York: Russell, 1962.

Marshall, L. E. " '*Words* Are *Things*': Byron and the Prophetic Efficacy of Language." *SEL* 25 (1985): 801–22.

Marshall, William H. "The Accretive Structure of Byron's *The Giaour.*" *Modern Language Notes* 76 (1961): 502–09.

———, ed. *Lord Byron: Selected Poems and Letters.* Riverside edition. Boston: Houghton, 1968.

———. *The Structure of Byron's Major Poems.* Philadelphia: U of Pennsylvania P, 1962.

Martin, L. C. *Byron's Lyrics.* Byron Foundation Lecture. Nottingham: U of Nottingham, 1948.

Martin, Philip W. *Byron: A Poet before His Public.* Cambridge: Cambridge UP, 1982.

Matthews, G. M. "*Julian and Maddalo*: The Draft and the Meaning." *Studia Neophilologica* 35 (1963): 57–84.

McConnell, Frank D., ed. *Byron's Poetry.* Norton Critical Edition. New York: Norton, 1978.

McFarland, Thomas. *Romanticism and the Forms of Ruin: Wordsworth, Coleridge, and the Modalities of Fragmentation.* Princeton: Princeton UP, 1981.

McGann, Jerome J. "The Book of Byron and the Book of a World." *The Beauty of Inflections: Literary Investigations in Historical Method and Theory.* 1985. Oxford: Clarendon–Oxford UP, 1988. 255–93.

———, ed. *Byron.* Oxford Authors. New York: Oxford UP, 1986.

———. *A Critique of Modern Textual Criticism.* Chicago: U of Chicago P, 1985.

———. *Don Juan in Context.* Chicago: U of Chicago P, 1976.

———. *Fiery Dust: Byron's Poetic Development.* Chicago: U of Chicago P, 1968.

———, ed. *Lord Byron: The Complete Poetical Works.* 5 vols. to date. Oxford: Clarendon–Oxford UP, 1980–

———. *The Romantic Ideology: A Critical Investigation.* Chicago: U of Chicago P, 1983.

Meisel, Martin. "Pictorial Engagements: Byron, Delacroix, Ford Madox Brown." *Studies in Romanticism* 27 (1988): 579–603.

Mellor, Anne K. *English Romantic Irony.* Cambridge: Harvard UP, 1980.

———, ed. *Romanticism and Feminism.* Bloomington: Indiana UP, 1988.

Moore, Doris Langley. *The Late Lord Byron: Posthumous Dramas.* London: Murray, 1961.

———. *Lord Byron: Accounts Rendered.* London: Murray, 1974.

———. *My Caravaggio Style.* New York: Lippincott, 1959.

Moore, Thomas. *Letters and Journals of Lord Byron with Notices of His Life.* 2 vols. London: Murray, 1830.

More, Paul E., ed. *The Poetical Works of Byron.* Rev. Robert F. Gleckner. Cambridge edition. Boston: Houghton, 1975.

Muecke, D. C. *The Compass of Irony.* London: Methuen, 1969.

Nicholson, Andrew, ed. *The Draft Manuscripts of Cantos VI and VII of Don Juan.* Garland Manuscripts of the Younger Romantics. New York: Garland, forthcoming.

Noyes, Russell, ed. *English Romantic Poetry and Prose.* New York: Oxford UP, 1956.

Pafford, Ward. "Byron and the Mind of Man: *Childe Harold* III–IV and *Manfred.*" *Studies in Romanticism* 1 (1961–62): 105–27.

Page, Frederick, ed. *Byron: Poetical Works.* Rev. John Jump. 3rd ed. Oxford Standard Authors. New York: Oxford UP, 1970.

Page, Norman. *A Byron Chronology.* Boston: Hall, 1988.

———, ed. *Byron: Interviews and Recollections.* Atlantic Highlands: Humanities, 1985.

Parker, Derek. *Byron and His World.* New York: Viking, 1969.

Peckham, Morse. "Toward a Theory of Romanticism." *PMLA* 66 (1951): 5–23.

———. "Toward a Theory of Romanticism: II. Reconsiderations." *Studies in Romanticism* 1 (1961): 1–8.

———. *The Triumph of Romanticism: Collected Essays.* Columbia: U of South Carolina P, 1970.

Perkins, David, ed. *English Romantic Writers.* New York: Harcourt, 1967.

———. *The Quest for Permanence: The Symbolism of Wordsworth, Shelley, and Keats.* Cambridge: Harvard UP, 1959.

Peterfreund, Stuart. "The Politics of 'Neutral Space' in Byron's *Vision of Judgement.*" *Modern Language Quarterly* 40 (1979): 275–91.

Pollard, H. G. "George Gordon Byron: Sixth Baron Byron." *The New Cambridge Bibliography of English Literature.* Ed. George Watson. 5 vols. Cambridge: Cambridge UP, 1969. 3: cols. 270–309.

Prokosh, Frederic. *The Missolonghi Manuscript.* New York: Farrar, 1968.

Prothero, Rowland E., ed. *The Works of Lord Byron: Letters and Journals.* 6 vols. London: Murray, 1898–1901. New York: Octagon, 1966.

Quennell, Peter, ed. *Byron, a Self-Portrait: Letters and Diaries, with Hitherto Unpublished Letters.* 2 vols. New York: Scribner's, 1950.

———. *Byron in Italy.* 1941. New York: Compass-Viking, 1957.

———. *Byron: The Years of Fame.* New York: Viking, 1935.

———. *Romantic England: Writing and Painting, 1717–1851.* New York: Macmillan, 1970.

Rajan, Balachandra. *The Form of the Unfinished: English Poetics from Spenser to Pound.* Princeton: Princeton UP, 1985.

Rajan, Tilottama. *Dark Interpreter: The Discourse of Romanticism.* Ithaca: Cornell UP, 1980.

———. "Romanticism and the Death of Lyric Consciousness." *Lyric Poetry: Beyond New Criticism.* Ed. Chaviva Hosek and Patricia Parker. Ithaca: Cornell UP, 1985. 194–207.

Rapf, Joanna E. "The Byronic Heroine: Incest and the Creative Process." *SEL* 21 (1981): 637–45.

Reiman, Donald H. "*Don Juan* in Epic Context." *Studies in Romanticism* 16 (1977): 587–94.

———. *Intervals of Inspiration: The Skeptical Tradition and the Psychology of Romanticism.* Greenwood: Penkevill, 1988.

———, ed. *The Romantics Reviewed: Contemporary Reviews of British Romantic Writers.* 9 vols. New York: Garland, 1972.

Richardson, Alan. *A Mental Theater: Poetic Drama and Consciousness in the Romantic Age.* University Park: Penn State UP, 1988.

Ridenour, George M. "Byron in 1816: Four Poems from Diodati." *From Sensibility to Romanticism: Essays Presented to Frederick A. Pottle.* Ed. Frederick W. Hilles and Harold Bloom. 1965. New York: Oxford UP, 1970. 453–65.

———. *The Style of* Don Juan. Yale Studies in English. New Haven: Yale UP, 1960.

Robinson, Charles E., ed. *Lord Byron and His Contemporaries: Essays from the Sixth International Byron Seminar.* Newark: U of Delaware P, 1982.

———. *Shelley and Byron: The Snake and Eagle Wreathed in Fight.* Baltimore: Johns Hopkins UP, 1976.

Roston, Murray. *Biblical Drama in England.* London: Faber, 1968.

Rudolf, Anthony. *Byron's Darkness: Lost Summer and Nuclear Winter.* London: Menard, 1984.

Russell, Bertrand. *A History of Western Philosophy.* New York: Simon, 1945.

Rutherford, Andrew. *Byron: A Critical Study.* Stanford: Stanford UP, 1961.

———, comp. *Byron: The Critical Heritage.* New York: Barnes, 1970.

Said, Edward W. *Orientalism.* New York: Random, 1978.

Sales, Roger. *English Literature in History, 1780–1830: Pastoral and Politics.* New York: St. Martin's, 1983.

Santucho, Oscar José. *George Gordon, Lord Byron: A Comprehensive Bibliography of Secondary Materials in English, 1807–1974.* Metuchen: Scarecrow, 1977.

Schaffner, Alfred. *Lord Byrons* Cain *und Seine Quellen*. Strassburg, 1880.

Shelley, Percy Bysshe. *Julian and Maddalo*. *Shelley: Poetical Works*. Ed. Thomas Hutchinson. Rev. G. M. Matthews. Oxford Standard Authors. New York: Oxford UP, 1970. 189–204.

———. *Shelley's Poetry and Prose*. Ed. Donald H. Reiman and Sharon B. Powers. New York: Norton, 1977.

Shilstone, Frederick W. *Byron and the Myth of Tradition*. Lincoln: U of Nebraska P, 1988.

———. "Byron's *The Giaour*: Narrative Tradition and Romantic Cognitive Theory." *Research Studies* 48 (1980): 94–104.

———. "A Grandfather, a Raft, a Tradition: The Shipwreck Scene in Byron's *Don Juan*." *Tennessee Studies in Literature* 25 (1980): 94–109.

———. "The Lyric Collection as Genre: Byron's *Hebrew Melodies*." *Concerning Poetry* 12 (1979): 45–52.

Simpson, David. *Irony and Authority in Romantic Poetry*. Totowa: Rowman, 1979.

Siskin, Clifford. *The Historicity of Romantic Discourse*. New York: Oxford UP, 1988.

Smiles, Samuel. *A Publisher and His Friends: Memoir and Correspondence of the Late John Murray*. 2 vols. London, 1891.

Spector, Jack J. *Delacroix:* The Death of Sardanapalus. New York: Viking, 1974.

Sperry, Stuart M. "Byron and the Meaning of *Manfred*." *Criticism* 16 (1974): 189–202.

Steffan, Truman Guy. "The Devil a Bit of Our *Beppo*." *Philological Quarterly* 32 (1953): 154–71.

———, ed. *Lord Byron's* Cain: *Twelve Essays and a Text*. Austin: U of Texas P, 1968.

Steffan, Truman Guy, and Willis W. Pratt, eds. *Byron's* Don Juan: *A Variorum Edition*. 2nd ed. 4 vols. Austin: U of Texas P, 1971.

Steffan, T. G., E. Steffan, and W. W. Pratt, eds. *George Gordon, Lord Byron,* Don Juan. New York: Penguin, 1989.

Storey, Mark. *Byron and the Eye of Appetite*. London: Macmillan, 1986.

Stowe, Harriet Beecher. *Lady Byron Vindicated: A History of the Byron Controversy*. . . . 1870. New York: Haskell, 1970.

Stürzl, Erwin A., and James Hogg, eds. *Byron: Poetry and Politics: Seventh International Byron Symposium*. Salzburg: Institut für Anglistik und Amerikanistik, 1981.

Sundell, Michael G. "The Development of *The Giaour*." *SEL* 9 (1969): 587–99.

Swingle, L. J. "On Reading Romantic Poetry." *PMLA* 86 (1971): 974–81.

Thomas, Gordon K. *Lord Byron's Iberian Pilgrimage*. Provo: Brigham Young UP, 1983.

Thorslev, Peter L., Jr. *The Byronic Hero: Types and Prototypes*. Minneapolis: U of Minnesota P, 1962.

——. *Romantic Contraries: Freedom versus Destiny*. New Haven: Yale UP, 1984.

Trapp, Frank Anderson. *The Attainment of Delacroix*. Baltimore: Johns Hopkins UP, 1970.

Trawick, Leonard M., ed. *Backgrounds of Romanticism: English Philosophical Prose of the Eighteenth Century*. Bloomington: Indiana UP, 1967.

Trueblood, Paul G., ed. *Byron's Political and Cultural Influence in Nineteenth-Century Europe: A Symposium*. Atlantic Highlands: Humanities, 1981.

——. *The Flowering of Byron's Genius: Studies in Byron's* Don Juan. Palo Alto: Stanford UP, 1945.

——. *Lord Byron*. 2nd ed. Boston: Twayne, 1977.

Vassallo, Peter. *Byron: The Italian Literary Influence*. New York: St. Martin's, 1984.

Vaughan, William. *Romantic Art*. New York: Oxford UP, 1978.

Wasserman, Earl R. "The English Romantics: The Grounds of Knowledge." *Studies in Romanticism* 4 (1964): 17–34.

Watkins, Daniel P. "Byron and the Poetics of Revolution." *Keats-Shelley Journal* 34 (1985): 95–130.

——. "The Ideological Dimensions of Byron's *The Deformed Transformed*." *Criticism* 25 (1983): 27–39.

——. "Politics and Religion in Byron's *Heaven and Earth*." *Byron Journal* 11 (1983): 30–39.

——. *Social Relations in Byron's Eastern Tales*. Rutherford: Fairleigh Dickinson UP, 1987.

——. "Violence, Class Consciousness, and Ideology in Byron's History Plays." *ELH* 48 (1981): 799–816.

Watson, J. R. *English Poetry of the Romantic Period, 1789–1830*. Longman Literature in English. London: Longman, 1985.

Weinstein, Leo. *The Metamorphosis of Don Juan*. Stanford: Stanford UP, 1959.

West, Paul, ed. *Byron: A Collection of Critical Essays*. Twentieth Century Views. Englewood Cliffs: Prentice, 1963.

——. *Lord Byron's Doctor: A Novel*. New York: Doubleday, 1989.

Whittingham, Selby. "Byron and the Two Giorgiones." *Byron Journal* 14 (1986): 52–55.

Wilkie, Brian. "Byron and the Epic of Negation." Wilkie, *Romantic Poets* 188–226.

——. "Byron: Artistry and Style." Elledge and Hoffman 129–46.

——. *Romantic Poets and Epic Tradition*. Madison: U of Wisconsin P, 1965.

Wilkie, Brian, and James Hurt, eds. *Literature of the Western World*. 2nd ed. 2 vols. New York: Macmillan, 1988.

Williams, Raymond. *The Country and the City*. New York: Oxford UP, 1973.

——. *Culture and Society, 1780–1950*. New York: Columbia UP, 1958.

Wilson, James D. *The Romantic Heroic Ideal*. Baton Rouge: Louisiana State UP, 1982.

Wilton, Andrew. *Turner in His Time*. New York: Abrams, 1987.

Witt, Mary Ann Frese, ed. *The Humanities: Cultural Roots and Continuities*. 3rd ed. 2 vols. Lexington: Heath, 1989.

Wolfson, Susan J. " 'Their She Condition': Cross-Dressing and the Politics of Gender in *Don Juan*." *ELH* 54 (1987): 585–617.

Woodring, Carl. "Nature, Art, Reason, and Imagination in *Childe Harold*." Elledge and Hoffman 147–57.

———. *Politics in English Romantic Poetry*. Cambridge: Harvard UP, 1970.

Woods, George B., ed. *English Poetry and Prose of the Romantic Movement*. Rev. ed. Glenview: Scott, 1950.

Wordsworth, Jonathan, Michael C. Jaye, and Robert Woof. *William Wordsworth and the Age of English Romanticism*. New Brunswick: Rutgers UP, 1987.

Wordsworth, William. *Convention of Cintra*. 1808. Facsim. ed. Ed. Gordon Kent Thomas. Provo: Brigham Young UP, 1983.

———. *The Poetical Works of Wordsworth*. Ed. Thomas Hutchinson and Ernest de Selincourt. London: Oxford UP, 1961.

———. The Prelude, *1799, 1805, 1850*. Ed. Jonathan Wordsworth, M. H. Abrams, and Stephen Gill. Norton Critical Edition. New York: Norton, 1979.

Yeats, W. B. *The Collected Poems*. New York: Macmillan, 1956.

Young, Ione Dodson, ed. *A Concordance to the Poetry of Byron*. 4 vols. Austin: Young, 1965.

Audiovisual Materials

Andrews, Anthony, and Simon Templeman, narrs. *The Romantic Spirit*. Landseer Film and Television Productions, 1982.

Byron, Shelley, and Keats. Sound filmstrip. Films for the Humanities, FFH 348, 1982.

Clark, Kenneth, writ. and narr. "The Fallacies of Hope." *Civilisation*. Dir. Michael Gill and Peter Montagnon. BBC, 1969. 12 programs. (Videocassette available Time-Life Films.)

———, writ. and narr. *The Romantic Rebellion: Romantic versus Classic Art*. Television series. 1973.

Colum, Padraic. "She Walks in Beauty." *Discoveries That a Poet Has Made in Poetry*. Library of Congress, LWO 2824, 1959.

Delacroix: The Restless Eye. Videocassette. RM ARTS/BBC, Home Vision Video Cassette, n.d.

English Romantic Poetry. Audiocassettes. With Claire Bloom, Anthony Quayle, Ralph Richardson, and Frederick Worlock. Caedmon, SWC-3005, 1971.

English Romantic Poetry and Painting: A Series. Sound filmstrip. United Learning, 1974.

Fletcher, Bramwell. *English Romantic Poets.* Audiocassette. Listening Library, LL305CX, 1971.

Gothic. Dir. Ken Russell. With Gabriel Byrne, Julian Sands, and Natasha Richardson. Virgin Vision, 1986.

Haunted Summer. Dir. Ivan Passer. With Alice Krige, Eric Stoltz, and Philip Anglim. Cannon Films, 1988.

Lady Caroline Lamb. Dir. Robert Bolt. With Sarah Miles, Richard Chamberlain, and Margaret Leighton. Tomorrow Entertainment/Pulsar Productions, 1972.

Martin, Graham, and Mark Storey. *English Romantic Poetry 1780–1820.* Audiocassette. Audio Learning, ELA 067, 1981.

Poems by George Gordon, Lord Byron. Sound filmstrip. Educational Filmstrips, 1970. 52 frames, 5 min.

The Portrait of George Gordon, Lord Byron. 16mm film. National Educational Television, 1958. 29 min.

The Prisoner of Chillon. Motion picture. Vikoa Entertainment, 1971. 15 min.

The Prisoner of Chillon. Sound filmstrip. Encyclopaedia Britannica Films, 1966. 48 frames.

The Romantic Age. Sound filmstrip. Thomas S. Klise, 1976.

The Romantic Age in English Literature. Slide program. Developed by Guidance Associates, White Plains, NY. Center for Humanities, 1980. 169 slides.

The Romantic Era. Sound filmstrip. Educational Audio-Visual, 1970.

Romanticism in Art and Music. Sound filmstrip. Educational Audio-Visual, 1972.

The Romantic Period. 16mm film. Coronet, 1957. 14 min.

Romantic Poetry. Sound filmstrip. Films for the Humanities, 1981. 95 frames, 30 min.

Salvesen, Christopher, and William Walsh. *The Romantics.* Audiocassette. Gould Media, A4, n.d.

A Selection of Hebrew Melodies, Ancient and Modern, by Isaac Nathan and Lord Byron. Audiocassette. U of Alabama P, 38685.3, 1988.

"She Walks in Beauty." Sound filmstrip. Brunswick Productions, 1969. 25 frames.

Treasury of Lord Byron. Audiocassette. Educational Frontiers, EF 8025, n.d.

The Younger Romantics. Videocassette. Films for the Humanities, FFH 1303, 1988.

INDEX OF NAMES

INDEX OF WORKS BY BYRON